ECONOMIC CHANGE

ECONOMIC CHANGE

Selected Essays in
Business Cycles, National Income,
and Economic Growth

BY SIMON KUZNETS

GREENWOOD PRESS, PUBLISHERS
WESTPORT, CONNECTICUT

Library of Congress Cataloging in Publication Data

Kuznets, Simon Smith, 1901–
    Economic change.

    Reprint. Originally published: New York : Norton,
1953.
        1. Economics—Addresses, essays, lectures.
2. Statics and dynamics (Social sciences)—Addresses,
essays, lectures. 3. Business cycles—Addresses,
essays, lectures. 4. National income—Addresses,
essays, lectures. 5. Economic development—Addresses,
essays, lectures. I. Title.
HB171.K85 1983   338.5'42   83-5609
ISBN 0-313-24007-8 (lib. bdg.)

First Edition

Reprinted with the permission of W. W. Norton & Company, Inc.

Reprinted in 1983 by Greenwood Press
A division of Congressional Information Service, Inc.
88 Post Road West, Westport, Connecticut 06881

Printed in the United States of America

10 9 8 7 6 5 4 3 2 1

CONTENTS

PREFACE

Of the eleven essays comprised in this volume, nine were published (two in Spanish) ; and two are manuscripts read as lectures, but never published. Minor changes were made: in some, by omitting a few paragraphs originally, but no longer, pertinent; in all, in an attempt to remove the more obvious infelicities of style. Short of arduous rewriting, which I could not undertake, the latter task could not be fully accomplished.

The volume omits, by design, the more technical papers in the fields of statistical analysis, national income, and business cycles; and the largely methodological papers on economic growth. The intent has been to include only essays dealing with wider problems, so that no matter how fragmentary the effort, slender the empirical base, or venturesome the hypotheses, they may still claim the attention of readers other than technical specialists.

The common concern of these essays is with economic change: the movement of economic processes over time, and their differences across space viewed largely as cumulated product of different past rates of change starting from different initial levels. They were written as the result of reflections and questions arising from active participation in prolonged quantitative and empirical studies. In essence, and despite the elaborateness of discussion in some, they are musings on larger themes. They are truly essays—the results of efforts to deal with complex problems by inadequate means, or to probe into wider implications for which adequate empirical data were not readily available, if available at all. Their order in the volume reflects, albeit roughly, the sequence of my own interests: from business cycles to national income to economic growth.

Of the papers presented here some were written over twenty

years ago, others quite recently. The main purpose of bringing them together in one volume is to make them more readily accessible to the interested reader. But this would not be warranted if cumulation of new events and changes in the bases of economic analysis rendered them largely obsolete. True, there is some obsolescence; and were the essays written today, some points would have been formulated differently. But, by and large, the ideas expressed, the findings suggested, and the questions raised, still seem relevant.

For assistance in preparing these papers for publication I am greatly indebted to Lillian Epstein. Thanks are due also to the various publishers for permission to republish articles already in print.

Simon Kuznets

December, 1952

Economic Change

1

EQUILIBRIUM ECONOMICS
AND BUSINESS-CYCLE THEORY *

I

The treatment of business cycles in their many aspects is a recent development in the history of economics. Of still more recent origin is the question as to the relation of business-cycle theory to economic theory. The question is of importance, and the refusal to face it is conditioned by a limited outlook either upon the scope and problems of theoretical economics, or upon the methods of business-cycle study.

The task of economic theory is to develop a generalized description of the basic processes of current economic life, to establish general relationships among the different factors in the present economic system. These generalizations are to be the tool, which should in combination with some specific data explain the appearance and general characteristics of an economic phenomenon; unless, of course, the latter is in the nature of a passing disturbance or is occasioned by factors outside the economic system. Thus the explanation of business cycles, in so far as they are not a passing disturbance or a result of non-economic factors, should be derived from generalized statements of economic theory. Business-cycle theory should be an integral part of general economic theory. This is the intellectual challenge which the problem of cycles presents to the system of theoretical economics.

Historically this challenge is recent since before the second half of the nineteenth century business cycles were hardly rec-

* Reprinted by permission from *The Quarterly Journal of Economics*, Vol. 44, May 1930, pp. 381-415.

ognized as a *bona fide* economic phenomenon. As long as the
fluctuations were conceived as business crises, they presented
no serious theoretical problem since crises could be treated as
temporary disturbances, as exceptions to the smooth course of
events postulated by economic theory. This view was strengthened both by the characteristics of the fluctuations and by the
implications of the system of theoretical economics. As F. E.
Trautmann points out,[1] one reason why classical economists
(Adam Smith, Ricardo, J. S. Mill) assigned to the problem of
business crises such a small place in their system of economic
science, was that most of the violent disturbances during the
years from 1763 to 1847 were associated with outside causes,
such as wars, technical changes, crops, speculative manias.
Acceptance of these characteristics of business fluctuations
during the early periods of modern business economy went
hand in hand with the theoretical impossibility of general
overproduction developed with much emphasis by J. B. Say.
It is true that the persistence of disturbances led some pessimistically inclined economists like Malthus, or critics of the
economic system like Sismondi, to pay more than fleeting attention to the problem and to insist that the simple explanations of Ricardian economics were misleading. But until the
regularity of the disturbances was established, until it was
made certain that the fluctuations are ever present and quite
pervasive, that they are not mere exceptions (even if unavoidable), these fluctuations presented no question, and their explanation was no challenge to theoretical economics.

Of course, even when cycles were recognized as an ever-
present phenomenon, they could still be explained by outside
causes rather than by economic factors. Thus, W. S. Jevons,
the first economist to insist on the rhythmical character of
business fluctuations (of which the crisis was only a culminat-
ing point), found it possible to explain business cycles not by
any economic cause, but by the influence of periodic fluctuations in the radiation of the sun. And while the task of tracing

[1] Das Problem der Wirtschaftskrisen in der Klassischen Nationaloekonomie, Munch, 1926.

these regular cycles generated by non-economic causes in the economic system still remained, this was a matter of incompleteness of inductive study, rather than a question of insufficiency of the theoretical system.

But the extended empirical investigations of the problem which appeared in the second half of the nineteenth century, especially from the pen of Clement Juglar, showed that the conception of business cycles as of strictly periodic swings due to outside causes was a misleading simplification; that business cycles were irregular; that their relation to outside factors such as climate was remote; and that their unfolding in economic reality allowed explanations by as many economic factors as were involved in the oscillations. As a consequence, business cycles grew in importance as a *bona fide* economic phenomenon, challenging understanding and calling for explanation with the aid of the essential principles of economics.

This organic relation between business-cycle theory and theoretical economics was stated by Böhm-Bawerk as early as 1898.[2] But the science was tardy in recognizing it, and has not yet come to the point where it would satisfy this formulated requirement. There continued to be a cleavage between economic theorists on one hand and the investigators of business cycles on the other. While the former continued to elaborate the concept of equilibrium and its manifestation, the latter continued to find additional factors that might account for the appearance of the fluctuations.

But lately the cumulative change in the two theoretical entities has brought about a renewal of the question of relationship. On the one hand, the empirical study of business cycles has grown by leaps and bounds, and shortly before the war reached a milestone in the first edition of W. C. Mitchell's Business Cycles. On the other hand, the criticism of the equilibrium scheme of economics as it was first developed by the classical school, then cardinally reconstructed by the marginal utility school, then made rigorous and refined by the mathe-

[2] See his review of Bergmann's treatise in the Zeitschrift für Volkswirtschaft Sozialpolitik und Verwaltung, vii, 132.

matical school, was increasing. It was urged that equilibrium economics simplified economic phenomena too much, that its abstraction from monetary institutions was a fatal vitiation of reality, that it did not explain economic development. From the point of view of business-cycle theory, a significant milestone in this formulation of its logical relation to static theory was Schumpeter's Theory of Economic Development. While in 1913 W. C. Mitchell unfolded the problem of business cycles to its full empirical extent, in 1914 Schumpeter presented a tentative theory of dynamic economics, in which business cycles became an integral part of the new theoretical system.

During the post-war years, the cleavage between pure economic theory and the study of business cycles was intensified by the development of a rather complex body of statistical techniques in the study of business fluctuations. But on the other hand, the need of a change became widely recognized, and the significance of business-cycle theory as part of a theoretical system of economics increasingly appreciated. In the latest post-war discussion, we find a striking change compared with the status of these two intellectual entities during the nineteenth century. From an empirical exception to the "normal" course of events, business cycles have become a cardinal economic problem propounded by many economists as a touchstone for economic theory. The present essay is an attempt to summarize and analyze these current developments.

It was in Germany, whose economists are interested in maintaining the continuity of scientific development, that the problem of the relation between this recently grown business-cycle theory and economic theory was examined anew in recent years.

II

In presenting the discussion that has developed during the past few years in Germany it is well to quote copiously, for this seems to be the best method of presenting a problem whose very formulation is important. We begin with the general statements made by Lederer.[3]

According to Lederer, pure economic theory cannot explain dynamic phenomena satisfactorily, because its static laws of value and price fail to take into consideration the type of social economy, the interrelations of different groups of economic agents. Pure theory, which can explain processes and factors of change (accumulation and interest) only as deviations from its static laws of supply and demand, must therefore be supplemented by another approach.

Such an approach would strive to clarify a specific form of economic system. It would start from the circulation process of the typical economy, describe it and establish its conditions. It would thus present the totality of economic phenomena, throw light on their movements and establish their social conditions. Each of these economic systems has its social side, whose recognition is necessary for the presentation of the economy as a social process. (Page 24.) . . . The investigation of types of social economy ties to the theory more organically than heretofore two problems: 1. The problem of the value of money: 2. The problem of conjuncture and of business cycles. (Page 22.)

While advocating a new theoretical system, viz., a general theory of circulation based upon the recognition of social structures, Lederer does not specify what should be the relation of pure theory to this new theoretical body. He is therefore unable to point more definitely to the logical peculiarity of pure theory which does not permit the inclusion of varying social conditions.

A more specific analysis, directly relevant to the question of the relation between business-cycle theory and the general

[3] Der Zirkulationsprozess als zentrales Problem der oekonomischen Theorie, Archiv für Sozialwissenschaft und Sozialpolitik, vol. lvi, heft 1, 1926, pp. 1-25.

system of economics, is developed in an article by A. Loewe.[4]

His point of view may be gathered from the following quotations:

> All the systems of economics since the Physiocrats have put in the center the concept of equilibrium. . . . This concept of equilibrium is logically bound up with the concept of a closed, interdependent system. It is only through independence from outside influences and through functional interconnection of the elements of the system, that the persistence of any state, i.e., of an equilibrium, is achieved. We can thus say that any system of economics which operates with the concept of equilibrium must necessarily be a closed interdependent system—in short, a static system. As such the theory of movement characteristic of this system is the movement by the method of variations.[5] . . .
>
> The general character and agreement in the periodic turn in movements of factors of circulation—these are the specific problems of business cycle theory which have to be solved within the closed interdependent system. *This solution should be possible of inclusion in a static system.* (Page 175.)

After presenting the task which the problem of business cycles requires general economic theory to perform, Loewe goes on to analyze current business-cycle theories to see whether the solutions they offer are within the bounds of the theoretical system of economics. For this purpose, he groups theories as follows:

1. *The anti-theoretical group.* To this belong all the explana-

[4] "Wie is Konjunkturtheorie ueberhaupt möglich," Weltwirtschaftliches Archiv, October 1926, pp. 163-197.

[5] By movements according to the method of variations Loewe understands changes from an equilibrium position which tend to be checked immediately by the forces that make for the restoration of the status quo ante. These movements are, then, passing deviations, temporary variations around the equilibrium.

tions that rely on error or refer to the anarchy of production as the general source of business cycles. These explanations assume that a businessman will not behave rationally, that his behavior does not follow the rules it is supposed to follow in the theoretical system of economics. To explain business cycles in such a way is obviously to deny the basic principle underlying all general economic theory. Examples of such hypotheses are those of Hardy or of Pigou.

2. *The group of circular reasoning.* To this belong all theories that begin by assuming a state of depression or a state of prosperity. These explanations then describe how from a given state of depression or prosperity the next stage in the business cycle develops, and how the unfolding of the cycle brings the economic system again to the state from which the explanation started. As examples Loewe cites Aftalion and Cassel.

The fault of such hypotheses is that they assume too much from the start. To fall within the limits of equilibrium economics, the explanation of business cycles must begin with a state of equilibrium and not with a state of economic affairs below or above it. It is the assumption of a depression or of prosperity as a starting point that allows the theories of this group to explain the next phase of the cycle. But the explanation is implied in the assumption.

3. *The group of generalizing theories.* To this belong all explanations that generalize a partial into a general disturbance (Sombart, Liefmann, Schumpeter, the quantity theorists). Thus, Schumpeter attributes business cycles to innovations introduced by business leaders. These innovations, appearing in waves, disturb the equilibrium of the static system. The question arises how a partial disturbance, caused by business leaders in one or two branches of economic activity, can cause general overproduction, a general rise in prices, and so on. From the point of view of equilibrium economics, a partial disturbance should be cancelled by an opposite change in some other part of the system.

4. *The theories of time discrepancy.* To this group belong all

hypotheses that explain business cycles as the result of a lag
of one group of economic changes behind another. The most
outstanding example is Irving Fisher's theory of the lag of
interest rates. Concerning this group Loewe says:

> The assumption of interdependence of the elements in
> the closed system imposes a limitation. Since each of the
> elements is equally dependent upon all the others, the
> time span which elapses from the start of a certain change
> (or disturbance) to its working out in all the elements of
> the system must be *equal* for each and all the elements.
> . . . The assumption of varying time spans for the re-
> action of the separate elements destroys general interde-
> pendence. (Page 184.)

5. *The theories of independent variables.* To this group
belong all theories that rely on factors outside the economic
system, such as climate, crop, technical progress. All these
theories are obviously non-economic theories of business cycles, since they present the fluctuations as essentially non-
economic phenomena, somewhat similar to seasonal variations.
To interpret business cycles in this way is to confess the failure of economic science to explain their appearance.

The bearing of this rather summary analysis of Loewe is
obvious. The conclusion is that all business-cycle theories, unless they attribute the fluctuations to some factors outside the
economic system itself, explain them in a way which denies
some basic assumption of theoretical economics—either the rationality of economic behavior or the strict interdependence
of the economic elements in the system. It is clear that, if
these explanations of business cycles throw light on the processes of reality, equilibrium economics is blocking this light by
denying the possibility of general overproduction. What, then,
is the use of equilibrium economics, what is its relation to
processes of economic change? [6]

[6] After this article had been completed, my attention was called to the
recent book by Dr. Marie Hirsch, Zur Theorie des Konjunkturzyklus,
Ein Beitrag zum dynamischen System (Tübingen, 1929). The author.

The challenge which has thus been offered by Loewe has been taken up in a treatise by Erich Carrel.[7] He denies any contradiction between pure economic theory and generalized reality as it is presented in business-cycle explanations. He goes further and denies the possibility of inductive verification of economic theory. Such attempts, he states, arise from a misconception of the nature and function of pure economic theory.

Our investigation of the nature of pure (exact) economic theory has shown us that the subject matter of this science is not an ideal system of "reality" nor any "state of economy," but the essence of "social economy" considered by itself, the pure "economy." We have established that the statements about relations made by pure theory are not statements concerning causal regularities, but about a causal relation of quantities. The judgments of pure theory relate to the essence or nature of social economy, but not to their existence in reality, not to the sociological, psychological or technical side of the actual relations which the essence may acquire in real life. The judgments of pure theory are absolute in their validity, not restricted in time, effective whenever the essence is materialized in actual life. (Pages 112-113.)

---

adopting the methodological approach of A. Loewe and J. Schumpeter, analyses some of the more recent business-cycle theories, bringing out clearly the static and the non-static elements in them. She then attempts to derive a theory of business cycles directly from certain dynamic principles, i.e., principles which constitute the basis of a dynamic economic system rather than of a static one. These principles are: 1. technical progress, 2. the process of accumulation, resulting from a discrepancy due to the existence of reserve labor between prices and costs (wages). The "reserve army" in turn results from the persistent working of the principle of technical progress.

The author's methodological approach does not depart from that of Loewe. Her analysis of business cycles does not fall within the scope of the present article.

[7] Sozialoekonomische Theorie und Konjunkturproblem, Muenchen und Leipzig, 1929.

What, then, is this essence of social economy? Pure theoretical economics deals with "the necessary relationships, with truths that are derived from scarcity and the economic principle i.e., the principle of rational economic action. The truth of the statements is given whenever the reasoning supplied is in the nature of a necessity of thought (Denknotwendigkeit)." (Page 85.)

If pure economic theory deals with necessary relations of quantities, derived from the operation of the economic principle in conditions of scarcity, if the theory is true without relevance to reality, one cannot challenge it on the ground that its manifestations in reality are so rare. Pure theory is realistic only in the sense that it deals with scarcity and rational economic behavior, both found in actual life. But beyond that, all the relations established in pure theory are in the nature of logical necessities derived from these two assumptions, and not generalizations either of the short, long, or any run of economic processes in real life.

III

The discussion by Carrel indicates that before the relation between business-cycle theory and economic theory can be discussed with profit, the subject matter and nature of theoretical economics should be agreed upon. For if general economic theory is an entirely different logical entity from the theory of any specific economic phenomenon, then the question is settled at the start. If theoretical economics is to preoccupy itself with the metaphysics of rational economic action under conditions of scarcity, never subject to test by reality, and is to be justified only by the "necessary character of the thinking involved," then the fact that the generalizations about reality presented by business-cycle theories contradict the most essential part of pure economic theory does not matter. The latter is an intellectual entity by itself.

One may doubt, however, that the economic theorists of today will subscribe to this characterization of their general systems. It is obvious, for example, that contemporary mathematical economists conceive their systems of equations as generalizations about relations that actually exist, and among factors that have frequent manifestation in real life. It is even assumed that these generalizations are immediately applicable to actual life, provided the necessary empirical data are given in their refined form. Economists of the marginal-utility school claim that their theories of value and of price present a true picture of the basic economic processes, and that the marginal productivity theory evolved from it has some significance in an analysis of reality as reflected in production, wage and other statistical indices. The theoretical system of Marshallian economics is certainly not supposed to be a metaphysical discussion of the essence of economy. Neither does Cassel's theory of prices purport to be one. Of course, one might say that none of these systems is an example of pure economic theory, but that would be quibbling about terms. The body of generalizations which appear under the name of economic theory in current treatises claims to describe the essential relations, the skeleton of economic processes of current reality. Nobody would claim that these generalizations should stand the test of comparison with passing events in their crude form. But they are supposed to yield the basic factors that underlie the flux of events, and should therefore form a system that would explain such a pervasive phenomenon as cyclical fluctuations.

But the current theoretical systems use the concept of equilibrium as a basic element. The mathematical economists continue to do so, as does Marshallian economics, or the simpler variants of the mathematical school, such as Cassel's. Indeed the usual procedure in the current theory of prices is to begin with: 1. the assumption of scarcity, 2. the assumption of economic rationality, 3. the general downward character of the demand function, 4. the general upward character of the supply function. (These two latter assumptions are in a way deducible from the principle of economic rationality applied in conditions of scarcity and multiplicity of goods and wants.) Enumerating the various factors operating on the side of supply and on the side of demand, they set up a system of equations that allows a solution for the unknown, i.e., for price. The concept of equilibrium is implied in the equation itself. The solution is given when there is a balance of supply and demand. The equilibrium of supply and demand becomes, then, the condition under which the price becomes determinate and under which all the relations become significant, since it is they that correspond to the materialized price.

This use of the concept of equilibrium, as a condition under which the problem of pricing becomes determinate, is in itself not objectionable. Strictly speaking, it means that every materialized price on the market implies a balance of supply and demand, for if there were no balance of supply and demand at this point the price would not have appeared, the transaction would not have been concluded. The only objection to such an inference is that the determinateness of the price is not absolute, i.e., that there is a range of prices within which the transaction could have taken place, and the balance of supply and demand become a fact. If one wishes to establish a system of equations by which each price at each moment is a function of certain factors in an equation, it is possible to do so. Such an interpretation may be charged with incompleteness, if some factors that have acted in bringing about the given single price are excluded. But there is otherwise no methodological objection to this use of the concept of equilibrium.

However, the current economic theories do not pretend to give only a schematic exposition of how each price arises from the numerous economic factors that underlie the surface of social economic phenomena. If they did, these systems would amount to nothing but lists of factors arranged on the side of supply or on the side of demand, lists of factors whose *interrelations* change with every single change of every single price on the market. They would amount, then, to what static economics should essentially amount to—a reduction of social phenomena to the individual acts that underlie them. But they would have no relevance to any *persistent* relations among factors.

It is exactly this persistence that is implied in the concept of equilibrium, as used at present in economic theory. The system of equations set up represents the system of interdependence which is supposed to yield stable equilibrium, and thus to reveal persistent relations among factors. This is true whether we have a fixed equilibrium or a moving equilibrium, an equilibrium of short or long run. It is supposed to yield a level to which the real economic system has a tendency to return after being disturbed by outside factors of a casual character.

The two aspects of the equilibrium system are interdependent; there is a persistent *state* of equilibrium conditioning the solution of the problem, and therefore the existence of persistent *relations*. If the state of equilibrium is unstable for reasons within the economic system, then the relations formulated in the equations are unstable also. Such a system may go through pervasive and considerable variations only if one postulates outside factors whose variations account for the changes in the constants and in the solutions of the equations. The relations, however, described by the structural characteristics of the equations are assumed not to vary with these variations in constants.

It is exactly against this implication of the concept of equilibrium and of fundamental interdependence that the criticism presented above is directed. The analysis of business-cycle theory by Loewe has indicated that any attempt to explain the pervasive fluctuations with the help of economic factors denies the assumption of general interdependence which is a direct implication of a concept of equilibrium. In the economic processes as described by business-cycle theories there are changes not only in the constants but also in the relations assumed to be persistent in equilibrium economics. Hence the curious situation that those economic theorists who pay attention to the problem of business cycles within their general economic treatises do not weave it organically into the system. Can one say that Cassel's theory of conjunctures is an integral part of his general theory of prices? Can one say that Pigou's theory of industrial fluctuations assumes the same kind of rational economic behavior as is assumed in the general Marshallian theory of the equilibrium of demand and supply?

From the point of view of business-cycle theory the concept of equilibrium and the implied general interdependence can be retained only in one of two ways: 1. by assuming that business cycles are a consequence of cycles in *outside* factors and that this variation in what might be called the economic constants does not essentially disturb the determinate fundamental relations among economic factors; or, 2. by assuming that the equilibrium concept applies to every instant of economic life, has no time span, intimates nothing concerning the sequence of economic events in time. The first way out is by and large a denial of the reality of all business-cycle theories which rest upon economic factors. The second way is a rather thorough limitation of the whole system. But even with such a limitation of the theoretical system to a list of factors, there would remain the question whether all the factors are included. Complete treatment is not assured by the fact that the system of equations includes as many equations as there are unknowns. One could provide a determinate solution with two factors on the side of supply and two factors on each side of demand, just as well as with twenty factors on each side. The exhaustiveness of a list of factors can be checked only by comparison with the changing reality. But such a check is available only to the economic theory of change, and the static equilibrium theory can find a final test of the completeness of its treatment only in the generalizations of dynamic economic theory.

However, a third way of preserving the reality of the equilibrium system in the full scope of its implications consists in saying that the concept applies to that section of reality which we obtain *after* we remove, by a process of analysis, the dynamic aspects of the changing events. H. L. Moore's approach to the equilibrium about the trend lines is a step in this direction.[8] Moore conceives the equilibrium as taking place among the ratio-deviations from lines of secular movements. In the second article he develops a theory of oscillations which are non-periodic, i.e., which are not cyclical, in their character. This latter theory therefore excludes from consideration not only the secular movements, which are taken for granted, but also cyclical fluctuations due to periodic causes. If therefore, the secular movements cannot be interpreted in terms of equilibrium forces and the cycles do not find sufficient explanation in the oscillations of an outside factor, does not the equilibrium system deal only with the non-periodic oscillations around a trend line?

It would be difficult to answer the question at present, when our knowledge of even the established processes of economic change is so scanty. But it may be observed that, in this approach, equilibrium economics gives up any attempt to explain processes of economic change. Instead of being a basic scheme which expounds persistent relationships and persistent levels—instead of being the groundwork for a general theory of economic change—it becomes in the order of intellectual attack a limiting condition, a point at which the service of dynamic theory in the explanation of changing reality ceases, since all the important processes of change have been accounted for, and what remains are non-periodic small changes, which could be treated by the method of variations.

If the equilibrium concept is to be assigned any reality as a persistent state, it may be applied only if cycles are reduced to a consequence of an outside factor, if secular movements are taken for granted. This conclusion already contains an answer to the other claim that is usually made for the equilibrium system of economics, viz., that it is only a first approximation, that it presents a simplified idealized system which facilitates

[8] "A Moving Equilibrium of Demand and Supply," Quarterly Journal of Economics, May 1925, pp. 357-371, also "A Theory of Economic Oscillations," ibid., November 1926, pp. 1-29.

our study of complex reality by setting off its variability, its dynamic character. In reality, as we have seen, the essential relationships established by equilibrium economics come into play only *after* all the factors of change are eliminated.

But it may still be asked whether the equilibrium theory cannot be conceived as an unrealistic though simplified system, which could be converted into a dynamic theory through the introduction of a complicating factor. The current generation of economists have been nurtured on the equilibrium concept; they may be trying to build up a new body of economic theory by starting with the concepts they were taught, and introducing the necessary complications to secure a better fit to reality. The modern developments in mathematical economics point towards that view. But that it is the road to follow, is greatly to be doubted.

Whatever the interpretation of the equilibrium approach, it seems to be a blind alley from the point of view of business-cycle theory. There are reasons for believing that it was the concept of stable or stably-moving equilibrium as the essential trait of economic reality that was largely, if not exclusively, responsible for those theories which attribute business cycles to one factor mainly. For whenever the concept of equilibrium is in the background of the discussion, it is sufficient for the solution of the problem of business cycles to point out *one* factor which accounts for the appearance of the oscillations. There is a definite predisposition to treat the whole problem as one of deviations from a preconceived picture of reality, rather than as a complex problem requiring exhaustive treatment.

To sum up: equilibrium economics in so far as it attempts to establish the concept of persistent equilibrium is running counter to all the generalizations of business-cycle theories, with the exception of those that would make cycles a simple consequence of periodic causes outside the economic system. Its idea of stable equilibrium has no counterpart in generalized reality, unless all the dynamic factors are taken for granted. Its main field of application is the analysis of each instantaneously given economico-social event into the underlying individual acts and attitudes. But even here it runs the danger of neglecting important factors, because it is satisfied with establishing a system of equations giving a determinate solution, without being able to check the solution. The whole intellectual procedure is well adapted to a science of controlled experiment, where isolation of factors is possible (to a considerable degree) and the timeless experiment provides an immediate check, but it is dangerous in a science whose subject matter is a changing flux of complex phenomena, bound historically and exhibiting only the loosest form of regular sequences.

The general system of economics, then, that will be capable of incorporating business-cycle theory, must begin by discarding the concept of equilibrium and the implied rigid interdependence of factors. It may still begin with the assumption of current economic theory about scarcity. But instead of accepting the next postulate, that of rationality in economic behavior, it must proceed to formulate a more realistic assumption, one that would recognize the extreme diversity of behavior which we observe in reality, and would treat both secular movements and cyclical fluctuations as parts of a normal state of economic phenomena. The following sections are devoted to a brief outline of such a scheme.

IV

The essential factor could be defined as time differences, i.e., time discrepancies in economic reactions of individuals or of groups. As we shall see, the recognition of these time differences introduces the congeries of social institutions in so far as they are of determinate significance in the economic system.

The question of time differences and its importance to the body of theoretical economics has been discussed in a penetrating article by P. N. Rosenstein-Rodan.[9] The gist of his

[9] "Das Zeitmoment in der mathematischen Theorie des wirtshaftlichen Gleichgewichtes," Zeitschrift für Nationaloekonomie, vol. i, Heft 1, May 1929, pp. 129-142.

discussion follows. The general theory of economic equilibrium, i.e., the pricing theory, assumes that there exists an equilibrium price for every commodity, and a certain general equilibrium price level for the whole economic system. The nature of changes in supply and demand is then such that every disturbance provokes a reaction which compensates it and restores the equilibrium. "If we distinguish the changes which cancel themselves out into an equilibrium we find the following six movements:

1. Demand ———→ price   2. Price ———→ demand
3. Supply ———→ demand   4. Price ———→ supply
5. Supply ———→ demand   6. Demand ———→ supply

"Since changes 5 and 6 are already included in 1-4, we can confine ourselves to the consideration of only 1-4." (p. 130.)

The assumption that these four movements lead towards an equilibrium implies that each of them will work itself out in one and the same time span; that in the same time span in which demand influences price, price also influences demand; that in the same time span in which supply influences price, price also influences supply, and so on. Otherwise there would not be any equilibrium. For when prices, for example, exercise their influence upon demand faster than upon supply, at the point of time when the price (the price change) has changed demand completely and supply only partly or not at all, the complete change of demand will influence the as yet incompletely changed supply, modifying the latter, so that the change in supply which was necessary to restore the equilibrium will be modified. Thus with the assumption of a varying rhythm of movements (a disproportionality of tempi) it would be only an accident if equilibrium were restored. On the contrary it is possible that equilibrium may never be attained, i.e., that, because of the non-simultaneous rhythm of movements, there may result a certain *perpetuum mobile* of changes.

Rosenstein-Rodan then goes on to show how the time element came to be omitted in equilibrium economics. It was implicitly assumed and even explicitly stated by Pareto that the whole equilibrium system and its implications rest upon the assumption of an equal rhythm of changes. He summarizes as follows:

> We saw that the effectiveness of the balancing mechanism of supply and demand presupposes that the four movements to be considered exert their influences in an equal time span. We must therefore analyze the combination of time coefficients in order to establish whether or not we arrive at an equilibrium. Three cases are possible: 1. The time coefficients are all equal: the equilibrium is attained directly. 2. They are not equal, but become equal after several transformation periods: equilibrium is attained only after a certain period. 3. They are not immediately equal and never become so: there is never an equilibrium. Before one speaks of an equilibrium, one must at least prove that the third case is impossible. The omission of time coefficients by Pareto rests on an untenable assumption of an identical rhythm of all economic phenomena; with Jevons, on a false psychological postulate and a logical error. (Page 140.) These defects lead to the conclusion that the assumption of a general equal interdependence of all economic quantities, which has been greatly emphasized by the mathematical economists, must be abandoned. In reality there is *no general interdependence, but only variable irreversible relationships of dependence. . . .* It is well known that none of the mathematical economists could follow through consequentially the supposition of general interdependence. It is definitely abandoned in the theory of open cycles. The further working out of the mathematical system will be bound up with the theory of open cycles. (Page 142.)

So much for the general criticism and the formulation of the principle of time-span differences. Referring to real markets, Rosenstein-Rodan expresses the opinion that some markets show an equal time span for the outlined reactions of price-demand and supply while others do not.

"When we follow up and analyze the time coefficients on separate markets, we see that there are some markets on which the time coefficients are approximately equal, so that there equilibrium is really attained (e.g., on the money market). This explains why the concept of economic equilibrium is so well known and so acceptable to us. But we also see that there are other markets in which the time coefficients vary (e.g., in the 'heavy' industries, where demand influences prices more quickly than prices influence supply). This explains why in reality we do not find a pervasive state of general equilibrium" (page 134).

Before dealing with the question whether time coefficients of economic reactions in different markets, i.e., in various branches of business activity, are equal, we distinguish two aspects under which a difference in time coefficients may appear in real life. These two aspects may be briefly characterized as (1) lag and (2) disproportionality.

The phenomenon of lag is familiar to all students of economic change. Suppose that a certain disturbance arises. While it may be known to all entrepreneurs in several branches of business activity, the reaction to this disturbance will not be equally prompt in all these branches. Some will react sooner, others later. Thus, even if the time span consumed in each of these branches by a proper response to a given disturbance is the same, the fact that the response did not begin at the same time will result in a lack of equilibrium. The time coefficient should therefore include not only the time during which a certain economic reaction is manifesting itself, but also the time elapsing from the moment the disturbance occurs to the moment the response begins. The phenomena of lead and lag are thus one possible aspect of differences in time coefficients.[10]

The second aspect of differences in time coefficients is that of disproportionality. When we say that the time span of the

[10] This distinction between the difference in the dating of the response and the actual time consumed by it was noted by Rosenstein-Rodan in a footnote, but not emphasized.

economic response to a certain disturbance is different in the various branches of activity, or on the opposite sides of demand and supply in the same field, we mean that if *equal time spans* are taken, the different economic reactions are disproportional, i.e., they are not quantitatively so matched that an equilibrium will be restored. The possibility of a lack of equilibrium due to the difference in time coefficients may thus be distinguished as due either to differences in timing of the reactions or to their disproportionality.

There may, however, be another kind of disproportionality which is also important in the study of economic changes. We mention it in the present connection, although its relation to the element of time differences is rather indirect. This disproportionality is significant, because, though not in itself a source of dis-equilibrium, it is a factor which accentuates considerably the results of time differences whose two aspects we have just mentioned.

Suppose that for some reason, such as the existence of lag, a casual disturbance in one field of economic activity, say, retail trade, has resulted in a temporary lack of equilibrium, in a process of change. This latter change constitutes in turn a disturbance in the field of wholesale trade, since the influence of the original disturbance upon the supplies of retailers will constitute also a change in the demand by retailers from wholesalers. The response by wholesalers to this change in the demand from retailers may be of an equal time span with the latter. The reactions that play about the wholesale price may all be of the same time span, and the equilibrium price may be restored for the time being. Nevertheless the reaction of the supply and demand may be disproportional as far as the absolute quantities are concerned. The wholesalers' supply may not be increased in the same measure as the retailers' demand; the retailers' supply may not increase in the same measure as did the demand of consumers. The equilibrium reactions may all work out in the same time span, but they are disproportional in *their absolute magnitudes*.

This difference in the quantitative aspects of the various economic reactions would not be important if there were no possibility of a continuous lack of equilibrium. But if a lack of equilibrium can manifest itself in one branch of activity for some time, this disproportionality in the amplitude of the reactions explains how a change in one economic field will result in a greater change in a related field. This factor is obviously of the utmost importance in any theory of economic cycles. In discussing the two aspects of time differences suggested above we must keep in mind the factor of quantitative disproportionality, as one that will magnify any inequality once arisen.

We may now attempt to answer whether in observable reality the time coefficients of economic reactions are equal, among different fields or within one field on the side of supply and on the side of demand. We may ask whether in real life there is lead or lag in the different economic reactions, and whether there is equality in the time spans during which the various economic reactions to a given disturbance work themselves out.

This question can be answered in only one way. If the accumulation of empirical data about economic life teaches us anything, it is that different economic processes have different timing and varying duration. Business-cycle theories base much of their explanation of cycles precisely upon the fact that, in response to a certain disturbance, some fields of economic activity react promptly and other fields lag. If we consider the reaction of only those fields which are bound together by the supply-demand relationship, what a variety in timing and duration of the reactions presents itself! Compare the promptness with which one and the same disturbing event, equally known to all the economic groups, is responded to by the retail trade and the wholesale trade, the manufacturers of producers' goods and of consumers' goods, the long-time and the short-time money market, the stock market, the mortgage market, and so on.

But even within one and the same field conditions rarely exist under which the responses of the supply and demand forces would take place during an equal period of time. Indeed, one might say that, in modern economy, the mere fact that one group of economic forces is on the supply side and the other on the demand side spells time differences in their reactions. Thus, in the merchandising fields, the supply side is as a rule more "wholesale" than the demand side. There is a world of difference between retailers whose specialized supply activities are the exclusive source of their incomes and consumers who spread their purchases and to whom purchasing is at most an auxiliary process. An analogous difference exists between wholesalers and retailers. And in the case of producers on one side and wholesalers or any other purchasers on the other, there is the difference resulting from the time-consuming productive processes. Indeed, knowing the diversity of productive and merchandising and selling processes, one doubts that equality of time coefficients is ever attained on any market.

We see, therefore that of the three possible cases enumerated by Rosenstein-Rodan, the first, the case of equal time coefficients, is improbable. The second and third cases are more likely. In the second an initial inequality of time coefficients is in time replaced by equality which permits attainment of an equilibrium. But even this conclusion is unrealistic, mainly because of the cumulation of random changes which occurs whenever there is original inequality of time coefficients.

V

Inequality of time coefficients implies that, while the reactions to a disturbance take place, some time passes after the disturbance has occurred before equilibrium is reëstablished (if at all). Now random disturbances always occur. This means that during the period it takes the system to respond to a given disturbance and to reëstablish equilibrium, new random disturbances arise and impinge upon the economic system, adding a new ripple the moment the economic system has reacted or is reacting to the preceding random change.

With unequal time coefficients of response, a given disturbance exercises its effect unchecked for some time after it has occurred. Because of the inequality of time coefficients the initial disturbance has not been completely counteracted. The next random change which occurs adds its strength to the original disturbance or offsets it in part; the next disturbance will be added to the preceding two, and so on. Unless there is absolute equality of time coefficients there will be cumulation of random changes.

Now the *cumulation of random changes becomes in certain conditions a source of prolonged oscillations*. This thesis, developed by a Russian statistician, Eugen Slutsky, has been discussed at length in a recent article by the present writer.[11] Briefly, the argument is:

The succession of random events may be conceived as a normal frequency distribution of changes strung along the line of time. Any normal frequency distribution includes a large number of items close to the average, and a smaller number of items which deviate considerably from the average. Since we conceive the random events as changes around the equilibrium, their average is zero. In a normal frequency distribution there will be a large number of absolutely small changes and a small number of absolutely large changes. While these large changes will be infrequent, they will occur. The occurrence of large changes tends to yield cycles because the process of cumulation will extend the influence of each large change much beyond the time at which it occurred. The large change will influence the cumulative sum or the moving average so long as it is not cancelled by a succession of small changes, or by one large change of an opposite sign.

Further, the random changes, by the very nature of random frequency, will come at times in clusters of changes of the same sign. It is highly improbable that for a substantial period of time each positive change will be immediately succeeded by a cancelling negative change. Changes will come in clusters of 2, 3, 4, 5, etc. items of the same sign. Large clusters will occur

[11] "Random Events and Cyclical Oscillations," Journal of the American Statistical Association, September 1929, pp. 258-275.

less frequently than small clusters, just as large changes are less frequent than small changes. But there will be large clusters, as there will be large single changes. And the effect of cumulation is to bind each of these clusters into a high or low plateau, and to extend its influence beyond the time period occupied by the cluster itself. The cumulation or averaging of a normal frequency distribution strung along the line of time will not result in a straight smooth line, but in oscillations which are an extension of the influence of large single changes or of large clusters of changes followed by a succession of smaller changes or of smaller clusters.

This brief exposition will make more comprehensible the summary of the statistical thesis given in the article quoted above:

1. Following Professor Slutsky's exposition, it was indicated that distributions of random causes, when summated, yield oscillations similar to those characteristic of economic data.

2. It was shown that this result is due to the smoothing and carrying over power of the summation process, and to the fact that in a frequency distribution of random character we are bound to find big clusters of deviations above or below the average, or single exceptional deviations. Of these, the process of summation or of moving averages tends to make cycles. (Page 273.)

The importance of this thesis to the business-cycle theory was stated in the same article as follows:

If cycles arise from random events, assuming the summation of the latter, then we obviously do not need the hypothesis of an independent regularly recurring cause which is deemed necessary by some theorists of business cycles. Indeed, if one can explain how, in certain processes of economic life, the response to stimuli is cumulative, then the whole discussion of a cause of business cycles becomes supererogation. If the business economy runs at a certain high or low plateau level, and the conditions of business behavior are such as to cumulate favorable or unfavorable random events, then we are bound to have a cyclical up and down swing sooner or later. It is to be seen that the so-called institutional explanations of business cycles deal mainly with the economic forces that make for cumulation, with forces that explain why a given random event is not immediately cancelled by an opposite reaction but allowed to exert its influence for some time to come, an economic counterpart of the statistical mechanism of moving average. (Pages 274-275.)

The preceding discussion makes the relevance of this statistical thesis still clearer. Once we consider differences in time coefficients of response, cyclical fluctuations follow as a normal consequence.

Thus any possibility of an equilibrium becomes exceedingly remote. For the inequality in time coefficients, even if only initial, leads to the cumulation of random causes, and thus in turn accounts for cyclical fluctuations. Under these conditions a persistent state of equilibrium is completely out of the picture.

In the statistical discussion in the article quoted, it was assumed that a continuous stream of random events impinges upon the economic system. Two complications may be introduced in order to secure greater conformity of the hypothesis to reality.

1. There is a certain direction in the disturbing changes, i.e., a trend movement. For example, such outside events as technical changes, have a certain trend: their economic significance or influence tends persistently in one direction, that of lowering costs. Changes in population also are not purely random in character: they tend in one direction, that of positive growth. We may conceive the disturbing changes as belonging to a distribution skewed in one direction, one that strung out along the line of time, presents deviations not from a straight

horizontal line, but from a line that runs either upwards or downwards.

This skewness, prevalence of changes of a certain character, stands for the presence of secular movements. While the cyclical oscillations may be ascribed to the cumulation of random causes when there is inequality of time coefficients, the secular movements are due to some trend in these causes that have to be established by inductive study.

2. The second complication is that we cannot treat the stream of disturbing changes as continuously random, for the simple reason that after the cumulation of these changes has gone on for some time and has yielded an upward or downward movement of some duration, this movement in itself becomes an important factor and begins to exercise an influence which overshadows the continued play of further random changes. Since there is a trend in the changes, it is easy to conceive of the disturbances cumulating into a prolonged upward or downward movement. But once this is given in a certain field of business activity, it provides the source of rather important disproportionalities, already discussed. It forms a prolonged disturbance the response to which in related branches of activity may be much larger than in the original branch itself. It is here that all the disproportionalities discussed by a number of business-cycle theories come into play, and help to explain how a comparatively mild movement, due to cumulation of random causes arising from an inequality of time coefficients, may develop into a cyclical swing of formidable magnitude.

VI

We are now at the end of our discussion and may glance back over the field traversed. In a brief introduction we pointed out how the question of the relation between general economic theory and business-cycle theory has grown to its present importance. The recent German discussion of the question was then surveyed. We next attempted to establish that the two ways in which equilibrium economics may be regarded as not in definite contradiction to reality would be either to conceive it as valid only for each instantaneously determined timeless and changeless cross-section of economic phenomena, or to apply it to that part of reality which remains after the elimination of secular movements and of cyclical swings. The viewpoint of Rosenstein-Rodan was then presented with its emphasis on the time characteristics of economic reactions, an element disregarded by equilibrium economics. It was shown that the consideration of this time element precludes almost completely the possibility of persistent equilibrium, since reality shows a diversity of the time coefficients in their twofold aspect of timing and duration. It was further shown how this inequality of time coefficients opens the way to the cumulation of random and biased disturbances and the appearance of prolonged oscillations as a usual form of economic changes. It was indicated that the element of absolute disproportionality discussed in business-cycle theories serves to magnify and prolong the amplitude of the cyclical oscillations. And it was pointed out that the existence of a skewness in the original distribution of disturbing changes may be conceived as standing for secular movements.

Thus the introduction of the element of time does away with the strict interdependence of economic quantities and the concept of equilibrium, and substitutes for it a consistent scheme that may be taken as basis for the general theory of economic changes. According to this scheme, the economy is not a stable system which reacts to random changes by cancelling them instantaneously or after a while. It is a loosely bound congeries of social institutions, which in response to random changes goes through a series of fluctuations, a congeries that has to be studied in the main aspects of the distinguishable elements, if any understanding of changes is to be attained.

The scheme, of course, is far from complete. But it synthesizes the recent developments in general economic and business-cycle theory, and, what is more important, calls upon economic theorists to follow a more promising direction than that indicated by equilibrium economics and its equational treatment of the system. The consideration of time differences and of the consequent disproportionalities obviously invites a close study of all the distinguishable elements of the economic system, since the establishment of the quantitative differences (i.e., of the inequality of time coefficients) will require a thoroughgoing description and distinction of the various groups of economic institutions. In order to know why and how the group of retailers respond more slowly than the group of wholesalers, to know why wages move more slowly than profits, one has to study the different social groups and their manifestations. The different types of reaction, conditioned by such factors as are studied in business-cycle theory, banking theory, monetary theory and so on—all these results of empirical study will have to be assembled and thoroughly organized into a generalized description of the various types of economic reaction. Connected with it will be the investigation of secular factors, i.e., of the *direction* of disturbing events in the different fields from which changes may come to influence the course of economic life.

The scheme presented may seem to involve a sacrifice of a number of definite achievements of equilibrium economics. Instead of a system we are likely to find ourselves with a chaotic description. Yet it should be kept in mind that we still retain, even though in qualified form, all relations of dependence of which equilibrium economics speaks. But for the notion of a stable or slowly varying equilibrium and the equational system of solving economic problems is substituted a general recognition of the importance of the time element—a recognition that permits the utilization of the results of various special investigations in a more complex and more realistic theory of economic change.

2

STATIC AND DYNAMIC
ECONOMICS *

Static economics deals with relations and processes on the assumption of uniformity and persistence of either the absolute or relative economic quantities involved. In contrast, dynamic economics deals with relations and processes on the assumption of change in either the absolute or the relative economic quantities. A narrower distinction is suggested by the analogy which Jevons employed so conspicuously with static and dynamic mechanics. In this sense, statics would deal with the relation of forces at the equilibrium level, dynamics with the same relations in the changes that lead towards equilibrium. But these two categories of Jevons are both types of static economics under the broader definition above. For our purposes, this broader definition is to be preferred.

While there may be agreement with this definition of static and dynamic economics, there is confusion as to the actual scope and relation of these two bodies. According to the economists of the past and to most of their followers of the present, static economics is a direct stepping stone to the dynamic system, and may be converted into the latter by the introduction of the element of change. Or, putting it technically, we have first to establish the factors and conditions of economic equilibrium, and only then can we study both the transitory and

* Reprinted by permission from the *American Economic Review*, Vol. XX, no. 3, September 1930, pp. 426-441. The present version omits the initial and the concluding few paragraphs.

the secular changes as deviations from that equilibrium. According to other economists, the body of economic theory must be cardinally rebuilt if dynamic problems are to be treated efficiently. The method of organization and possibly even the factors to be considered in the economics of change are entirely different from those of traditional economic theory. It is to this question of the proper relation between traditional theory and the problems of economic change that the discussion below is devoted.

I

This relation might be perceived by examining the function which static theory has heretofore performed. What has been the scope of its problems, the precise nature of its analysis and explanations?

Traditional economic theory is primarily a reduction of social phenomena to the individual actions of which they are compounded. It selects social phenomena such as prices, wages, interest, capital, wealth, profits, etc., and states: Here are phenomena that we observe and distinguish because each possesses characteristics not repeated in the others. What are the factors that determine these phenomena? Static economics seeks the answer to this question either in some other social phenomenon or, eventually, in the activities of individuals. Thus, the marginal utility theory explains the social phenomenon of price largely in terms of the individual's valuation of sacrifice and satisfaction. With the labor value theory it is productive efforts of individuals that lie at the base of price relations. Wages are explained in terms of the individual's subsistence cost; interest, in terms of reward for abstinence or waiting; and so on. In the more recent variants, welfare economics leads directly from the social phenomena to individual choices and valuations, while price economics, in its circle of reasoning from present to past prices, emphasizes the individual's or firm's actions as the important link.

Two features of this type of explanation should be noted in

order to present a fuller picture of at least the kernel of static economics.

(1) Of the three groups of factors that actually condition any economic phenomenon—man, nature, and the state of the arts—only man and his activities are given a prominent place. Nature and the state of the arts are assumed to be unchanging and unresponsive, and man is the active unit in social phenomena. But on this assumption, static economics becomes essentially: (a) a theory of human behavior, which in its generalizations deals with matters so vague as to be susceptible of interpretive distortion and not susceptible to exact inductive tests; (b) a social philosophy, since its main task is the reduction of the complex and often incomprehensible social phenomena to the much more comprehensible terms of the activity of each and every individual. The Robinson Crusoe tales of classical economists were naïve in that they overlooked the socially conditioned character of the individual's actions; but they did represent truly the main function of static economic theory, the reduction of the social phenomenon to the level of the individual.

(2) Further, traditional economics made use of individual activity as the unit underlying social phenomena so as to show how the several social phenomena, so different on the surface, are directly related. The same active element of individual activity which made a determinate social event possible within the assumed fixity of goods and of the state of the arts, also bound together the various social phenomena, such as wages, profits, interest, amount of capital, number of workers, and every other factor in the problem. The great service of the mathematical school particularly consists in bringing out clearly this interdependence among the various economic entities.

In addition to enumerating different social phenomena and demonstrating their reducibility to the factor of individual activity which binds these phenomena together, static economics deduces or assumes certain features of these phenomena, which it treats as self-evident. Such features are, *e.g.,* the equality of prices, and the mobility of capital and labor. One of the reasons for the intricacy of static economic theory is the reconciliation of a single principle of individual activity with the variety of social phenomena, under conditions in which the constituent factors possess definite characteristics. Consider the ingenuity which had to be used in reconciling the labor theory of value with the equality in the rate of profit among various industries, or on the task of squaring the theory of pleasure and pain with the behavior of prices of reproducible goods.

The reduction of social phenomena to the individual activities that determine them, the demonstration that the various economic entities are interconnected through these activities, and display persistent characteristics amidst the variety of their concrete manifestations—this analysis is the kernel, the essence of static economic theory. It is primarily an intellectual construction which shows how the "social" arises from the "individual."

Of course, the treatises on theoretical economics did not confine themselves solely to this analysis. The other parts of the discussion, in so far as they constitute theory (*i.e.*, excluding historical introductions, concrete illustrations, etc.), consist mostly of the application of the static schemes worked out. Among the uses to which these schemes have been put, three groups may be distinguished.

(1) Tracing the significance of certain "interventionist" changes, such as taxes, tariffs, etc. The Physiocratic *tableau économique* had, as one of its major purposes, the location of the source from which taxes might properly be drawn, and appraisal of the significance of both internal and external barriers of trade. And taking a jump in time, one might say that the primary application of the schemes of mathematical economics has been in connection with the problems of tariffs, taxes, and monopoly. Reference should also be made to the rôle which the discussion of probable effects of the repeal of the Corn laws in England played in working out the integrated theoretical system of Ricardian economics.

(2) The problem of ethical judgment. Since the distinguishable social phenomena are expressions of the activity of various social groups, and the problem of distribution is one of the apportionment of the social product, the ethical significance of the analysis of static theory is obvious. For the reduction of the social phenomena to individual or group efforts passes an implicit judgment on the ethical rightness of the social order under discussion.[1] The strength of this element in the Marxian analysis is quite obvious, even though the analysis is supposed to form a scientific system, *i.e.*, a system oriented only to persistent tendencies defined as truth by the rules of scientific inquiry. The obvious usefulness of static analysis from the ethical point of view is stated explicitly by J. B. Clark in his *Distribution of Wealth.*

(3) The problem of change. This use of static schemes is especially interesting in the present connection, because it constitutes an approach to dynamic economics by a direct complication of the theoretical system heretofore developed. This is usually attempted in the form of postulating the source and some general feature of a process of change, and then working out the implication within the static system. The most conspicuous example of such an attempt is probably the analysis of long-run economic development undertaken by Ricardo which used the Malthusian principle of population. Malthus' law of population growth (and possibly the accumulation of capital as a secondary process) was almost the only general notion of change that Ricardo had explicitly in view, although in the process of arriving at its consequences he had to pass judgment on other probable changes to the extent of declaring them subordinate to this one important principle of population growth. But the procedure is typical of other attempts. Thus the numerous single factor explanations of business cycles are of the same logical character: they postulate the existence of the static system on the one hand, the influence of one disturbing factor on the other, and "deduce" the cyclical swings

[1] This does not apply to static systems which stay completely on the level of prices (H. J. Davenport or some of the Mathematical School).

as the working out of the single disturbing factor. And, just as Ricardo assumes all other secular tendencies to be subordinate to growth of population according to the Malthusian law, so these business cycle economists assume all the other factors making for cyclical oscillations subordinate to the one disturbing factor they choose to emphasize. Closer analysis will show, however, that such uses represent a departure from some of the cardinal principles of static economics.[2]

It is important to note that these uses of the static scheme in application to the solution of problems of change, have been among the earliest and most unsuccessful. The long-time forecast of Ricardo is one of the glaring examples of failure which is likely to follow an application of the scheme to dynamic problems in the only way in which a static scheme can be applied with definite results, viz. by posing changes of one and only one factor. The inadequacy of business cycle explanations, based on attempts to modify static theory to make it agree better with a changing and fluctuating reality, has long since become patent.

If traditional economic theory is essentially a study of the relations between individual activity and the resulting social phenomena, both taken at a given instant of time (or under stable conditions), what is the content of dynamic economics? We can say less about dynamic economics, since it is not as yet developed. A tentative description, however, may be attempted.

The major preoccupation of dynamic economics is with the study of changes in the social phenomena over historical time. It deals with social phenomena, without descending to the level of individual activity, unless it can be established that changes in individual behavior are important factors in the movements of social phenomena over time. The task of dynamic economics is first and foremost that of ascertaining the exact course of social changes, and of distilling, if possible,

[2] See the article by the present writer, "Equilibrium Economics and Business Cycle Theory," *Quarterly Journal of Economics*, May, 1930, pp. 381-415. Reprinted in this volume, pp. 3-31.

some general characteristics of these changes either in a given social phenomenon in the course of time, or in the relations among various social phenomena. Such changes, once established, must be explained. It is at this point that dynamic economics may reconsider some of the factors used by static economics to explain how a social phenomenon "arose" or was "determined," and thus it may again consider the element of individual activity. But in dynamic economics, as far as one can see at present, this recourse to explanation in terms of individual activity is not the essence of the theoretical scheme as it is in traditional economic theory, since individual activity (human nature) instead of being the unifying principle, becomes only one of the several factors in social change.

II

How can the relations between the individual and society established in static economics be used in any analysis of economic movements? Of what use will the static interconnections among the various groups of social phenomena be in the study of economic change?

This question has been discussed in the article referred to above, but a restatement of the answer may be given here.

We saw that static economics emphasizes the activity of men as determining social phenomena, men acting in conditions fixed by a given state of nature and the technical arts. But in any discussion of changes over time, the state of the arts and of nature do not remain stable, and the study of these changing conditions becomes in itself one of the major tasks of dynamic economics. It is not enough, as it is done in static economics, merely to note differences in quality among land areas or in the state of the technical arts among industries. Nature and the technical arts must be considered in greater detail in order to see what determines the course of changes which take place in them. In dynamic economics it is important to grasp clearly the congeries of conditions formed by the technological elements in the economic system.

This study of the conditioning factors is, however, only supplementary to the discussion of static economics, and it is exactly as such that traditional economists conceive dynamic economics. In this use the static scheme remains the base of the study of changes, for the rules of human behavior and the interrelations among economic entities retain their character, and changes take place only in the technical conditions of human activity.

Yet we can hardly use the generalizations concerning individual behavior evolved in static economics to solve its problem of decomposing the social phenomena. Just as one must assume the other factors (land and the state of arts) inert and stable, one must also posit individual activity as ruled exclusively by motives that make it extremely mobile, allowing it to fill out the space left by the conditioning factors, thus making possible an unequivocal determination of the social phenomena. In reducing social phenomena to individual activity, one can not allow any significant variations in the motives and types of response of the latter, unless the analysis is to be left incomplete by reducing social phenomena to unconnected social groups rather than to the mobile, all-connecting, individual unit (see Cairnes's "non-competing" groups, as an example of an incomplete analysis).

This rigidity, which must be attributed to the factor of human behavior in static economics, makes the scheme unsuitable for explaining changes in social phenomena. With its full acceptance, the sources of change would have to be sought in non-human factors exclusively, since the behavior of individuals within society is assumed to be ruled by unchangeable rules in response to the stimuli provided by the changing reality.

This stricture relates to the human element as presented by the static scheme. One may also take exception to the assumption that there is close interdependence among the various social phenomena—the "closed" character of the static system. It is essential in dynamic theory to assume not only that the absolute economic quantities change, but also that

their relations change. Just as it would be unwise to accept a
rigidly defined norm of human behavior when seeking changes
in the pattern of economic behavior caused by changing environment, so also would it be unwise to accept the cardinal
assumption of rigid interdependence among social phenomena
in a study attempting to establish changes in this dependence.
Such an acceptance would imply that the movements themselves can take place only in the conditioning constants, an
unnecessary limitation of the scope of dynamic economics.

Thus far we have considered the confining influence of the
static scheme when used as a base for the explanation of problems of dynamics. But it has been tacitly assumed that while
reducing the social phenomena to individual activities, static
economics succeeded in describing and analyzing all important
varieties of social phenomena, including the habits of various
social groups. Even though in its analysis it is confined to the
acceptance of only one type of economic behavior, static theory
may have encompassed various types of social behavior in its
qualifications. We assumed so far that static economics has
done a complete and exhaustive job, and is limited in its use
only on the score of the essential rigidity assumed in its analysis, rather than on the score of incompleteness.

But static analysis is necessarily incomplete, since it cannot
deal with varieties of behavior of even the most important
social groups. This is in a way an unavoidable consequence
of the static point of view. The demand for realism requires
consideration of the outstanding, most important differences in
the economic-social phenomena, and the tracing of these differences either to differences in human behavior or to differences
in conditions, or to both. But exposition and analysis presented
in static economics are essentially those of social philosophy,
propositions that are not subject to precise check. The central
problem is to reduce the complex known to the simple familiar.
The usual practice is to take certain traits of social phenomena
that stand out unmistakably and clearly, known by direct observation only and try to explain them as manifestations of
familiar, indisputable tendencies in human behavior.

The dangers of incompleteness in such a performance are patent, since the static character of the problem does not permit exact observation. Any observation of reality is necessarily a measure of change, and it is impossible to secure, in empirical terms, the static picture of a complex reality. The analysis of the static scheme necessarily presents only a meager list of factors to explain any observed course of changes.

So far only past economic theory has been discussed. But what of the static theory of the future? One hesitates to say anything definite. It may develop a broader concept of economic behavior and may succeed in distinguishing the habits of various socio-economic groups. It is possible that mathematical economics in its current phase will work out various types of equilibria and succeed in taking account of differences in response both to given stimuli and to judgments of the future. This will mean that present theory will be enriched by empirical data derived from observation of reality. But as long as static economics remains a strictly unified system based upon the concept of equilibrium, and continues to reduce the social phenomenon to levels of rigidly defined individual behavior, its analytic content will remain of little use in a system of dynamic economics.

Current critics of economic theory often point out its lack of realism, and suggest that a closer observation of actual life and the utilization of additional inductive materials will remedy the situation. But it is important to realize that as long as static theory remains a *system* (as distinct from a set of descriptive chapters) centered in the concept of equilibrium, with individual activity as the unit, it will necessarily remain a distorted picture of *changing* reality. It can be made more plausible but it will always be a scheme of social philosophy or of evaluation of disturbances in a system assumed to be persistent and timeless. The realistic diversity of social groups and of types of conditions is hardly compatible with the rigidity and analytic value of an equilibrium scheme.

To sum up: it is true that the element of empirical generalization and analysis contained in traditional economic theory is of some value for the purpose of explaining problems of change. The singling out of the most important groups of social phenomena, the attempt to show their interconnection, the broad generalization about human behavior and the interaction of individuals, the groups of conditioning factors singled out, all these parts of a static scheme are usually derived from observation of economic life and are thus likely to yield results of some value. But the static scheme in its entirety, in the essence of its approach, is neither a basis, nor a stepping stone towards a proper treatment of dynamic problems. It may provide some clues for dynamics, but its list of factors is incomplete, its emphasis is misleading, and its essential analytic part, its principle of organization must be discarded if the otherwise difficult problem of analysis of economic change is not to be made deceptively simple in the short run, and all the more difficult of handling in the long run.

III

The distinction drawn above between static and dynamic economic theory is useful in itself, as distinguishing sharply between two types of approach, two different sets of problems. But it is also useful for its implications. These implications concern questions which have led to some discussion lately, and it is hoped that the distinction drawn may clarify matters. The first implication concerns the use of the quantitative method; [3] the second, the seemingly unsatisfactory service of quantitative studies in throwing light upon social problems.

Each theoretical system contains empirical elements drawn into certain relationships by statements of a higher order general validity. Static economics contains some empirical elements, many of which appear in qualifications rather than as content of generalizations. But inductive and especially quantitative study can have only limited significance for static economics.

[3] See *e.g.*, The round table discussion, *Proceedings* of the American Economic Association, no. 1, March, 1928, pp. 28-46.

Statistical studies have often been characterized, especially by the adherents of the mathematical school, as complements to economic theory. If by economic theory we understand the static scheme, statistical study may provide it with starting points and with qualifications of its general statements about social phenomena, but never with a complement, and very rarely with a check. It is obvious that the basic task of static economics, e.g. the translation of a given set of prices to underlying individual valuations, is impossible as a problem of inductive quantitative research. The curves of supply and demand deduced from statistical data are summaries of historical experience, and are not free from dynamic changes, thus making it impossible to measure the manifestations of the balance of supply and demand with which static theory deals. Even were it possible to isolate exhaustively the dynamic elements in a time series or in any other set of data, in order to provide either a measurement or a test of the static scheme, it would first be necessary to know fairly definitely what the dynamic elements are—and we do not know them. All our quantitative data refer to a changing reality, and therefore any possibility of using them in the static scheme, other than for illustration, is contingent upon our precise knowledge of dynamic processes. This, to repeat, does not apply to the purely descriptive or illustrative material used to specify and qualify the general statement of economic reality with which static economics may start. But as far as the connections and relations drawn by static economics, *i.e.*, the analytic part itself is concerned, quantitative research can be neither a complement, a test, nor a basis for application.

In the case of dynamic economics the situation is almost the exact opposite. Whereas in conventional economic theory of the past, the theorist generalized about phenomena that were fairly well within the scope of his individual observation, and were, superficially at least, self-evident, in the study of changes such unarmed observation is of minor importance. One can observe in a general fashion the growth of industry or fluctuations of business conditions; one can sense the existence of broad change: but all too soon it becomes obvious that the projection of a few broad movements which an economist can observe during his generation is scant basis for the study of changes. One may arrive at the theoretical need for dynamic economics by an armchair analysis of the static scheme, for its limitations are obvious even when compared with generally observed reality. But in order to progress, dynamic economics must measure the changes that are its raw material.

The task of establishing general tendencies, is much more formidable in dynamic economics than it ever was in static economics. The former had to wait until the methods of establishing the stable and recurring elements in the manifold variety of everyday facts were sufficiently developed to yield that inductive material with which the dynamic economic theory has to deal. It is in this connection that the importance of the quantitative method in dynamic economics emerges most clearly. Without the means to measure changes, dynamic economics would be reduced to a search for the laws of history similar to that of the early Historical School. The study of qualitative changes can deal only with the broad aspects and clearly distinguished fields of activity. It can never measure the degree of change, and thus bars attempts at establishing general movements within homogeneous fields where the promise of valid generalizations is the greatest.

The quantitative approach not only enriches the body of inductive knowledge with which dynamic economics starts, but it also gives promise of a preliminary transformation of the variegated stuff of changing reality into more or less established inductive generalizations. It is small wonder, therefore, that the development of dynamic economics had to wait for the creation of a body of analytic methods for dealing with quantitative data, and that, unlike static economics, it lays such heavy emphasis upon statistical research.

In the discussion around the quantitative method, adherents of the classical or mathematical approach are quite right in dwelling upon the limited contribution of this method in the present stage of development of economic theory. To the essential function of traditional economic theory, that of showing the individual factors underlying social phenomena, and the interrelations which the activities of individuals driven by certain motives impose upon the various fields of economic performance, quantitative research is of little relevance. In a system of social philosophy, only some starting points and a notion as to the limited character of the conclusions can be derived from statistical, and other empirical, studies. It is in dynamic economics that the latter are important, for there they provide significant records of observed reality.

This leads us to the other implication—the unsatisfactory character of quantitative method from the point of view of conventional economic theory. It is clear that to the economists of the past century and to most of the economists of today, the static scheme of economics provided a tool that no quantitative research can replace. The system of social philosophy which is built up in the form of a theoretical economic system answers questions as to the probable effect of interventionist changes, provides a basis for discussion of ethical implications, permits the passing of judgment upon the desirability of this or that public measure. True, the basis of these judgments is precarious, for the simple reason that they concern proposed changes in real life, and that the theoretical scheme upon which such judgments are based may well neglect or misconceive the weights of the real forces. But with all its limitations the system assures the possibility of giving definite answers. In connection with any practical question, the proponent of a scheme of static economics is capable of building up *ad hoc* the necessary amount of specific inductive data, and by applying the laws of interconnections among phenomena and of response of individual activity to certain changes can obtain definite answers.

To such uses of a theoretical scheme, be its result a verdict of moral rectitude passed on a social order, or a forecast that a definite tax will be shifted in a certain way, or an argument that the burden of foreign debts is borne in such and such a way, there is no parallel in studies produced at present by the application of quantitative methods. Dynamic economics is, as yet, in the stage where it is more important to establish facts and to bring out the broad underlying tendencies than aim at establishing persistent relations to be used for prognoses of the future, tracing social implications, etc. So far quantitative research is mostly a process of accumulating partial inductive inferences, and the theoretical system of dynamic economics can be built up only piece by piece. Within some fields there has already accumulated a sufficient body of generalizations to make possible tentative applications. But even in the oldest, the field of business cycles, the body of organized inductive materials is far from sufficient. In other fields accumulation has hardly been started.

The theoretical economists of today are, therefore, quite right when they attack the quantitative approach as irrelevant to static theory and as of doubtful fruitfulness. It is an unsatisfactory approach if one wishes some basis for providing definite answers to questions of social desirability or social effects of a certain change. Such a criticism, however, overlooks two considerations. First, in preparing the ground for solving practical problems, the quantitative method cannot be neglected. Many an economist would profit by knowing the different factors at play and the various groups of changes already marked out by quantitative investigators. Second, the potential fruitfulness of the method will materialize only after the body of inductive data has been accumulated and analyzed and after the ground has been prepared for whatever systematic construction is to take place.

3

RELATION BETWEEN CAPITAL GOODS AND FINISHED PRODUCTS IN THE BUSINESS CYCLE *

INTRODUCTION

The present essay examines at length the relation between the demand for finished products and the demand for capital goods,[1] as it was first formulated by J. M. Clark [2] and has since found considerable currency in business-cycle theory. The formulation given by Clark and adopted, fully or partly, by others, suggests: that the demand for capital goods is likely to move with the *rate of change* in the demand for finished

---

* Reprinted by permission from *Economic Essays in Honor of Wesley Clair Mitchell*, Columbia University Press, New York 1934, pp. 211-267.

[1] The terms "finished products" and "capital goods" are used in the present discussion not in an absolute sense, but as relative to each specific link in the buying-selling relations that run through the economic system. Capital goods are thus raw materials, machinery, buildings, and any other commodity which an entrepreneur needs to produce what from his standpoint is the finished product. What are finished products to a given entrepreneur may obviously be capital goods to another entrepreneur. Similarly, "production" is used in the broadest sense, to include not only manufacturing and extracting industries, but also transportation, trade, and service.

[2] First stated in "Business Acceleration and the Law of Demand," *Journal of Political Economy*, XXV (March, 1917), 217-35; also in *Economics of Overhead Costs* (University of Chicago Press, 1923), pp. 389-94; and most recently in *Strategic Factors in Business Cycles* (National Bureau of Economic Research, 1934), pp. 33-35, 41-44. See also the controversy with Ragnar Frisch, *Journal of Political Economy*, October, December, 1931, April, 1932.

products, rather than with the *absolute volume* of the latter; that, for this reason, fluctuations in the demand for capital goods are likely to precede changes in the demand for finished products and exhibit a wider amplitude; that the relation thus stated accounts for such attributes of the business cycle as the lead and wider amplitude of cycles in producers' goods as compared with the swings in consumers' goods; and, finally, that the interaction of demand for finished products and of the demand for capital goods provides an effective explanation of the business cycle, given an initial change in the rate of movement of the demand for finished products.

Before being examined, the hypothesis must be stated more precisely than is usually the case; and its application to the behavior of demand for various types of capital goods must be clearly shown. Such an exposition is attempted in the first section of the essay. The second and third sections are devoted to an analysis of the basic features of the hypothesis in the light of a general knowledge of economic institutions. A more extended treatment of one of the problems arising in the discussion in the second section, and a statistical test of the hypothesis are presented in Appendices A and B respectively. The fourth, and final section summarizes the analytical discussion of the second and third sections and the statistical evidence of Appendix B.

I. Schematic Presentation of the Relation of Demand for Capital Goods to the Demand for Finished Products

ASSUMPTIONS OF THE DISCUSSIONS

In formulating the relation between demand for finished products and demand for capital goods in accordance with the Clark hypothesis, rigid assumptions will be made, some in order to clarify the exposition, and others in order to remove the influence of factors that are not considered an integral part of the theoretical scheme developed. The assumptions adhered to throughout this section are as follows:

1. The demand for both finished products and capital goods is measured in value units, at constant price levels.

2. Each illustrative case below deals with a single group of capital goods, related not to the total value of demand for finished products, but only to that part of this latter demand which is satisfied by the utilization of the particular group of capital goods in question. For the sake of brevity, the part of the finished product attributable to the capital goods in question is referred to below by the general term "finished product."

3. A cyclical swing in the demand for finished products is assumed, as one of a series of similar swings.

4. The demand for new units of capital goods becomes apparent concurrently with the demand for finished products.

5. Replacement demand for capital goods becomes apparent at the completion of the time unit during which consumption of the capital goods has taken place: i.e., at the beginning of the next time unit.

6. Both demand for finished goods and demand for capital goods are satisfied within the time unit in which such demand becomes apparent. Thus, demand for finished products and for capital goods becomes identical with their production.

7. There is a necessary ratio between the stock of capital goods and current production (demand for finished products); and this ratio remains constant in time.

Obviously, assumptions 2 to 5 are in the nature of specifications intended to render the schematic exposition below unambiguous. Assumptions 1 and 6 express a definite and conscious neglect of some important factors in determining the demand for capital goods—price changes, the period of production, credit availability, and so forth. Assumption 7 is basic to Clark's hypothesis, and is a cornerstone in the derivation of that peculiar relation between demand for finished products and the demand for capital goods which renders it particularly important in business-cycle theory.

CAPITAL GOODS OF ETERNAL LIFE

We begin with a group of capital goods which have eternal life and, therefore, infinite use over time. Land of a certain type may serve as a good practical example, although actually, of course, the period of service of no capital good is interminable. For such capital goods the replacement demand is zero, and the demand takes the form of a demand for additional units only. The relation between the demand for such capital goods and the demand for finished products thus shows clearly the effect of changes in the latter upon the demand for additional units of *any* capital good.

Case Ia

DEMAND FOR CAPITAL GOODS OF INFINITE USE IN TIME
(DEMAND FOR ADDITIONAL UNITS ONLY OF ANY CAPITAL GOOD)

Assumption: Stock of capital goods is to current production (demand for finished products) as 10 is to 1.

Time Unit	Demand for Finished Products	Changes in Demand for Finished Products	Stock of Capital Goods Needed (2) x 10	Stock of Capital Goods Available (Beginning of Time Unit) a	Capital Goods Consumed	Total Demand for Capital Goods (4)−(5)	Replacement Demand for Capital Goods b	Demand for Additional Units of Capital Goods (7)−(8)
(1)	(2)	(3)	(4)	(5)	(6)	(7)	(8)	(9)
1	92	0	920	920	0	0	0	0
2	96	4	960	920	0	40	0	40
3	100	4	1,000	960	0	40	0	40
4	108	8	1,080	1,000	0	80	0	80
5	114	6	1,140	1,080	0	60	0	60
6	114	0	1,140	1,140	0	0	0	0
7	108	—6	1,080	1,140	0	—60	0	—60
8	100	—8	1,000	1,080	0	—80	0	—80
9	96	—4	960	1,000	0	—40	0	—40
10	92	—4	920	960	0	—40	0	—40

a Equal to stock in column 4 in preceding time unit, minus the entry in column 6 during preceding time unit.

b Equal to entry in column 6 during preceding time unit.

In Case 1a, the demand for capital goods moves quite differently from the demand for finished products from which it has been derived. The absolute magnitude of the demand for capital goods is ten times as large as that of net changes in demand for finished products (columns 3 and 7). The turning points in the demand for capital goods precede those in the demand for finished products; the absolute amplitude of the former (as measured by the total change from trough to peak to trough) is appreciably wider than the absolute amplitude in the latter (320 and 44); and, finally, the relative amplitude of changes in the demand for capital goods (as measured by percentage rise and decline from peak) is much wider than the relative amplitude of changes in demand for finished products (400 percent and 37 percent).

Under the assumptions of Case 1a, the absolute magnitude of the demand for capital goods and the timing and amplitude of its changes are determined by two factors: (1) the ratio of the stock of capital goods to the demand for finished products; (2) the character of changes in the demand for finished products. The variations in the ratio will affect the absolute magnitude and the absolute amplitude of changes in the demand for capital goods, but not the timing of these changes, nor the relative amplitude of fluctuations. Thus, if, in the example above, a ratio of 1 to 1 were assumed instead of the ratio 10 to 1, the values in column 7 would be 0, $+4$, $+4$, $+8$, etc., instead of 0, $+40$, $+40$, $+80$, etc. The absolute magnitude of the demand for capital goods, and the absolute amplitude of its fluctuations would be one-tenth as large. But the turning points in the new series of demand for capital goods and the percentage amplitude of fluctuations would be the same as in the example.

The timing and relative amplitude of changes in the demand for capital goods are, under the conditions of Case 1a, affected only by the character of changes in the demand for finished products. As one or another function of time is used to characterize variations in this latter demand, the comparative timing and relative amplitude of changes in the demand for capital goods are predetermined. We could choose any one of a large number of such functions and compare its movement with the movement of its first differences: the comparison would yield the relation of demand for finished products and for capital goods in regard to timing and relative amplitude of changes in both.

In the example above, a time unit was used without specifying whether it was a decade, a year, a month, or a week. However, both the changes over time in the demand for finished products and the constant ratio of the stock of capital goods to the volume of current production may be affected by the size of the time unit employed to measure changes in the two types of demand. This appears clearly in the illustrative case below, in which we assume a time unit twice as long as that in Case 1a, and reproduce only columns 1, 2, 3, 4, and 7 of Case 1a.

CASE 1b

DEMAND FOR CAPITAL GOODS OF INFINITE USE IN TIME
(DEMAND FOR ADDITIONAL UNITS OF ANY CAPITAL GOOD)

Assumption: The time unit taken is twice as long as in Case 1a.

Time Unit	Demand for Finished Products	Changes in Demand for Finished Products	Stock of Capital Goods Needed	Demand for Capital Goods
(1)	(2)	(3)	(4)	(5)
(1+ 2)	188	0	940	0
(3+ 4)	208	20	1,040	100
(5+ 6)	228	20	1,140	100
(7+ 8)	208	—20	1,040	—100
(9+10)	188	—20	940	—100

The lengthening of the time unit of observation has resulted in a smaller ratio of the stock of capital goods to volume of current production. Consequently, the magnification of changes in the demand for capital goods has been cut in half. Similarly, while the absolute amplitude of changes in the demand for capital goods is wider in Case 1b than in Case 1a (400 instead of 320), the absolute amplitude of changes in the demand for finished products has widened still more (80 instead of 44). The timing disparity between changes in the two types of demand disappears completely. The relative amplitude of changes in the demand for capital goods is the same in both cases, but the relative amplitude of changes in the demand for finished products is somewhat narrower in Case 1b than in Case 1a (35 percent instead of 37 percent).

A similar calculation might be made with a time unit shorter than that used in Case 1a. One obvious change would be the rise in the ratio of the stock of capital goods to the current volume of production, resulting in a corresponding increase in the ratio of the absolute magnitude of the demand for capital goods to changes in the demand for finished products; and, similarly, in an increase in the ratio of the absolute amplitude of changes in demand for capital goods to the same amplitude in demand for finished products. But the timing relationship of the two types of demand, and the ratio of their relative amplitudes, would depend directly upon the character of the interpolating function used to read off the ordinates of the demand for finished products along a more detailed time scale.

As noted above, the scheme so far developed applies to the demand for additional units of any capital good, be it durable equipment such as machinery or buildings, raw materials, or inventories of finished goods in the hands of producers or distributors. Various types of capital goods differ in the size of the constant ratio to the demand for finished products. But the size of this ratio does not affect the peculiar relation that exists between changes in the two types of demand in respect of timing and relative amplitude. Therefore, if the assumption of the constancy of the ratio is accepted, fluctuations in the demand for additional units of *any* capital good are likely to precede and be of a much wider relative amplitude than the fluctuations in primary demand. If this be the essence of Clark's hypothesis, the important differences in behavior of demand among various types of capital goods do not originate in the demand for additional units, but in replacement demand.

FULLY CONSUMABLE CAPITAL GOODS

In respect of replacement demand, two groups of capital goods may be distinguished: in one, industrial and trade stocks, replacement demand is equal to the production of the finished product; in the other, such as buildings and machinery, no such simple and direct relation exists between replacement demand and output of the finished product. The first group may, in turn, be subdivided into: (*a*) all those capital goods the stock of which is in a ratio of 1 to 1 to the volume of current production; (*b*) those capital goods for which this ratio is above 1.

In group (*a*), we find capital goods that are fully consumed within the period of production. For such goods, the replacement demand is equal to the volume of current production within the immediately preceding time unit; while the demand for additional units of capital goods is equal to the successive changes in the demand for finished products. As a result the two types of demand move in an exactly similar fashion, as appears in Case 2.

Cases 2 and 1a illustrate the limits within which the acceleration and magnification of the demand for capital goods may range. In Case 1a, demand for additional units only was present, and the *rate of change* in the demand for finished goods was the dominating factor. In the present case, total demand for capital goods reproduces exactly the *absolute volume* of the demand for finished products. All other cases will obviously lie between the two extremes of Cases 1a and 2. It should be noted that both limiting cases are rarely represented in reality: there are practically no concrete capital goods of infinite life, and there are very few capital goods that are held in stock in an amount just sufficient for the next period of production.

CASE 2

DEMAND FOR FULLY CONSUMABLE CAPITAL GOODS

Assumption: Stock of capital goods is to current production as 1 is to 1.

Time Unit	Demand for Finished Products	Changes in Demand for Finished Products	Stock of Capital Goods Needed	Stock of Capital Goods Available (Beginning of Time Unit)[a]	Capital Goods Consumed	Total Demand for Capital Goods	Replacement Demand for Capital Goods[b]	Demand for Additional Units of Capital Goods
(1)	(2)	(3)	(4)	(5)	(6)	(7)	(8)	(9)
1	92	0	92	0	92	92	92	0
2	96	4	96	0	96	96	92	4
3	100	4	100	0	100	100	96	4
4	108	8	108	0	108	108	100	8
5	114	6	114	0	114	114	108	6
6	114	0	114	0	114	114	114	0
7	108	—6	108	0	108	108	114	—6
8	100	—8	100	0	100	100	108	—8
9	96	—4	96	0	96	96	100	—4
10	92	—4	92	0	92	92	96	—4

[a] Equal to stock in column 4 in preceding time unit, minus the entry in column 6 during preceding time unit.

[b] Equal to entry in column 6 during preceding time unit.

PARTLY CONSUMABLE CAPITAL GOODS—DIVISIBLE UNITS

Physical consumability or perishability should not be confused with economic consumability or perishability. For a large group of capital goods destruction in the process of production is fully equal to current production, but a stock is always left at the completion of the production process. The physical identity of this stock changes constantly, of course, but its economic identity remains the same. Such capital goods, comprising largely raw materials and finished goods in the hands of producers and distributors, belong obviously to group (*b*). The movement of the total demand for this group is illustrated in Case 3.

In the particular example in Case 3, significant differences appear between the movements in the demand for finished products and those in the demand for capital goods (columns 2 and 7). The peak and trough in column 7 are reached earlier than in column 2, while the absolute and relative amplitude of changes in the former are wider than in the latter. But some of these results are obviously dependent upon the particular changes assumed in the demand for finished products and upon the specific size of the ratio of the stock of capital goods to current output.

A general analysis of this case is presented by Ragnar Frisch,[3] who assumes that replacement demand is equal to the volume of finished products in the immediately preceding unit of time. We may therefore quote his conclusions, substituting for his terms "consumer-taking" and "capital-production" our broader pair of terms "demand for finished products" and "demand for capital goods."

> Formula . . . indicates the two parts of which total demand for capital goods is made up. In the first place we have the part . . . that represents demand for replacement purposes. This part is (under our simplified assumption) proportional to the size of the demand for finished products. In the second place, we have the part . . . representing demand for expansion purposes (additional

[3] See "The Interrelation between Capital Production and Consumer-Taking," *Journal of Political Economy*, XXXIX (October, 1931), 646–54. Frisch assumes that replacement demand is proportional to the stock of capital goods existing at any given moment of time, and hence proportional to the volume of demand for finished products (consumer-taking) in the immediately preceding unit of time. In studying Frisch's conclusions it must be remembered that they are applicable only to the type of capital goods involved in Case 3, a type best exemplified by stocks of distributive trades, but not applicable to durable, fixed equipment, the replacement demand for which is obviously not related directly to current output.

CASE 3

DEMAND FOR PARTLY CONSUMABLE CAPITAL GOODS
(DURABLE AS A WHOLE, BUT IN DIVISIBLE, FULLY CONSUMABLE UNITS)

Assumption: Stock of capital goods is to current output as 2 is to 1.

Time Unit	Demand for Finished Products	Changes in Demand for Finished Products	Stock of Capital Goods Needed	Stock of Capital Goods Available (Beginning of Time Unit)^a	Capital Goods Consumed	Total Demand for Capital Goods	Replacement Demand for Capital Goods^b	Demand for Additional Units of Capital Goods
(1)	(2)	(3)	(4)	(5)	(6)	(7)	(8)	(9)
1	92	0	184	92	92	92	92	0
2	96	4	192	92	96	100	92	8
3	100	4	200	96	100	104	96	8
4	108	8	216	100	108	116	100	16
5	114	6	228	108	114	120	108	12
6	114	0	228	114	114	114	114	0
7	108	—6	216	114	108	102	114	—12
8	100	—8	200	108	100	92	108	—16
9	96	—4	192	100	96	92	100	—8
10	92	—4	184	96	92	88	96	—8

^{a} Equal to stock in column 4 in preceding time unit, minus the entry in column 6 during preceding time unit.
^{b} Equal to entry in column 6 during preceding time unit.

units). This part is (under the present simplified assumption) proportional to the *rate of change* of the demand for finished products.

Thus there are two forces that act upon total demand for capital goods. If demand for finished products is increasing, but at a constantly decreasing rate, the first of these two forces tends to increase and the second tends to slow down total demand for capital goods. Which one of the two forces shall have the upper hand depends upon the *manner* in which the increase in the demand for finished goods slows down, and it depends also on the *rate of depreciation.* [Frisch appears to use interchangeably the terms "rate of depreciation" and "rate of replacement."] If the rate of depreciation is very small, the second force represents always the most important influence. In the limiting case where there is no depreciation at all, the second force (the rate of change in demand for finished products) is the dominating one, and, even if the rate of depreciation is not very small, there may be certain points of time where the second force is dominating, namely, those points of time where the change in the demand for finished products is very slow. If the rate of depreciation is very high, the first force (the size of the demand for finished products) is nearly always the dominating one. The necessary and sufficient condition that demand for capital goods shall be increasing (decreasing) at a given moment of time is . . . that the acceleration (the rate of change of the rate of change) of the demand for finished products, plus the product of the depreciation rate and the rate of change of the demand for finished products, shall be positive (negative).

PARTLY CONSUMABLE CAPITAL GOODS—INDIVISIBLE UNITS

We consider now the group of capital goods the replacement demand for which stands in no definite relation to the current volume of output. This presumably is the characteristic of such indivisible units of durable equipment as machinery and buildings, which are not consumed within any one production period and whose physical wear and technological obsolescence are little affected whether the machines and buildings are used twenty-four hours a day or are not used at all. If this is sufficiently near the truth, then the period of life of such fixed equipment is uninfluenced by current output, and retirements and replacements are not related definitely to the volume of current output. Additional assumptions are thus needed concerning replacement demand to render its movement determinate.

The first assumption is that the period of the equipment's

life is constant. If the contribution of a unit of durable equipment to the output of finished products is properly measured, the ratio of the stock of equipment to current output shows the number of time units in the fixed period of the equipment's life. Thus, the replacement demand for such capital goods is the same as the installation of these goods as many time units ago as are given in the ratio of the stock of these capital goods to current production. If this ratio is 10 to 1, then the life period of the capital good in question is 10 time units, and the replacement demand in the year 1930 will equal the volume of installation in 1920 (if time units be years).

An additional assumption must be made, therefore, concerning the movements of the installation of such durable capital goods in the past. Case 4 illustrates the application of the assumption that past installation of the capital goods was at a constant volume.

The addition of a constant replacement demand to the variable demand for additional units of capital goods changes this latter series but little. The disparity in timing between the total demand for capital goods and the demand for finished products is, under such conditions, still the same as in Case 1a; and so is the difference in the absolute amplitude of changes in the two types of demand. True, the relative amplitude of changes in the demand for capital goods is damped by the addition of a constant quantity. But obviously, no matter how much we reduce the ratio of the stock of capital goods to current output and thus shorten the life of the capital goods in question, we can never make the relative amplitude of changes in total demand for capital goods narrower than that in the demand for finished products. For, as the period of life is reduced, replacement demand begins to reflect changes in installation within the period of the cycle assumed in the illustrative example above. The limiting case is that of fully consumable capital goods, with a life period of one time unit, in which the relative amplitude is as wide as, but is not narrower than, the relative amplitude in the demand for finished products.

Were secular growth assumed in past installation of capital

CASE 4

DEMAND FOR PARTLY CONSUMABLE CAPITAL GOODS
(DURABLE, IN INDIVISIBLE UNITS)

Assumptions: Stock of capital goods is to current production as 10 is to 1. Installation of capital goods in the past at a constant volume.

Time Unit	Demand for Finished Products	Changes in Demand for Finished Products	Stock of Capital Goods Needed	Stock of Capital Goods Available (Beginning of Time Unit) [a]	Capital Goods Consumed	Total Demand for Capital Goods	Replacement Demand for Capital Goods [b]	Demand for Additional Units of Capital Goods
(1)	(2)	(3)	(4)	(5)	(6)	(7)	(8)	(9)
1	92	0	920	828	92	92	92	0
2	96	4	960	828	92	132	92	40
3	100	4	1,000	868	92	132	92	40
4	108	8	1,080	908	92	172	92	80
5	114	6	1,140	988	92	152	92	60
6	114	0	1,140	1,048	92	92	92	0
7	108	—6	1,080	1,048	92	32	92	—60
8	100	—8	1,000	988	92	12	92	—80
9	96	—4	960	908	92	52	92	—40
10	92	—4	920	868	92	52	92	—40

[a] Equal to stock in column 4 in preceding time unit, minus the entry in column 6 during preceding time unit.
[b] Equal to entry in column 6 during preceding time unit.

goods, similar secular growth would appear in replacement demand, and thus in the total demand for capital goods. This secular movement may affect the timing of the turning points in the demand for capital goods, provided it is of sufficient magnitude either upward or downward. The secular change is, however, unlikely to affect the absolute or relative amplitude of fluctuations in the total demand for capital goods, as compared with the same demand derived on the basis of a constant replacement volume; unless the secular movement itself is not uniform, or unless the cycle in the demand for additional units of capital goods is not symmetrical.

However, a constant volume of past installation of capital goods is incompatible with assumption 3 above, that the cycle in the demand for finished products is one of a series of exactly identical swings. A strict application of the assumption, in view of the perfect regularity of cycles in the demand for finished products, would call for cycles in replacement demand synchronous with those in the demand for additional units of capital goods. Besides such synchronism, it is also interesting to observe the effect of a timing disparity between cycles in replacement demand and those in demand for additional units of capital goods. Case 5 illustrates various possibilities of relative timing of these cycles.

The timing of the cycle in replacement demand affects conspicuously the fluctuations observed in total demand for capital goods. In Combination I, which assumes synchronism between the cycles in the two components of total demand for capital goods, the latter shows the same timing as the demand for additional units; wider absolute amplitude (560 instead of 320), but narrower relative amplitude (somewhat above 200 percent as over against 400 percent). On the contrary, when the correlation in time between the cycle in replacement demand and that in demand for additional units is negative (Combination II), total demand for capital goods shows a swing almost inverse to that in the demand for finished products. Combination III, which assumes about a quarter-cycle lag in demand for additional units over replacement demand, shows shifts in the timing of changes in total demand for capital goods: the peak is reached in time unit 5 instead of time unit 4, and the trough does not appear until time unit 10 instead of time unit 8.

Were we to assume an average volume of replacement demand smaller than that given in Case 5, the influence of its cycles on the variation in the total demand for capital goods would obviously be smaller. The effects of such a change, as well as of an additional assumption of a secular movement in

CASE 5

DEMAND FOR PARTLY CONSUMABLE CAPITAL GOODS
(DURABLE, IN INDIVISIBLE UNITS)

Assumptions: (1) Stock of capital goods is to current production as 10 is to 1. (2) Volume of installation of capital goods in the past varies as total demand for capital goods in column 7 of Case 4. (3) Various timing relations between the cycle in replacement demand as given by assumption 2, and the cycle in the demand for additional units (Combinations I, II and III).

			COMBINATION I		COMBINATION II		COMBINATION III	
Time Unit	Demand for Finished Products	Demand for Additional Units of Capital Goods	Replacement Demand	Total Demand for Capital Goods (3)+(4)	Replacement Demand	Total Demand for Capital Goods (3)+(6)	Replacement Demand	Total Demand for Capital Goods (3)+(8)
(1)	(2)	(3)	(4)	(5)	(6)	(7)	(8)	(9)
1	92	0	92	92	152	152	12	12
2	96	40	132	172	92	132	52	92
3	100	40	132	172	32	72	52	92
4	108	80	172	252	12	92	92	172
5	114	60	152	212	52	112	132	192
6	114	0	92	92	52	52	132	132
7	108	—60	32	—28	92	32	172	112
8	100	—80	12	—68	132	52	152	72
9	96	—40	52	12	132	92	92	52
10	92	—40	52	12	172	132	32	—8

replacement demand, can be clearly seen, and call for no further discussion.

SUMMARY OF THE SCHEMATIC ANALYSIS

We may now summarize the schematic presentation of the hypothesis as follows:

1. The extent to which the absolute amplitude of changes

in the demand for finished products becomes magnified in the absolute amplitude of changes in the demand for *additional units* of capital goods is determined exclusively by the size of the constant ratio of the stock of capital goods to the volume of current production. The comparative timing and the comparative relative amplitude of changes in these two types of demand depend only upon the character of changes assumed in the demand for finished products, but are not affected by the size of the constant ratio just mentioned.

2. The replacement demand for capital goods is either related to the volume of current production, with a ratio of the stock of capital goods to current production of one; or it is related to current production, but with this ratio larger than one; or it stands in no direct relation to the volume of current production. In the latter case the volume of replacement demand may be determined by assuming a constant period of useful life of the capital good in question and a given volume of its installation in the past. This volume of installation may be assumed to be large or small as compared with the volume of demand for additional units of capital goods; constant, or cyclically variable; and the cycles in installation may be assumed to time in variously with cycles in the demand for additional units.

3. If replacement demand is related to current output, then the total demand for capital goods will differ as we assume a different ratio of stock of capital goods to current output. If the ratio is 1 to 1, changes in total demand for capital goods will be an exact replica of changes in the volume of demand for finished products. If the ratio is larger than one, the absolute amplitude of changes in total demand for capital goods will be proportionately wider than that of changes in demand for finished products. And as the ratio becomes larger, there will be a tendency for total demand for capital goods to move in closer accordance with changes in demand for additional units.

4. If the volume of replacement demand is substantial compared with the demand for additional units and is subject to

variations, the relation of fluctuations in total demand for capital goods to those in demand for finished products will depend upon the extent of correlation in time between changes in replacement demand and those in the demand for additional units. If this correlation is positive, total demand for capital goods will undergo changes similar to those in the demand for additional units. If the correlation is negative, changes in the demand for finished products are not likely to be reflected in the total demand for capital goods.

II. DEMAND FOR ADDITIONAL UNITS OF CAPITAL GOODS

QUALIFICATIONS OF THE HYPOTHESIS

The statistics available for two groups of capital goods, "inventories" and "fixed assets," indicate a substantial ratio of their stock to monthly volume of current production. Hence, if these ratios may be assumed to be constant in time, demand for additional units of these capital goods will move with the rate of change in the demand for finished products, and exhibit the phenomena of acceleration and magnification illustrated in Case 1a above. And if replacement demand is negligible as compared with the volume (both positive and negative) of the demand for additional units, total demand for capital goods will tend to behave as it does in column 7 of Case 1a. The main question, however, relates to the validity of assuming the ratio of stock of capital goods to current production to be constant in time. This question is discussed in the present section on the assumption that replacement demand is negligible, i.e., on terms most favorable to the hypothesis under analysis.

We may begin by a summary of the qualifications of this hypothesis which were suggested by J. M. Clark in his various writings (see references under note 2). These qualifications are as follows:

1. Elastic credit facilities are necessary, if the theoretical need for capital goods is to be translated into effective demand.

2. The time relationship between cycles in the demand for

finished products and in the demand for capital goods may be affected by the size of the replacement rate relative to the size of changes in the rate of movement of the demand for finished products.

3. On the other hand, fluctuations in the demand for capital goods may be intensified by: (a) variations in the rate of scrapping, which may be more rapid during good times than during bad; (b) violent swings in the profits of industrial undertakings.

4. There may be lags, errors of estimate, etc., in entrepreneurial judgment, which may prevent the demand for capital goods from following promptly changes in the rate of change in the demand for finished products.

5. There may be on hand an oversupply of capital goods, which may delay changes in the demand for such goods.

Of these qualifications, the second is disposed of by the assumption in the present section of a negligible volume of replacement demand. The others fall into two groups: (1) those not necessarily related to the premise of a large ratio of stocks of capital goods to current production, constant in time; (2) others, definitely related to this premise. Obviously, it is the second group of qualifications that is of theoretical importance in the present connection.[4] The purpose of the present discussion is to demonstrate that qualifications 5 and 3b are both related to the size of the ratio of the stock of capital goods to the volume of current production; and that, consequently, the theoretical scheme so far developed on the lines of Clark's model is incomplete until these qualifications are given their proper weight as an integral part of the scheme.

[4] This should not be taken to mean that the other qualifications, especially the first, are of little importance in determining whether or not effective demand for capital goods will move as indicated by the hypothetical schemes. Elasticity of credit and errors of judgment are all-important. But since they are not related directly to the assumptions involved in our discussion, they are in the nature of additional factors, rather than an integral part of the present, admittedly one-sided, theoretical scheme.

RESPONSE OF ENTREPRENEURS TO CHANGES IN DEMAND
FOR FINISHED PRODUCTS

When the ratio of stock of capital goods to current output is high, and replacement demand is small, acceleration and magnification of demand for capital goods are likely to take place. But is the theoretical need for additional units of capital goods, resulting from a positive change in the rate of demand for finished products, sufficient under such conditions to induce in the entrepreneur an effective demand for these additional units? If the constant ratio is 10 to 1 or 20 to 1, a rise in the demand for finished products of 5 percent calls for orders by the entrepreneur of capital goods the value of which is ten or twenty times the value to be realized from increasing sales by 5 percent during the next time unit. The entrepreneur knows that if the 5 percent rise in demand proves to be temporary, he is likely to be burdened with additional equipment for some time to come. At this point his ability to express effective negative demand becomes important. If the increase in the demand for finished goods proves to be short-lived the entrepreneur may reduce his replacement demand or maintenance charges, and thus cut down his stock of capital goods. But we assume throughout this section that replacement demand is negligible; and under such conditions an increase of productive equipment may necessitate a cessation of purchasing of new equipment for a considerable period, while all through that period burdensome overcapacity is gradually worked down.

Other factors disregarded, there will thus be a natural tendency for the entrepreneur to hesitate in committing himself to an increase in his stock of durable capital goods in response to a rise in the demand for finished products. This hesitancy will be the greater, in proportion as the replacement demand is smaller, and as the ratio of the value of capital goods to the value of services they render in satisfying demand for finished products is higher. It is at this point that a consideration of the time unit in which variations in demand are reckoned in the hypothesis becomes of importance. If monthly units are used instead of annual ones, the ratio of the stock of capital goods to current services jumps twelvefold, and the replacement part of the demand for capital goods (as well as the maintenance charges) shrinks into insignificance. If the capital good lasts twenty years, will the monthly demand for it reflect in a 240-fold fashion changes in the rate of increase or decline in the monthly volume of the demand for finished products?

Once the question is put in this form, the importance of the answer for evaluating the hypothesis as an effective explanation of business cycle phenomena becomes clear. If it is assumed that changes in demand for finished products over periods as short as months or quarters are, other factors being equal, likely to be translated into effective demand for additional units of capital goods, then, provided replacement demand is negligible, the hypothesis becomes important for explaining business cycles of a duration of from four to eight years. But this assumption is unrealistic, since the entrepreneur will be unlikely to commit himself on the basis of changes in demand that extend only over such a short period of time. On the other hand, if it is argued that changes in the demand for finished products must occur over a considerable period of time, say a year or two, before they can form a stimulus sufficient to induce an effective demand for additional units of capital goods, then the hypothesis obviously assumes a change in the demand for finished products which in its own turn calls for an explanation.[5]

Furthermore, let it be assumed that the demand for additional units of capital goods responds promptly and fully to

[5] The importance of this point may be illustrated by quoting the argument developed by Clark in his final reply to Ragnar Frisch: "Thus, if we take as our initial fact a moderate decrease in the rate of growth of consumer demand (such as needs no particular explanation), this may result—with a lag—in a positive decline in rate of production of durable producers' or consumers' goods. This in turn reduces purchasing power, unless offset by opposite movements elsewhere, and results in a positive decrease in consumers' demand, presumably extended to more commodities than those originally affected. And this in turn further extends and intensifies the shrinkage in production of durable goods, etc. This may serve as an answer to a criticism of this theory, made by Dr. C. O. Hardy before the American Statistical Association last December, to the effect

changes in the demand for finished goods. As a result, the stock of capital goods is built up during the rising phase of the swing in the demand for finished products. What happens during the declining phase? Since replacement demand is negligible, the entrepreneur is unable to express fully his negative demand for additional units of capital goods, with the result that when the next upward swing in the demand for finished products begins, it is likely to occur in the face of a considerable oversupply of capital goods. Such an oversupply, a necessary corollary of the full response of demand for capital goods according to the scheme, will prevent this scheme from operating during the next cycle. Thus, under the assumption of a negligible replacement demand, the relation between the demand for capital goods and the demand for finished products as established in Case 1a above, is likely to be effective only during the rising phase of the first cycle.

THE NECESSARY CHARACTER OF OVERCAPACITY

This argument brings into discussion the second factor that is likely to prevent the ratio of the stock of capital goods to current output from being constant in time, viz., overcapacity. It was seen above that there is apt to be an inverse relation be-

---

that the theory presupposes a cyclical alternation of expansions and contractions in consumer demand, and leaves these movements to be explained. As stated above, the actual contractions (and the more rapid expansions), if they do not arise as original movements produced by 'outside causes', can be explained as results of an intensifying mechanism whereby a fluctuation in the rate of growth may be converted into alternations of rapid expansion and absolute contraction, through the interaction of the two sets of forces indicated. It may also be mentioned that other enabling causes, such as elastic credit, are necessary to this result, even on a strict theoretical basis; not to mention the many forces which, whether theoretically necessary or not, play a part in the actual process." (See *Journal of Political Economy*, October 1932, pp. 692-93.)

Obviously, this argument envisages a prompt response in the demand for capital goods to short-time changes occurring in the demand for finished products. Otherwise, the self-perpetuation and reinforcement of the original movement in consumer demand could occur only if the initial change were very substantial and thus in turn in need of explanation.

tween the size of this ratio and the probability that such demand for additional units for capital goods as is indicated in the schematic exposition will become effective. It may now be stated that there is likely to be a positive relation between the extent of overcapacity in those industries the demand for whose products is variable, and the size of the ratio of the stock of capital goods to current production.

Capacity may be defined and measured in various ways, two of which are important for the present discussion. One takes into account the possibility of intensive utilization of available factors of production during short periods of time. Another would disregard the possibility of an intensive utilization of equipment during short periods of time, and measure needed capacity on the basis of average possible performance over long stretches of time. The difference between the two types of definition is obviously determined by the variation in the length of the period for which sustained performance is measured.

If changes in demand for finished products over short periods of time be assumed to affect demand for capital goods, and they are so assumed in the Clark hypothesis, it is overcapacity from the point of view of the performance possible over short periods of time that is to be considered. Such overcapacity is likely to be the rule. Clearly, if demand for industry's finished products is known to be variable, there is likely to be such planning of capacity as to allow higher levels of performance for short periods of time. It is unlikely that in the case of durable capital goods such supply will be allowed as could satisfy the average volume of demand only under conditions of intensive utilization sustainable but for short periods of time. Thus, in planning the capacity of a department store, it is improbable that a plant will be provided which could satisfy the *average* volume of demand only with such intensive utilization of all factors of production as prevails during the week of the Christmas or the Easter rush. Rather, the capacity of the plant provided will be determined by performance needed under average conditions through the year; with the result that at all other times, except Christmas and Easter, overcapacity will exist in the sense of the possibility of a much greater volume of performance over short periods of time, than is actually being rendered by the plant. The more variable the demand for the finished products, the larger is likely to be the extent of such overcapacity in durable capital goods.

Moreover, even when we measure capacity on the basis of performance sustainable over longer periods of time, it is still likely that in industries with variable demand there will be an oversupply of the more durable capital goods. If there is a possibility of raising the rate of utilization of productive factors over short periods of time, cutting down costs per unit and increasing profits per unit; and if the cost of the more durable capital goods, per unit of finished product, is a small fraction of the total cost per unit—there will be an incentive to provide a supply of capital goods that will be excessive, even when peak rate of utilization possible over short periods is disregarded.

The factors making for such an incentive appear clearly in the following hypothetical example. Let us assume that an entrepreneur faces a potential demand during the coming three time units of 100, 200, and 300 units of his finished product, at constant prices. Let us further assume that no variations in the intensity of the utilization of the capital goods are possible; and that the factors of production may be divided into three cost groups: that of durable capital goods, other more variable productive factors, and profits (residual). Then, if for each time unit the supply of durable capital goods and of other factors of production is exactly sufficient to satisfy the demand for the finished products, cost per unit and total profits are as follows:

Time Unit	Demand for Finished Product	Cost of Durable Capital Goods per Unit of Finished Product	Other Costs per Unit	Profits per Unit	Total Profits
(1)	(2)	(3)	(4)	(5)	(6)
1	100	5	89	6	600
2	200	5	89	6	1,800
3	300	5	89	6	1,800

But the supply of durable capital goods cannot be varied from one time unit to the next: it has to be fixed for the whole period. At whatever level it will be fixed, this level will determine how much of the demand for the finished products can be satisfied. If total profits (the sum of entries in column 6) are to be maximized, it may be seen that durable capital goods will have to be provided to permit production of 200 units of finished products. Total production for all three time units will then be 500 (instead of the 600 possible), and total profits will be maximized at 2,500.

Let us now assume that, for a single time unit, a more intensive utilization of all the factors of production is possible, so that 5 percent more demand may be supplied at the same total cost. If this assumption be added to the preceding ones, the cost of capital goods for that single time unit will drop to 4.76 per unit, the cost of other productive factors to 84.76 per unit, and the profits per unit will rise to 10.48. Under such conditions, what supply of durable capital goods will maximize total profits? A brief computation will show that it would pay the entrepreneur to provide a stock of durable goods to satisfy the largest demand possible at any single time unit, that is, to provide durable goods capable of producing under average conditions 286 units, or under the condition of intensive utilization exactly 300 units; with the result that substantial overcapacity exists during two of the three time units.

The specific results of the example above are due to the specific figures employed. But some of the tendencies shown are general in character and may be formulated as follows:
(1) if no variation in the rate of utilization of productive factors is possible, the durable equipment will be provided up to the point where gains from satisfying a larger volume of the demand for finished products will begin to be offset by losses involved in the increase of the constant cost per unit for the times when the demand is low; [6] (2) if a more intensive utilization of productive factors is possible for a time unit in which the demand is large, the stock of *durable* capital goods provided is likely to be larger than under case (1) above.

[6] For an exact formulation and solution of the problem, see Appendix A.

In industries with variable demand for their finished products, the stock of capital goods provided, even as determined under (1), will spell short-run overcapacity and may possibly mean some long-run overcapacity. But variations in intensity of utilization of productive factors over short periods of time may be considered in their effect on even the variable costs (which, of course, by this very fact cease to be fully variable). In that case, those durable capital goods whose cost per unit of output is but a small fraction of the total per unit cost, will tend toward excess capacity, even when capacity is figured for an average rate of utilization over longer periods of time. It is important to note that both short- and long-run overcapacity will tend to be positively correlated with the variability of the demand for the industry's finished products.

If overcapacity of durable capital goods is thus a normal condition of industries [7] supplying products of variable demand, the relation between changes in this demand and in the demand for additional units of durable capital goods may be unlike that suggested by the schematic exposition of the first section. Orders for additional units of durable capital goods need not revive earlier than demand for finished products. A large fraction of the rise in the demand for finished products being satisfied by a fuller utilization of the already existing stock of capital goods, it is not necessary that the rise in the demand for additional units of capital goods be of wider amplitude than that in the demand for finished products. Similarly, with the retardation in the increase of the demand for finished products, it is not necessary that there follow a decline in the demand for additional units of capital goods.

Thus, the positive relation between the variability of demand for the industry's finished products and the tendency toward oversupply of durable capital goods destroys the valid-

[7] The argument above disregards the rise in prices of finished products, which would result if potential demand were not fully satisfied. The assumption of constant prices of finished products was definitely adopted in order to allow the determination of the capacity planning policy of a single entrepreneur, under competitive conditions.

ity of the hypothesis which renders changes in the demand for additional units of durable capital goods dependent upon the *rate of change* in the demand for finished products. But the same relation contributes to a wider amplitude of cycles in the demand for capital goods and a possible lead in these cycles. This occurs through the influence of overcapacity on the sensitivity of business profits to fluctuations in the volume of production, that is, in demand for finished products. Overcapacity obviously increases the magnitude of overhead costs in the industry, and thus adds to the weight of factors that make for extreme fluctuations in profits with variation in the volume of output. In this indirect way the high ratio of the stock of durable capital goods to current production does make for a wider amplitude of fluctuations in the demand for capital goods, and may serve to create a lead in this demand over the demand for finished products.

III. REPLACEMENT DEMAND FOR DURABLE CAPITAL GOODS

THE VARIABILITY OF REPLACEMENT DEMAND

It was seen above that, on the assumption of negligible replacement demand, the scheme of acceleration and magnification of the demand for capital goods is of dubious validity beyond the rising phase of the first cycle in the demand for finished products. A considerable volume of replacement demand for capital goods thus becomes a *sine qua non* for the continuous operation of the hypothesis under analysis. But the assumption of a sizeable replacement demand means the introduction of a factor which, for the important group of durable capital goods in indivisible units, is, at first glance, unrelated to variations in the demand for finished products, and hence uncorrelated with the demand for additional units of capital goods. It may be shown statistically that in most industries, especially those of some maturity, replacement demand is of considerable magnitude as compared with the demand for additional units of capital goods. Hence, as long as we adhere to the premise of a rigid life period, total demand for capital goods is determined not only by the demand for additional units, but by another important factor uncorrelated with the latter, the volume of installation of capital goods in the past.

The assumption of a constant life period, however, can hardly be accepted at its full value. True, productive units whose life period averages twenty years are rarely retired after only five years of service, and are rarely continued in use for fifty years. But the average life period is a central tendency of a distribution with dispersion along the scale of life periods. Empirical studies of the phenomena in question are difficult and rare. But the available evidence indicates that the life period of productive equipment is subject to wide dispersion.[8]

It is obvious that the longer the average period of life of a unit of productive equipment, the larger (in absolute time units) is likely to be the variation in the actual life of the single productive units of this particular type. Thus, even for units whose average life period is only seven to ten years, the deviations from the average are likely to be sufficiently great to affect the course of replacement demand in the business cycle. A constant period of life may be predicated only when the factors of physical wear and technological and economic obsolescence are considered in their secular aspects. When cyclical fluctuations in the cost of equipment and volume of activity are considered, it may be seen that they affect the entrepreneur in his choice as between further retention of old equipment and replacement of it by new units.

The factors that influence such a choice by entrepreneurs are numerous. The present and prospective cost of equipment per efficiency unit, the present and prospective volume of demand for finished products—these are but summary factors that cover a multitude of specific elements. In the present connection, however, we are interested only in such of them as

[8] See the study by Robley Winfrey and Edwin B. Kurtz, "Life Characteristics of Physical Property," *Bulletin* 103, Iowa Engineering Experiment Station, June 17, 1931.

are definitely correlated with changes in the demand for finished products. Does a rise in the volume of this demand imply a foreshortening of the life period of some of the existing units of productive equipment, and thus spell a larger volume of replacement demand than would otherwise have been the case?

INFLUENCE OF THE DEMAND FOR FINISHED PRODUCTS ON THE REPLACEMENT DEMAND FOR CAPITAL GOODS

The answer to the question above depends to some extent upon the adaptability of the stock of productive equipment to the production of various specific finished products, and upon the nature of the increase in the demand for the latter. If the existing units of productive equipment are of such specific character as to be serviceable in the production of only a single type of finished product, and if the increase in the demand for finished products involves a shift in the specific character of the goods demanded, the case will obviously be that of a sudden increase in the obsolescence rate. Under such conditions, there will appear not only a demand for additional units of capital goods, but the replacement demand will also rise above the average volume prevalent during a longer period of time.

This case is, however, in the nature of a secular change from one product to another, or from one industry to another. It is mentioned here because it is important to remember that many an increase in the demand for finished products takes the form of a shift in the specific character of the commodities demanded; and that with such prevalence of secular shifts associated with increases in consumers' demand, the effect on the demand for productive equipment, whenever that happens to be of a uni-purpose type, is both through the demand for additional units and through a rise in the replacement demand. But the conditions presented by such cases are incompatible with the basic assumption of the whole discussion, viz., the homogeneity over time of both types of demand, with only quantitative changes allowed.

However, even within the restricted conditions of our discussion, there may still be positive relation between changes in the demand for finished products and changes in replacement demand. The entrepreneur's choice between retention and retirement of old equipment depends largely upon the net volume of savings that may materialize from the shift. If the net volume of savings is proportional to the volume of current production (i.e., demand for finished products), any increase in the latter, other factors being disregarded, will raise the replacement rate; and any decline will tend to decrease the replacement rate. This effect appears clearly in the illustrative example below.

Let us assume that a machine capable of turning out 10,000 units of finished products costs $100,000 and has an average period of life of twenty years, with a straight-line depreciation rate of 5 percent and an interest charge on the capital invested of 4 percent. The average interest charge throughout the life of the machine will be $2,000 per year, since the amount of capital invested in the machine shrinks each year as the depreciation reserve is built up along a uniformly rising straight line. The depreciation rate is purely an obsolescence cost, that is, it expresses the loss sustained annually in not replacing the present machine by a new one that embodies the results of technical progress. If we assume further that the life of the machine remains constant (in spite of technical progress), and that its cost remains at $100,000, the effect of technical progress will be to permit savings in the expenditures on other productive factors. Since the depreciation allowance per year is $5,000 and the interest rate is 4 percent, the annual savings of technical progress may be seen to be $\frac{\$7,360}{20}$ or $368 (which, for twenty years, discounted at a 4 percent rate, yields a present value of $5,000).

The machine works at 60 percent capacity, which is "normal" for the industry, and thus turns out annually 6,000 units of finished products. The total annual cost contribution of the machine is $7,000, or $1.17 per unit of finished product. At the rate of technical progress embodied in the depreciation allowance, the annual rate of savings is $368, or about 6.13 cents per unit.

On the basis of the assumptions made, it would not pay to replace the old machine until it had completed its twentieth year of service, for at the beginning of the twentieth year of service the cost of the machine for that year, to be met whether or not the machine is used or discarded, is $7,000, of which $5,000 is allowance for obsolescence and $2,000 interest charges. At the beginning of the twentieth year, i.e., nineteen years after the old machine has been installed, the total savings from replacement for the coming year would be somewhat below $7,000 (it will be $368 $\times$ 19 or exactly $6,992). Thus the savings for the coming year from discarding the old machine and installing a new one would not equal the cost of the old machine, still to be covered; or, which is the same, the additional cost resulting from the introduction of the new machine. Provided the enterprise in question considers its past and future commitments, it will not replace the old machine until the end of its full period of life, a situation true so long as the rate of technical progress and the volume of output of finished products are in accordance with the assumptions made above.

But let us now assume that the forecast demand for finished products during the coming year has changed, the entrepreneur expecting a production of 8,000 units instead of only 6,000; and that this rise will be confined to that one year. If the rate of technical progress is still the same, the entrepreneur in the possession of a nineteen-year-old machine faces the following situation. The charges for a new machine for the coming years will be $7,000, added to the same charges for the old machine; the savings from the new machine at the beginning of the same year will be about $1.16 per unit (6.13 cents $\times$ 19). Were the expected production of finished products only 6,000 units, it would not pay to replace the old machine. But with an output of 8,000, total savings for the coming year from the introduction of a new machine would be above $9,000, while the additional cost is only $7,000. Hence it would pay to replace the old machine, even if it is only nineteen years old. Indeed, it would pay to replace a machine only eighteen years old, but not one seventeen years old.

Thus, if demand for finished products increases, and if gross savings from the introduction of new units of capital goods are proportional to the volume of current output, replacement demand will rise, even though the increase in the demand for finished products is considered temporary and even though overcapacity exists that may render demand for additional units of capital goods unnecessary. Under conditions assumed above, those units of capital goods that are sufficiently near the end of their average period of life to be affected by the change in prospective savings from installation of new units will tend to be replaced earlier than would have been the case were there no increase in the demand for finished products. Similarly, a decline in the latter, temporary though it may be, will mean a decline in such savings from the installation of new productive units as are proportional to the volume of current production; and will thus tend to retard replacement of old units of capital goods.

This effect of changes in the demand for finished products on replacement demand for capital goods is magnified, if entrepreneurs extrapolate into the future at least part of the change in the former demand. It was suggested in the second section that the translation of changes in the demand for finished products into demand for additional units of capital goods is considerably qualified by the existence of overcapacity and the unwillingness of entrepreneurs to make long-term commitments on the basis of short-term changes. But it is not inconsistent to assume that a given increase or decline in demand for finished products is likely to be extrapolated in greatly reduced form into the future. If this is done, the influence of a given change in the demand for finished products on the replacement demand for capital goods is still greater than that suggested by the example above. Thus, if in this example we assume that the entrepreneur expects half of the increase to continue beyond the coming year, it would pay him to replace a machine only seventeen years old, and even one shortly beyond its sixteenth year.

LIMITATIONS OF THE CONCLUSIONS

The conclusions arrived at in the argument above are contingent upon three assumptions: (1) constant rate of technical progress; (2) the willingness of entrepreneurs to maintain constant overcapacity; (3) a constant volume of output of finished products, as a basis of the depreciation allowance. The effect of omitting the second assumption is obviously the same as the effect of considering the existence of overcapacity in studying the relation of the demand for additional units of capital goods to changes in the demand for finished products. As in the latter case, the existence of overcapacity would nullify at least in part, effects of changes in the demand for finished products. This first obvious limitation of the conclusions arrived at needs no further discussion. The second is that following from assumption (3) of the argument.

It is unlikely that in figuring the depreciation or obsolescence rate the volume of the current output will be assumed at a constant level. More likely, the depreciation allowance will be based upon an average volume of activity, expected as a mean of a fluctuating level of output of finished products. If this is the case, a rise or decline in this level, within the limits of the variation expected, would not call for any such revision of the duration of life as is implied in the example above. Similarly, if the depreciation rate is established on the basis of an expected secular rise in the volume of activity (and in growing industries this is likely to be the case), to that extent an extrapolated rise in the volume of demand for finished products will fail to have any effect on the replacement demand, provided that this rise is within the range of the expected secular growth. Only in so far as changes in the demand for finished products are outside the range of expected variations about the mean volume of current output, which were taken into consideration when the depreciation allowance was fixed, will these changes have any influence on the replacement demand for capital goods.

With these limitations, the conclusions arrived at above concerning the effect of changes in demand for finished products on replacement demand for capital goods are valid. Within these limits, net changes in the demand for finished products will give rise to similar net changes in replacement demand. The total volume of replacement demand will then vary with the total volume of the demand for finished products, or rather with the deviations of that latter demand from the range of variations expected about the mean embodied in the depreciation rate. It is important to note that the total volume of replacement is not governed by the *net change* in the demand for finished products, but by its *volume*. The case is thus somewhat akin to Case 2 in the first section. In this case, as we have seen on the basis of Frisch's conclusion, no necessary relation exists between the total demand for capital goods and the net changes in the demand for finished products.

IV. SUMMARY AND CONCLUSIONS

Throughout, the hypothesis under analysis was discussed in terms of an individual entrepreneur in competitive conditions; and it was held that the increased demand for finished products could be satisfied only through the increased utilization of certain specific capital goods. The removal of these assumptions would impair still further the validity of the hypothesis. A monopolistic entrepreneur's response to a prospective rise in the rate of demand for his finished products is likely to be still more qualified than that of an entrepreneur under competitive conditions, if for one reason only: the former, unlike the latter, can delay the satisfaction of the demand for finished products and still avoid losing it completely, provided that this demand is by its technical nature deferable and cumulative. Similarly, if it is assumed that not only the given specific type of durable goods can be used to meet a temporary increase in the demand for finished products, but that some substitution of other, less durable productive factors is possible, the entrepreneur's response to a change in the demand for finished products is likely to depart still more from the course suggested by the hypothesis.

But even under the assumptions of competitive conditions and of the impossibility of substitution for the specific type of durable capital goods, it was seen that:

1. There tends to be an inverse relation between the readiness of entrepreneurs to act upon temporary changes in the demand for finished products and the size of the ratio of the stock of capital goods to volume of current output.

2. There tends to be a positive relation between the variability of the demand for finished products and oversupply of those durable capital goods whose ratio to their contribution to current output is high and whose relative share of costs in the finished products is low.

3. By the very nature of the hypothesis, replacement demand must be substantial if the acceleration and magnification of changes in demand for finished products as they are reflected in the demand for capital goods are to take place continuously.

4. This substantial replacement demand is subject to variations of its own. In the case of highly durable capital goods these variations in replacement demand are partly a reflection of changes in the volume of past installation of the durable goods, partly a reflection of variations in the obsolescence rate due to changes in the volume of demand for finished products. The latter factor causes the volume of replacement demand to move with the volume of demand for finished products. But none of these factors makes for a direct correlation between the volume of the total demand for capital goods and the *rate of change* in the demand for finished products.

How far these particular factors, related to the basic assumptions of the hypothesis, serve to qualify it, cannot be approximated by a discussion in general terms, and one turns naturally to statistical evidence. But the latter reflects the effect of all qualifying factors, not only of those directly related to the premises of the hypothesis under discussion. A detailed statistical test presented in Appendix B shows quite clearly that while changes in the demand for capital goods lead changes in the demand for finished products, the range of this lead is far short of that suggested by the hypothesis; and that while the amplitude of cyclical fluctuations is wider in the demand for capital goods than for finished products, the disparity is much smaller than one would expect on the basis of the hypothesis. Now, the lead and wider amplitude of cycles in the demand for capital goods may be easily explained on grounds other than those provided by the hypothesis. The speculative character of the demand for durable capital goods, which involves a commitment by the entrepreneur for years ahead and a possible delay in delivery by the duration of the process of production; the influence of changes in the volume of demand for finished products upon the obsolescence rate; the effect of fluctuations in the interest rate upon the valuation of capital goods by entrepreneurs—such factors make for the acceleration and magnification of changes in the demand for capital goods. The value of a specific explanation, such as is offered by the hypothesis, is obviously contingent upon the extent to which the tendencies it describes are unimpeded in reality by other factors. But the statistical test indicates that these other factors nullify to a considerable extent the effect of the forces suggested by the hypothesis.

The foregoing statements should not be interpreted to mean that the relation established by Clark between the demand for capital goods and the demand for finished products is completely invalid as a tool in understanding business-cycle phenomena. This relation is inadequate as a self-sufficient theory of cyclical fluctuations. It is but partially effective as an explanation of the wider amplitude and the lead of cycles in the demand for capital goods. But it is valuable in as much as it indicates an important factor making for secular overcapacity of durable capital goods, which in turn has a bearing upon business-cycle phenomena; and it is valid as an explanation of the movement of the demand for capital goods under the following limiting conditions: when there is little over-capacity and no hesitation on the part of entrepreneurs to in-cur commitments—a situation that occurs sometimes in the later part of the expansion phase of cycles in rapidly growing industries.

APPENDIX A: THE DETERMINATION OF STOCKS OF DURABLE CAPITAL GOODS ON THE ASSUMPTION OF A VARIABLE DEMAND FOR FINISHED PRODUCTS [9]

This Appendix deals with the case of an entrepreneur who forecasts the potential demand for his finished products at time units $0, 1, \ldots i \ldots k$, the demand in value units being $n_0, n_1 \ldots n_i \ldots n_k$. If the stock of durable capital goods, x, is measured in units corresponding to units of finished product (i.e., in units of \$1,000, if it takes \$1,000 of capital goods to produce \$1.00 of finished products), the level at which x will be fixed for the whole time period from time unit 0 to time unit k, will determine how much of the potential demand for finished products can be satisfied.

Let us further designate

g—margin per value unit of finished product of the yield over all costs except those contributed by the durable capital goods

d—depreciation rate plus the interest charges on the capital invested in durable capital goods

p_i—profit per value unit of the finished product.

Then, when x is larger than n, the equations for time units $0, 1 \ldots k$, are:

$$p_0 n_0 = g n_0 - dx$$
$$p_1 n_1 = g n_1 - dx$$
$$\cdot \quad \cdot \quad \cdot \quad \cdot \quad \cdot \quad \cdot \quad \cdot$$
$$p_k n_k = g n_k - dx$$

The problem of finding the value of x which will maximize total profits can then be formulated mathematically, on one condition: that $n_0, n_1, n_2, \ldots n_k$ are in increasing order of their magnitude.

[9] I am indebted to Lucile Kean and Arthur Stein of the National Bureau of Economic Research, for assistance in the solution of this problem.

Given $k + 1$ functions of x of the type:
$$p_i n_i = g n_i - dx$$
when $n_i = $ or $< x$ or:
$$p_i n_i = g n_i - dx - g\,(n_i - x)$$
when $x < n_i$.

The numbers $n_0, n_1 \ldots n_i \ldots n_k$, g and d are given constants.

To find the value of x for which the sum $P\,(x)$ of these $k + 1$ functions is a maximum. The solution is given as follows:

When $n_k <$ or $= x$,
$$\frac{P\,(x)}{g} = n_0 + n_1 + n_2 \ldots n_i + n_k + x\left(0 - \frac{(k + 1)\,d}{g}\right).$$

When $n_{i-1} = $ or $< x$, and $x < n_i$
$$\frac{P(x)}{g} = n_0 + n_1 + n_2 \ldots n_{i-1} + x\left[(k+1-i) - \frac{(k+1)d}{g}\right].$$

When $x < n_0$
$$\frac{P\,(x)}{g} = x\left[(k+1) - \frac{(k+1)\,d}{g}\right].$$

The function $\dfrac{P\,(x)}{g}$ is a maximum when $P\,(x)$ is a maximum.

It is a broken line, beginning at the origin with a line segment of positive slope for the interval $(0 < x < n_0)$; then a line segment of a slope algebraically less for the interval $(n_0 < x < n_1)$; and so on. Eventually the slope becomes negative, and the line segment for $(n_k < x)$ crosses the x axis, the whole making a kind of arch, or "convex open polygon." The maximum value is taken on at the juncture of the two line segments where the slope changes from positive to negative.

The slope is given by the bracket
$$\left[(k + 1 - i) - \frac{(k + 1)\,d}{g}\right].$$

If the slope for $(n_{i-1} <$ or $= x < n_i)$ which is $\left[(k + 1 - i) - \dfrac{(k + 1)\,d}{g}\right]$ is positive, while the slope for $(n_i <$ or $= x <$

n_{i+1} which is $\left[(k-i) - \dfrac{(k+1)d}{g}\right]$, is negative, then

$x = n_i$ gives the maximum.

Or in general if

$$\frac{k-i}{k+1} \leq \frac{d}{g} \leq \frac{k+1-i}{k+1}$$

$x = n_i$ gives the maximum.

From the expression just arrived at, one can, given d, g, and k, ascertain the position value in the series $n_0, n_1 \ldots n_k$ at which x will give a maximum of profits, provided that the series of values of n is arranged in the increasing order of magnitude. Thus if $k = 9$ (i.e. the entrepreneur can forecast demand for 10 points of time), if $d = 6$, and $g = 12$, the profits will be maximized if a stock of capital goods will be provided that can satisfy a demand for finished products equal to the median value of the array of points of forecast demand.

APPENDIX B: STATISTICAL TEST OF THE HYPOTHESIS

The statistical test presented below is not designed to declare the hypothesis under analysis right or wrong: no statistical test, in itself, can enable one to render such a categorical judgment. But it ought to show the extent to which the tendencies suggested by the hypothesis are allowed to operate in at least one section of the world of reality.

The analysis below falls into two parts, the division being determined primarily by the character of the data studied. First, annual series on the volume of railroad equipment permit the study of both comparative timing and comparative amplitude of fluctuations in the demand for finished products and the demand for capital goods; second, a few monthly series on industrial equipment and construction are analyzed with emphasis exclusively on the study of comparative timing.

DEMAND FOR RAILROAD TRANSPORTATION SERVICES AND THE DEMAND FOR RAILROAD EQUIPMENT

Measuring Theoretical Demand for Additional Units of Railroad Equipment. Data on railroad equipment and services,

available annually from 1890 to date, relate to the number of
freight cars, passenger cars, and locomotives in service; the
number of freight ton-miles and passenger car-miles attained
during the year; orders for freight cars, locomotives, and passenger cars placed by railroads; and, from 1904 to date, average capacity of freight cars in service and average tractive
power of locomotives in service. With the help of these data
we can measure theoretical demand for additional units of
railroad equipment, expected on the basis of the hypothesis
tested; and actual demand, as indicated by orders placed.

Theoretical demand for additional railroad equipment can
be gauged by multiplying net changes in the demand for services by a constant ratio of the stock of equipment to current
volume of services (or by dividing it by the reciprocal of this
ratio). Changes in demand for services are given by successive
differences of the annual series of freight ton-miles and of
passenger car-miles, the implied assumption being that the railroads have succeeded each year in satisfying the demand for
their services. To ascertain the ratio of the stock of equipment to volume of services is somewhat more difficult. This
ratio is assumed constant in time, and in translating this
assumption into the conditions of the statistical experiment,
it is obviously reasonable to allow secular movements in the
ratio. Hence, for each year we divided: (1) freight ton-miles
by the number of freight cars in service at the beginning of
the year; (2) freight ton-miles by the number of locomotives
in service at the beginning of the year (freight transportation
being so much more important in the utilization of locomotives
than passenger traffic, it was considered justifiable to neglect
the latter); (3) passenger train- or car-miles by the number
of passenger cars in service at the beginning of the year. The
resulting three series were smoothed by freehand lines, the
smoothness of the lines being indicated by the fact that over
a period of more than forty years there are only two turning
points in the case of freight cars, and three turning points for
locomotives and passenger cars, respectively. The result was
the reciprocal of the secularly moving ratio of stock of equip-

ment to volume of services for each of the three types of railroad equipment.

These secular ratios, however, cannot be applied directly to successive changes in the demand for transportation services, because these ratios relate *existing* stock of equipment to current services, while the demand for additional units of equipment is a demand for *new* units, i.e., for *current* product of technical progress. The difference in efficiency between the average equipment unit in service and the new equipment unit that can be purchased depends obviously upon two factors: (1) average age of existing equipment; (2) rate of technical progress in the equipment unit. The first factor was approximated by assuming a period of twenty years as the life of freight cars and locomotives (corresponding to the prevalent depreciation rate of 5 percent) [10] and by establishing the percentage rate of growth in the stock of equipment in service. The second factor was given by the series of average capacity of freight cars and average tractive power of locomotives in service. The combination of the two factors indicates the approximate lag in time of the ratio of *existing* equipment to volume of service behind the ratio of *new* equipment to volume of service. Thus, for freight cars, in order to estimate the theoretical demand for additional equipment for a given year, we used the secular ratio of existing equipment to freight ton-miles for the tenth year ahead, for all changes in demand for services that occurred between 1890 and 1908; the ninth year ahead for changes in 1909 and 1910; eighth year ahead for the change in 1912; seventh year ahead for changes during the period 1913-20; and sixth year ahead for changes from 1921 to date. For locomotives, the tenth year ahead was used for all changes from 1891 to 1920; and the eleventh year ahead for changes from 1921 to date. For passenger cars, the technical improvement in capacity of the unit itself was negligible; and for this group the secular ratio of *existing* equipment to

[10] See Bureau of Internal Revenue, *Depreciation Studies* (Preliminary Report, January, 1931), p. 33. A similar period of average life is found also by R. Winfrey and E. B. Kurtz, *op. cit.*

volume of services for a given year was applied to the net change in passenger car-miles for the same year (change from the preceding year) to obtain theoretical demand for additional passenger cars. The resulting three series of theoretical demand for additional units of railroad equipment are fair approximations as far as their absolute volume is concerned, and are quite precise in the indication of their annual changes. They are presented in columns 2, 5, and 8 of Table I.

Measuring Actual Demand for Railroad Equipment, Total and Adjusted for Replacements. Columns 3, 6, and 9 of Table I present the series on total orders for railroad equipment. These may be compared directly with theoretical demand for additional units of equipment in order to ascertain the extent to which *total actual* demand for these three groups of capital goods was affected by *net changes* in the volume of service rendered. But before making this comparison it would be better to explain the derivation of the third set of series in Table I, viz., that of total orders for equipment adjusted for replacements.

Net changes in equipment in service represent the total installation of equipment minus the number of old units discarded. If we assume that all orders placed are eventually filled (i.e., that cancellations are negligible), then total orders represent total installation, but with a certain lead, since it takes some time to fill an order. A comparison of net changes in freight cars, locomotives, and passenger cars in service with the series of total orders for them indicates a high degree of concomitance, but with an approximate lag of the former over the latter of one year. Allowing for this lag, and subtracting from total orders the net change in equipment in service, we obtain an annual estimate of number of units withdrawn from service.

This annual estimate of withdrawals shows marked fluctuations from year to year, partly because the actual lag of installation behind orders is not always one year, partly because there are cyclical fluctuations in the withdrawals of old units of equipment. Fluctuations arising from an imperfect correction for the lag of installation behind orders should be neglected, while short-time changes in withdrawals of old equipment units cannot be segregated. Consequently, it was thought best to confine changes in withdrawals to secular movements only. In so far as replacement demand is then identical with withdrawals, the estimate of replacement demand is shown by a smooth line passing through the annual differences between total orders and net changes in equipment in service, the latter taken one year later than the former (i.e., total orders for year ending June 30, 1890 as compared with the net change in equipment from June 30, 1890 to June 30, 1891).

In obtaining this smooth line representing replacement demand, we neglected, in the case of locomotives and passenger cars, the great increase in withdrawals that began about 1922 and reflected the decline in the stock of equipment in service. Were the smooth line allowed to represent this rise in withdrawals, it would mean that replacement demand was estimated on the assumption that the stock of equipment is not declining—an assumption which would materially distort the estimates of actual demand for additional equipment. As it is presently estimated, actual demand for additional equipment, presented in columns 4, 7, and 10 of Table I, implies two assumptions: (1) that replacement demand moves along a smooth line; (2) that in the last decade of the period, replacement demand is not allowed to rise, thus reflecting the secular downturn in the volume of equipment in service.

Finally, withdrawals are primarily of *old* equipment units, while orders are for *new* equipment units. If we then equate withdrawals with replacement demand, and subtract the number of units withdrawn (read off a smooth line) from total orders to obtain orders for additional units of equipment, the operation implies that replacement demand reflects the technical improvement of equipment units and the progress in the efficiency of handling them. There is considerable justification for such a definition of replacement demand, as over against another definition that would render the volume of replace-

TABLE I

THEORETICAL DEMAND COMPARED WITH ACTUAL ORDERS FOR ADDITIONAL UNITS OF RAILROAD EQUIPMENT, 1891-1930

	FREIGHT CARS (IN THOUSANDS)			LOCOMOTIVES			PASSENGER CARS		
Year	Theoretical Demand for Additional Units of Equipment	Total Orders for Equipment	Orders for Equipment Minus Replacements	Theoretical Demand for Additional Units of Equipment	Total Orders for Equipment	Orders for Equipment Minus Replacements	Theoretical Demand for Additional Units of Equipment	Total Orders for Equipment	Orders for Equipment, Minus Replacements
(1)	(2)	(3)	(4)	(5)	(6)	(7)	(8)	(9)	(10)
1891	50.1	47.6	20.4	1,449	1,389	929	2,136	1,073	938
1892	72.6	84.3	53.9	2,054	1,770	1,270	915	2,381	2,216
1893	53.3	58.3	24.7	1,481	1,724	1,189	1,718	2,143	1,943
1894	—129.9	23.2	—13.6	—3,553	315	—255	—863	299	64
1895	47.0	40.3	0.3	1,274	727	127	—841	370	100
1896	95.3	77.6	34.4	2,557	877	247	1,432	533	223
1897	—1.7	29.3	—17.1	—47	737	77	202	468	118
1898	171.5	103.8	54.2	4,575	1,176	486	602	894	504
1899	85.1	146.0	93.2	2,267	1,998	1,278	1,187	1,213	783
1900	155.4	127.4	71.4	4,160	2,433	1,683	824	1,491	1,021
1901	46.4	159.4	100.2	1,248	2,676	1,901	1,960	1,810	1,305
1902	84.4	214.0	151.5	2,285	3,620	2,820	1,831	1,909	1,369
1903	128.5	157.7	92.1	3,502	3,699	2,874	1,735	2,441	1,871
1904	10.2	66.0	—2.8	281	2,098	1,248	1,349	1,429	829
1905	91.7	186.6	114.7	2,541	4,002	3,127	1,693	2,436	1,806

Year							
	2,009	3,209	4,005	4,142	3,042	3,154	249.3	3,445
1907	151.0	241.7	4,255	4,017	3,092	2,613	2,255	1,565
1908	−127.6	40.5	−3,666	1,666	716	−712	688	−32
1909	2.9	75.6	83	1,507	532	648	2,810	2,065
1910	246.7	199.3	6,991	3,697	2,702	3,995	3,178	2,413
1911	−8.4	55.2	−233	2,129	1,114	2,200	1,763	978
1912	68.2	143.6	1,900	2,227	1,192	1,571	2,240	1,435
1913	249.3	169.6	6,796	3,372	2,322	1,354	2,090	1,265
1914	−84.2	144.5	−2,313	1,335	270	1,268	1,909	1,064
1915	−72.0	52.3	−1,990	814	−266	−2,744	862	−2
1916	405.5	101.9	11,263	2,238	1,143	2,149	1,311	438
1917	192.4	36.9	5,357	3,095	1,977	1,235	597	−293
1918	61.9	100.5	1,727	2,153	1,020	−3,392	0	−900
1919	−240.8	22.1	−6,745	216	−932	2,756	288	−622
1920	264.9	84.2	7,470	1,992	829	2,771	1,776	856
1921	−592.9	23.3	−16,430	240	−938	−1,845	240	−690
1922	183.2	180.2	5,118	2,604	1,411	−917	2,388	1,453
1923	410.6	94.5	11,537	1,980	777	2,688	2,220	1,280
1924	−133.5	142.8	−3,769	1,416	203	941	2,556	1,611
1925	138.7	78.3	3,937	996	−227	1,488	1,620	670
1926	162.3	56.3	4,627	1,200	−33	1,373	1,320	370
1927	−82.9	59.0	−2,374	660	−578	−191	1,220	270
1928	21.8	37.0	627	348	−895	−528	1,776	826
1929	75.0	98.3	2,170	1,044	−204	840	1,260	310
1930	−341.0	42.0	−9,904	396	−857	−2,702	636	−314

Years 1891-1916—ending June 30; 1917 to date—ending December 31.
All data relating to equipment from *Statistics of Railways*, published annually by the Interstate Commerce Commission.
Data on orders: 1891-1918 from John E. Partington, *Railroad Purchasing and the Business Cycle* (Washington, 1929); 1919 to date from *Survey of Current Business*.

ment demand in any given year equal only to the *efficiency equivalent* of the old units withdrawn. However, were we to adopt this latter definition, the values in columns 4, 7, and 10 would be between the present values of these columns and the values in columns 3, 6, and 9, respectively. This change would not affect the timing of the changes in the actual demand for additional units of equipment. The conclusions as to amplitude that are arrived at below are true whether we use columns 3, 6, and 9, or the values given now in columns 4, 7, and 10, and would thus be true for any intermediate value-pairs.

Actual and Theoretical Demand for Railroad Equipment: Comparison of Timing. In order to study timing, we had to mark off the peaks and troughs. The data being annual, and thus concealing the more conspicuous fluctuations that would be apparent in monthly series, it was decided to define each actual decline and rise as constituting a cycle and to date the peaks and troughs accordingly. The only two declines not treated in this fashion were the minor ones from 1905 to 1906, in theoretical demand for passenger cars, and from 1922 to 1923, in total orders for passenger cars. Table II assembles the dates of peaks and troughs in the series listed in Table I; and in addition shows the dates of peaks and troughs in the absolute volume of freight ton-miles and passenger car-miles, these having been determined by inspection with due consideration to the secular movement of the series.[11]

The first question in connection with timing is whether actual orders for equipment tend to follow *net changes* (theoretical demand) or the *absolute volume* of the demand for services. In terms of Table II, the question is whether the

[11] This consideration of the secular movement changes but little the dates of peaks and troughs, as compared with those based on the series in their original form. Thus of the peak dates in Table II for freight ton-miles all but one (that for 1903) mark years followed by absolute declines in the original series. The same is true of passenger train- and car-miles, in which only the peak of 1896 is not followed by an absolute decline in the original

TABLE II

DATES OF PEAKS AND TROUGHS IN THE VOLUME OF
TRANSPORTATION SERVICE AND IN THE DEMAND AND
ORDERS FOR RAILROAD EQUIPMENT, 1891-1930

Year	Freight Ton-Miles Transported	Theoretical Demand for Additional Units of Freight Cars and Locomotives	Total Orders, and Orders Minus Replacements, Freight Cars	Total Orders, and Orders Minus Replacements, Locomotives	Passenger Train-Miles and Passenger Car-Miles Transported	Theoretical Demand for Additional Passenger Cars	Total Orders, and Orders Minus Replacements, Passenger Cars
(1)	(2)	(3)	(4)	(5)	(6)	(7)	(8)
1891	..	..	..	..	..	..	..
1892	..	P	P	P	..	T	P
1893	P	..	..	..	P	P	..
1894	T	T	T	T	..	T	T
1895	..	..	..	..	T	..	..
1896	P	P	P	P	P	P	P
1897	T	T	T	T	T	T	T
1898	..	P	..	..	..	..	..
1899	..	T	P	..	..	P	..
1900	..	P	T	..	..	T	..
1901	..	T	..	..	..	P	..
1902	..	..	P	..	..	..	..
1903	P	P	..	P	..	..	P
1904	T	T	T	T	..	T	T
1905	..	..	..	..	..	..	..
1906	..	P	P	P	..	..	P
1907	P	..	..	..	P	P	..
1908	T	T	T	..	T	T	T
1909	..	..	..	T	..	..	..
1910	P	P	P	P	..	P	P
1911	T	T	T	T	..	..	T
1912	..	..	..	..	..	..	P
1913	P	P	P	P	.	..	..
1914	..	T	..	..	P	..	..
1915	T	..	T	T	T	T	T
1916	..	P	P	..	..	P	P

TABLE II—*Continued*

DATES OF PEAKS AND TROUGHS IN THE VOLUME OF TRANSPORTATION SERVICE AND IN THE DEMAND AND ORDERS FOR RAILROAD EQUIPMENT, 1891-1930

Year	Freight Ton-Miles Transported	Theoretical Demand for Additional Units of Freight Cars and Locomotives	Total Orders, and Orders Minus Replacements, Freight Cars	Total Orders, and Orders Minus Replacements, Locomotives	Passenger Train-Miles and Passenger Car-Miles Transported	Theoretical Demand for Additional Passenger Cars	Total Orders, and Orders Minus Replacements, Passenger Cars
(1)	(2)	(3)	(4)	(5)	(6)	(7)	(8)
1917	..	..	T	P	P	..	..
1918	P	..	P	..	T	T	T
1919	T	T	T	T	..	..	..
1920	P	P	P	P	P	P	P
1921	T	T	T	T	..	T	T
1922	..	..	..	P	T	..	..
1923	P	P	T	..	..	P	..
1924	T	T	P	..	..	T	P
1925	..	..	..	T	..	P	..
1926	P	P	T	P	P	..	..
1927	T	T	P	..	..	..	T
1928	..	..	T	T	T	T	P
1929	P	P	P	P	P	P	..
1930	..	..	..	..	..	..	..

dates in columns 4 and 5 show a better conformity to dates in column 3 than to those in column 2; and whether the dates in column 8 show a better conformity to those in column 7 than to those in column 6.

In four cases, column 3, expressive of the *net changes* in freight ton-miles, shows a lead over column 2, expressive of the *absolute volume*. A peak in column 3 in 1892 precedes the corresponding peak in column 2 in 1893; similarly, there is a peak in column 3 in 1906, in column 2 in 1907; a trough in column 3 in 1914, in column 2 in 1915; a peak in column 3 in 1916, in column 2 in 1918; and besides, there are two addi-

tional cycles in column 3 (1897-99 and 1899-1901) absent in
column 2. Looking at column 4, i.e., dates of orders for freight
cars, we find that in 1892 and 1906 the peaks in orders coincide with the movement of the *net change* (column 3) rather
than with the movement of the absolute volume (column 2);
but that in the trough of 1915, changes in orders coincide with
the movement of absolute volume, while the showing for 1916
is indeterminate. The same conclusion is arrived at from inspection of column 5, the dates of changes in orders for locomotives. Thus, out of the four test years, two seem to support
the hypothesis, one seems to contradict it, and one is indeterminate. But it is highly significant that in the two years in
which orders for freight cars and locomotives seem to follow
the *net change* rather than the *absolute volume* of freight ton-
miles, there are also peaks in the orders for passenger cars,
although no such peaks are to be expected according to the
hypothesis on the basis of net changes in passenger car-miles
(compare column 8 and column 7). This clearly suggests that
some factors were in operation to establish a peak in orders
for all railroad equipment in the years 1892 and 1906, factors
not directly related to net changes in volume of transportation
service. Of the two additional cycles in column 3, neither finds
an exact replica in freight-car or locomotive orders.

Comparing columns 6 and 7, we find five years in which
peaks and troughs in the net change (theoretical demand)
precede those in absolute volume, viz., the trough of 1894,
peak of 1910, peak of 1916, trough of 1921, and peak of 1926;
and, besides net changes show additional cycles not apparent
in the absolute volume, viz., 1897-1900, 1900-1904, and 1921-24.
Of the five years in which the theoretical demand for passenger
cars precedes that in the absolute volume of passenger car-
miles, actual orders follow the movement of theoretical demand in three years; and of the seven additional turning
points which column 7 shows, two find a counterpart in column
8. But the support which this showing lends to the hypothesis
is again weakened by the fact that these years (1894, 1916,
1921, 1904, and 1910) happen to be years of peaks and troughs

in orders for all types of railroad equipment, and are years of turning points in general business conditions.

Similar conclusions are suggested by the following summary table, in which the actual number of coincident turning points is related to the maximum possible. For each pair of series the maximum possible number of coincidences is given by the sum of the smaller number of peaks and the smaller number of troughs.

	Number of Coincident Peaks and Troughs	Maximum Possible Number of Coincident Turning Points	Percentage of Actual to Maximum
Freight Ton-miles and Orders for Freight Cars (columns 2 and 4)	14	21	66.7
Theoretical Demand and Orders for Freight Cars (columns 3 and 4)	15	25	60.0
Freight Ton-miles and Orders for Locomotives (columns 2 and 5)	14	21	66.7
Theoretical Demand and Orders for Locomotives (columns 3 and 5)	15	21	71.1
Passenger Car-miles and Orders for Passenger Cars (columns 6 and 8)	6	15	40.0
Theoretical Demand and Orders for Passenger Cars (columns 7 and 8)	11	19	57.9
Theoretical Demand for Freight Cars, Locomotives and Passenger Cars (columns 3 and 7)	12	22	54.5
Orders for Freight Cars, Locomotives and Passenger Cars (columns 4, 5, and 8)	12	19	63.2
Orders for Freight Cars and Passenger Cars (columns 4 and 8)	14	19	73.7
Orders for Locomotives and Passenger Cars (columns 5 and 8)	12	19	63.2

Thus, with the exception of passenger cars, there is little evidence that orders for railroad equipment follow net changes in transportation service, rather than the absolute volume of the latter. But orders for all types of railroad equipment seem to move in greater consonance than is justified by the correlation of net changes in the various types of transportation service. However, in view of inadequacy of annual data for the purpose of studying timing, the conclusions above should be taken with caution.

Actual and Theoretical Demand for Railroad Equipment: Comparison of Amplitude. The measures of amplitude of changes in theoretical demand for additional units and in actual orders for railroad equipment are assembled in Table III. The evidence may be summarized as follows:

TABLE III

AMPLITUDE OF CYCLICAL CHANGES IN THEORETICAL DEMAND AND ACTUAL ORDERS FOR RAILROAD EQUIPMENT

Freight cars in thousands; other equipment in units.

	Peaks		Troughs		Total
		Average Value of		Average Value of	Amplitude
Series	Number	Series	Number	Series	(3)–(5)
(1)	(2)	(3)	(4)	(5)	(6)
A. ALL TURNING POINTS					
I. *First Half of Period (1891-1910)*					
I-1. *Freight Cars*					
Theoretical Demand for Additional Units	7	155.7	6	–19.6	175.3
Total Orders	6	174.3	5	57.3	117.0
Orders minus Replacement	6	116.2	5	–0.3	116.5
I-2. *Locomotives*					
Theoretical Demand for Additional Units	7	4,285	6	–578	4,863
Total Orders	5	3,137	4	1,169	1,968

TABLE III—*Continued*

AMPLITUDE OF CYCLICAL CHANGES IN THEORETICAL
DEMAND AND ACTUAL ORDERS FOR RAILROAD
EQUIPMENT

Freight cars in thousands; other equipment in units.

Series	Peaks Number	Average Value of Series	Troughs Number	Average Value of Series	Total Amplitude (3)-(5)
(1)	(2)	(3)	(4)	(5)	(6)
Orders minus Replacement	5	2,367	4	400	1,967
I-3. Passenger Cars					
Theoretical Demand for Additional Units	6	2,151	6	286	1,865
Total Orders	5	2,360	4	721	1,639
Orders minus Replacement	5	1,866	4	245	1,621
II. Second Half of Period (1911 to date)					
II-1. Freight Cars					
Theoretical Demand for Additional Units	6	261.3	6	−190.4	451.7
Total Orders	8	117.1	8	47.2	69.9
Orders minus Replacement	8	19.1	8	−49.9	69.0
II-2. Locomotives					
Theoretical Demand for Additional Units	6	7,310	6	−5,311	12,621
Total Orders	6	2,218	6	790	1,428
Orders minus Replacement	6	1,050	6	−356	1,406
II-3. Passenger Cars					
Theoretical Demand for Additional Units	5	1,987	5	−1,514	3,501
Total Orders	5	1,932	5	817	1,115
Orders minus Replacement	5	1,033	5	−69	1,102

TABLE III—*Continued*

AMPLITUDE OF CYCLICAL CHANGES IN THEORETICAL
DEMAND AND ACTUAL ORDERS FOR RAILROAD
EQUIPMENT

Freight cars in thousands; other equipment in units.

Series	Number	Peaks Average Value of Series	Number	Troughs Average Value of Series	Total Amplitude (3)–(5)
(1)	(2)	(3)	(4)	(5)	(6)
III. *Full Period (1891 to date)*					
III-1. *Freight Cars*					
Theoretical Demand for					
Additional Units	13	204.4	12	–105.0	309.4
Total Orders	14	141.6	13	51.1	90.5
Orders minus Replace-					
ment	14	60.7	13	–30.8	91.5
III-2. *Locomotives*					
Theoretical Demand for					
Additional Units	13	5,681	12	–2,944	8,625
Total Orders	11	2,636	10	940	1,696
Orders minus Replace-					
ment	11	1,649	10	–54	1,703
III-3. *Passenger Cars*					
Theoretical Demand for					
Additional Units	11	2,076	11	–532	2,608
Total Orders	10	2,146	9	774	1,372
Orders minus Replace-					
ment	10	1,450	9	71	1,379
B. COINCIDENT TURNING POINTS ONLY					
Full period (1891 to date)					
1. *Freight Cars*					
Theoretical Demand for					
Additional Units	8	203.7	7	–155.9	359.6
Total Orders	8	142.8	7	37.1	105.7
Orders minus Replace-					
ment	8	65.1	7	–36.6	101.7

TABLE III—*Continued*

AMPLITUDE OF CYCLICAL CHANGES IN THEORETICAL
DEMAND AND ACTUAL ORDERS FOR RAILROAD
EQUIPMENT

Freight cars in thousands; other equipment in units.

		Peaks		Troughs	Total
		Average		Average	Ampli-
		Value of		Value of	tude
Series	Number	Series	Number	Series	(3)–(5)
(1)	(2)	(3)	(4)	(5)	(6)
2. Locomotives					
Theoretical Demand for					
Additional Units	9	4,702	6	–4,454	9,156
Total Orders	9	2,588	6	956	1,632
Orders minus Replace-					
ment	9	1,691	6	52	1,629
3. Passenger Cars					
Theoretical Demand for					
Additional Units	4	2,587	7	–1,144	3,731
Total Orders	4	1,699	7	569	1,130
Orders minus Replacement	4	982	7	–88	1,070

1. The amplitude of changes in actual orders for equipment, whether total or adjusted for replacements, is much narrower than that of changes in theoretical demand for additional units of equipment. Taking the full period covered by the data and all the turning points, we find that for freight cars the amplitude of changes in actual orders is less than one-third as wide as that of fluctuations in theoretical demand; for locomotives about one-fifth; and for passenger cars about one-half. Taking coincident turning points only, we find the amplitude of changes in actual orders for freight cars to be again less than one-third as wide as that of changes in theoretical demand; for locomotives, less than one-fifth; and for passenger cars, less than one-third.

2. As between the two halves of the period covered, the amplitude of changes in actual orders for equipment narrows

from the period 1891-1910 to the period 1911-30, while the amplitude of changes in theoretical demand widens between the same two periods. As a result the difference in the amplitude of changes between actual orders and theoretical demand is much more appreciable in the later half of the period covered than in the earlier.

3. Generally, the difference between actual orders and theoretical demand in standing at turning points is much more striking at the troughs than at the peaks. This difference undergoes the same secular change within the period as was noted for total amplitude under (2) above.

Thus, the statistical evidence indicates that the magnification of changes in the demand for equipment, expected on the basis of the hypothesis tested, fails to materialize by a wide margin.

Qualifications of the Statistical Analysis. Before concluding this analysis of data on railroad equipment, it may be useful to suggest some of the deficiencies of the data and their possible bearing upon the validity of the conclusions.

1. Data refer to orders, unadjusted for cancellations, withholding of specifications, or requests for delay in shipments. The magnitude of these forms of cancellation is unknown, but judging by the evidence of such industries for which cancellations for recent years are reported, their size cannot be large as compared with new orders.

2. On the other hand, orders for equipment reflect only a part of the total demand for new equipment, and probably the more variable one, since railroad repair shops build new cars and locomotives. The fraction of equipment built by the roads themselves is, however, small, amounting in recent years to slightly less than 10 percent. Still, this factor, which exaggerates the amplitude of fluctuations in orders, may be sufficient to offset the correction for cancellations.

3. Also, freight ton-miles and passenger car-miles represent actual volume of transportation services rather than demand for them. In years of contraction, the two are likely to be identical, but in years of expansion it is quite possible for

demand to outrun the volume of services which the railroads
can provide. (This is especially true of the two earlier decades
of the period covered.) Thus the amplitude of changes in
theoretical demand may understate the intensity of fluctuations
that would be obtained if data on the volume of demand for
railroad services were available.

4. There is a possibility that the series relating to orders
are subject to error, since the original data reported in the
journals may be incomplete. However, for the years after
1890, such errors in annual data are likely to be small.

The balance of these considerations is to leave unaffected
the conclusions in regard to comparative timing and amplitude of changes in theoretical demand and actual orders. If
anything, it appears to strengthen the impression of disparity
in amplitude between theoretical demand and actual orders
for railroad equipment.

TIMING OF CYCLICAL CHANGES IN THE OUTPUT OF
FINISHED PRODUCTS AND IN THE DEMAND FOR
CAPITAL GOODS (MONTHLY SERIES)

In studying comparative timing of series bearing upon the
hypothesis under consideration, the main question is whether
the lead of changes in the demand for capital goods over those
in output of finished products is of the range suggested by the
hypothesis. In order to answer this question precisely, monthly
series are needed relating to the output of finished products
and to the demand for capital goods used in attaining that
output. Such series are available only for recent years and are
few in number. In the ones available, cyclical turning points
have been determined by inspection, and the dates are presented in Table IV.

The index of manufacturing production of the Federal Reserve Board may be considered, from the standpoint of cyclical
timing, an adequate reflection of the volume of finished products, in the production of which such capital goods as industrial structures and machine tools play an important part.
Similarly, woodworking machinery, a series that relates pri-

marily to machines used in sawmills, may properly be compared with the index of lumber production. The comparison indicates that the demand for capital goods moves more in accordance with the absolute volume of the output of finished products than with the net changes in this output. In total manufacturing production, net change shows a substantial lead over absolute volume in four cases (1920, 1922, 1924-25, and 1926), and in each, both contracts awarded for industrial construction and new orders for machine tools tend to synchronize with the volume of manufacturing production. Similarly, in lumber output, net changes show substantial lead over absolute volume in three cases (1921-22, 1925 and 1926), and, in all three, new orders for and shipments of woodworking machinery tend to synchronize with the absolute volume of lumber output.

This evidence is subject to one qualification: the series reflecting demand for capital goods are all in dollar values at changing prices, while the series relating to production of finished products are either in quantity units or in dollar values at constant prices. It may be suggested that the turning points in the demand for capital goods would occur earlier, were the series expressed in quantity units or in dollar values at constant prices. This suggestion is, however, at least partly disposed of by the evidence of the series of woodworking machinery shipments in quantity units (see column 10 of Table IV), the turning points in which do not differ appreciably from those in new orders and shipments in dollar values at changing prices.

The evidence presented in Table IV, slender as the statistical basis is, added to the negative conclusions with regard to timing derived from the annual series on railroad equipment, indicates that while the cycles in the demand for capital goods may lead those in the output of finished products, the lead is not of the range suggested by the hypothesis.

TABLE IV

DATES OF CYCLICAL TURNING POINTS IN SERIES REFLECTING PRODUCTION of FINISHED PRODUCTS AND DEMAND FOR CAPITAL GOODS

| TURNING POINT | INDEX OF MANUFACTURING PRODUCTION, F.R.B. | | CONTRACTS AWARDED, INDUSTRIAL CONSTRUCTION ($) | NEW ORDERS, MACHINE TOOLS ($) | LUMBER PRODUCTION, F.R.B. INDEX | | WOODWORKING MACHINERY | | |
| | Absolute Values | Net Changes | | | Absolute Values | Net Changes | New Orders ($) | Shipments ($) | Shipments (units) |
(1)	(2)	(3)	(4)	(5)	(6)	(7)	(8)	(9)	(10)
Peak	Jan.-Feb. 1920	January 1920	January 1920	January 1920	February 1920	September 1919	No data	June 1920	No Data
Trough	April 1921	November 1920	March 1921	July-Sept. 1921	January 1921	Dec. 1920-Jan. 1921	January 1921 (?)	July 1921	No Data
Peak	May 1923	May or Oct. 1922	May 1923	March 1923	November 1923	Dec. 1921 or May 1922	March 1923	March 1923	January 1923
Trough	July 1924	May 1924	May 1924	June 1924	July 1924	Jan. or May 1924	June 1924	July 1924	July 1924
Peak	October 1923	Dec. 1924 or Dec. 1925	July 1926	October 1926	December 1925	January 1925	Oct. 1925 or Mar. 1926	Mar. 1926	April 1926
Trough	November 1927	Dec. 1926 or Oct. 1927	December 1927	September 1927	Apr. 1927 or July 1928	December 1926	July 1927	July 1927	November 1927
Peak	June 1929	June 1929	July 1929	May 1929	July 1929	March 1929	January 1929	April 1929	April 1929

Index of manufacturing production, lumber output (F.R.B.) corrected for seasonal variations. Other series do not appear subject to any appreciable seasonal swing.

Data from Federal Reserve Board, and Survey of Current Business.

4

SCHUMPETER'S BUSINESS
CYCLES *

The scope of the treatise is so wide that any thorough summary of its contents would exceed the limits of the present review. Such a summary would also be difficult because of the character of Professor Schumpeter's discussion. Some of the chapters are themselves summaries of the author's earlier writings, and would need expansion rather than condensation. Other parts are running commentaries upon specific situations, with a wealth of allusions, incisive sidelights, references to existing literature, and theoretical suggestions. Such discussion cannot be summarized effectively. In still other parts, the author's meaning is elusive in that the reader is uncertain what limits of confidence Professor Schumpeter assigns to his statements and what in detail is the basis upon which they are made—a comment of particular application to the discussion of the dating of cycles and the presence or absence of cycles in a given series.

One must therefore select for review only a few of the numerous problems treated in the two volumes. The presentation below deals with three topics that seem to the writer to be of wide bearing and to call for critical evaluation: (a) the relation between distribution of entrepreneurial ability and the cyclical character of economic change; (b) the four-phase scheme of the business cycle and its bearing upon statistical

* Reprinted by permission from *American Economic Review*, Vol. XXX no. 2, June 1940, pp. 250-271. The first three paragraphs have been omitted. This article is a review of Joseph A. Schumpeter's *Business Cycles*, Vols. I and II, New York: McGraw-Hill, 1939.

analysis; (c) the three types of cycles distinguished. I shall first attempt to present Professor Schumpeter's view on these three topics, and then formulate the questions which, in my view, are raised by his discussion.

I

To Professor Schumpeter, business cycles are pulsations of the rate of economic evolution. Economic change in general is attributed to three groups of forces: external factors, for example, the demand of governments for new military weapons; the factor of growth, by which the author means the continuous gradual changes in population and in the volume of savings and accumulation, changes that do not require drastic shifts in the combination of productive factors and thus may be attained by the ordinary, run of the mill economic agent addicted to an habitual and adaptive type of activity; and innovations which represent material changes (or as Professor Schumpeter defines them, changes of first order) in the production functions. It is innovations that are of strategic importance in the evolution of capitalist economy, innovations that are usually introduced by new rather than by old firms, by new men rather than by those who already occupy prominent niches in the functioning system.

Business cycles are recurrent fluctuations in the rate at which innovations are introduced into the economy, in the intensity with which entrepreneurs exercise their *sui generis* function of overcoming obstacles to new combinations. The reason for this discontinuity in the rate of innovations and in the intensity of entrepreneurial endeavor, of the bunching of innovations at one time and their comparative scarcity at others, lies in the distribution of entrepreneurial ability. This ability to dare, to initiate, to overcome obstacles to innovations is, like many other abilities, distributed along a curve which suggests that there are few individuals endowed with such ability to any great degree and many who are equipped only to imitate and follow the pioneering efforts of the few. If then we envisage, in a state of equilibrium, the action of the first entrepreneur, one of high ability, we shall see that his action will be followed by a swarm of imitations, increasing in volume as time passes and as the innovation becomes a more accepted pattern of action.

This uprush of innovation, accompanied by expanding credit, rising prices, rising interest rates, a relatively constant volume of total output but usually a shift in favor of producers' goods, constitutes the period of rise in the first approximation to the business cycle. It terminates as soon as the disturbance of the equilibrium has proceeded far enough to upset the existing relations of prices, costs and quantities, thus making it impossible to formulate rationally calculated plans for the future. This terminus is reached all the sooner because innovations are usually concentrated at any given time in one or few industrial areas, and the increase in risk and uncertainty is made more effective by the exhaustion of innovation opportunities. At the turn, the rate of innovation slackens and a period of readjustment ensues in which entrepreneurs take stock and the economy recedes to a new equilibrium level, a level which both growth and innovations make higher than that from which the expansion started. During this period of recession credit volumes, prices and interest rates decline but total output is likely to average larger than in the preceding prosperity.

This first approximation, the primary model, thus accounts for a two-phase cycle, a departure upward from equilibrium level and a recession to a new equilibrium level. But conditions under which entrepreneurial activity takes place in reality must next be considered: the errors of forecast; the speculative tendencies of individuals; the thousand and one peculiarities of economic institutions that are likely to prolong and exaggerate a movement once initiated. These surface factors, which, in Professor Schumpeter's view, often claim the attention of business-cycle students to the exclusion of the fundamental process of innovation, may and do intensify the rise during the prosperity phase beyond the level to which it would have been carried by the stream of innovations proper; and during recession they reënforce the deflation, carrying it often below the equilibrium level into depression. When this occurs, the economy returns to equilibrium whenever the forces of depression spend themselves, a point determined largely by the peculiarities of the secondary factors that produce the abnormal contraction. But the equilibrium reached by recovery is not necessarily identical with that which would have been attained had the depression not taken place.

The combination of the first and second approximations yields a four-phase cycle of prosperity, recession, depression, and revival. The upper turning point is determined essentially by the primary model, whereas the revival point is determined largely by secondary factors. But whatever the difference in the causation of prosperity and recession as over against depression and revival, the four-phase model of the cycle must constitute the paramount guide in the statistical study of time series. Cyclical units should be defined not from trough to trough or peak to peak but from the beginning of prosperity, the point where the series begins to rise above the normal level to the end of revival, the point where the series again reaches the new normal. Professor Schumpeter dates the terminal points of the cycles that he distinguishes in accordance with this rule, and advocates for time-series analysis a method, originally proposed by Ragnar Frisch, that calls for establishing points of inflection. Under certain conditions these points of inflection are in the neighborhood of equilibrium levels and their establishment will thus serve to ascertain the terminal dates of the cycles, if not the turning points that divide prosperity from recession and depression from revival. Since inflection points suggest equilibrium levels in cyclical movements only if the rate of cyclical rise or decline diminishes as the curve pulls away from the equilibrium line, Professor Schumpeter accepts this condition as consonant with the theoretical significance of normal levels.

Neither the primary, nor the secondary, model implies necessarily one type of cycle only, *i.e.*, a cycle of approximately the same duration and intensity. On the contrary, differences in the magnitude of various innovations suggest that there may be several kinds of cycles differing in duration and in amplitude as the innovations with which they are associated differ in magnitude and the time they require to attain their proper place in the economy. Presumably the same is true of the secondary factors: they may and do differ with reference to the span of time during which they produce their exaggerating effect upon expansion and liquidation. It is thus theoretically plausible to expect cycles of varying duration and intensity, their types and their interrelations to be determined largely by observation.

Professor Schumpeter finds that in order to account for the cycles that can be observed historically and statistically during the last century and a half three types of cycles should be distinguished: long waves of about fifty years in duration (Kondratieffs); intermediate waves of about eight to nine years in duration (Juglars); and short waves of about forty months in duration (Kitchins). Unfortunately nowhere in the two volumes is there a chronology stating the terminal dates of the various types of cycles distinguished by Professor Schumpeter for the three countries with which he deals in his historical and statistical sections. But the historical outlines in Volume I are concerned with establishing the Kondratieffs and the Juglars in the three countries before the World War; and in the detailed discussion of the years since 1919 there are a few specific indications of the dates of some Kitchins.[1]

[1] I have attempted to construct a chronology of the Kondratieffs with the following results:

Prosperity	Recession	Depression	Revival
Industrial Revolution Kondratieff, 1787-1842: Cotton Textile, Iron, Steam Power			
1787-1800	1801-1813	1814-1827	1828-1842
Bourgeois Kondratieff, 1842-1897: Railroadization			
1843-1857	1858-1869	1870-1884-5	1886-1897
Neo-Mercantilist Kondratieff, 1897 to date: Electricity, Automobile			
1898-1911	1912-1924-5	1925-6-1939	

The dates of the first and second Kondratieff are established from the

The concurrence of these three types of cycles, each christened by the name of the economist who was chiefly responsible for claiming validity for it, accounts, according to Professor Schumpeter, for the diversity in the duration and amplitude of cycles observed in time series; and it explains why some "depressions," such as those of 1825-30, 1873-78, and 1929-34, were so long and so deep—a result of coincidence in phase of at least two of the three types of cycles. But all three types of cycles are due to the same fundamental set of causes, described by the primary model; in all we should expect four or two phases as the secondary factors are or are not sufficiently effective to produce depressions and revivals. As to the relations among these three types of cycles, two observations are made by Professor Schumpeter. First, the theoretical model requires that "each Kondratieff should contain an integral number of Juglars and each Juglar an integral number of Kitchins" (p. 172). The immediate consequence of this is that the first years in the prosperity phase of each Kondratieff coincide with Juglar and Kitchin prosperities; and the same is true of the immediately preceding revivals. Second, "barring very few cases in which difficulties arise, it is possible to count off, historically as well as statistically, six Juglars to a Kondratieff and three Kitchins to a Juglar—not as an average but in every individual case" (p. 174). This empirical conclusion, however, is not called for by the theoretical scheme; indeed the latter would lead us to expect irregularity in the number of the shorter type cycles comprised within each cyclical unit of longer duration.

---

discussion for Great Britain; that of the third from the discussion for the United States. The specific dates for the three countries are presumably somewhat different, but the differences are likely to be minor. It should also be noted that Professor Schumpeter considers that the first Kondratieff is not clearly shown in Germany. The table above was checked by Professor Schumpeter who has kindly suggested a few changes in its original version.

Professor Schumpeter also provides dates for Juglars. They are presented as roughly corresponding to the dates in Thorp's *Business Annals*, with due allowance for the difference in terminology.

II

This summary, bare and oversimplified as it is, reveals the significance of Professor Schumpeter's theoretical scheme and empirical findings. The close connection in this scheme between business cycles and the general process of evolution of capitalist economy; the direct bearing of the theoretical model of the cycle, with its equilibrium levels and its four phases, upon the statistical analysis of time series; the specificity of the three-cycle scheme, in the duration, interrelation and concurrence of the three cycle types—all contribute to an impression of a well integrated intellectual structure that elegantly spans the gap between controlled imagination and diversified reality.

But further reflection and even a partial scrutiny of the evidence presented in the two volumes raise a host of crucial questions and disturbing doubts. In selecting some of these for discussion, we may begin with the association claimed to exist between the distribution of entrepreneurial ability and discontinuity in the making of innovations—in other words, their "bunching." What precisely is the necessary connection between scarcity at any given time of high entrepreneurial ability (and the plenitude of imitators) and the bunching of innovations? Given an infinite supply of possible innovations (inventions and other new combinations), why need entrepreneurial genius defer the next pioneering step until his preceding one has been so imitated and expanded that the upsetting of the equilibrium stops even him in his tracks? If imitators are ready to follow as soon as the entrepreneurial genius has proved the innovation successful, the disturbance of equilibrium at that time is certainly not sufficient to bar this genius from turning to new feats and thus initiating an uprush in another industry. Why should we not conceive these applications of high entrepreneurial ability, whether represented by one man or several, as flowing in a continuous stream, a stream magnified in a constant proportion by the efforts of the imitators?

A close reading of Professor Schumpeter's text, both in this book and in his earlier treatise on the *Theory of Economic Development,* indicates that he expects high entrepreneurial ability to pause after the innovation and descend to the lower level of its imitators. The theory definitely calls for discontinuity *over time* in the operation of entrepreneurial ability. Such discontinuity cannot be derived from a distribution of entrepreneurial ability *at any given moment of time,* except on one assumption—namely, that the ability called for is so scarce that it may be completely absent during some periods of time while present at others. But this implies cycles in the supply of entrepreneurial ability, whether the supply be conceived in terms of individuals or of phases in the life of various individuals. I am not sure that Professor Schumpeter would view this assumption as valid.

Further reading and reflection suggest two possible alternative explanations of the bunching of innovations. The first is that *by definition* an innovation so disturbs existing economic relations that its introduction on a significant scale (*i.e.,* by the first entrepreneur plus the imitators) will necessarily prevent any other innovation from being successful so long as a process of readjustment has not taken place. This answer means, of course, that an innovation, by definition, is tantamount to a two-phase cycle, *i.e.,* it is defined as the kind of change that produces, upon its introduction, a phase of prosperity and of recession. And correspondingly, an entrepreneur *sui generis* is one who by definition introduces innovations that by definition result in a two-phase cycle. Hence by definition there is a necessary association between two-phase cycles and the *existence* of entrepreneurs. This, however, is such an obvious tautology as to be inacceptable as a significant interpretation or extension of Professor Schumpeter's position.

The second answer, suggested by Professor Schumpeter references to the concentration of innovations in restricted industrial areas and by the emphasis in his historical discussion of technological changes, is that the discontinuity or bunching in the rate of innovation rests essentially upon discontinuity or bunching in the supply of possible new combinations, particularly of technological inventions. This, in essence, assumes cyclical fluctuations in the rate at which producers of the technical basis for innovations contribute to the stock of possible new combinations from which entrepreneurs can choose. Thus, it may be said that in the last quarter of the eighteenth century in England there were several major inventions (cotton textiles, iron and steel, steam engine); that thereafter it was not until the 30's of the nineteenth century that another big group of inventions, connected with steam railroads, became accessible to the entrepreneur; and that as a result we have a two-phase cycle of prosperity in the last quarter of the eighteenth century and of recession in the next quarter.

Whether or not this be a proper extension of Professor Schumpeter's theory, the argument that technological and other opportunities for economic innovation are not necessarily continuous over time has some plausibility. There may be periods of hiatus with no big potential change on hand to stimulate and motivate the driving power of entrepreneurial genius. But this generalization, viewed as a basis for a primary model of business cycles, is subject to severe qualifications. Discontinuity of opportunity can be assumed only with reference to the most momentous innovations such as steam power, electricity, etc., *i.e.*, innovations that bear upon Kondratieff cycles. We can hardly expect significant fluctuations in the stock of innovation opportunities of the type that are associated with the Juglar or the Kitchin cycles. Furthermore, even with reference to the major innovations that may be associated with fifty-year spans, there is some indication that the long lapse between the appearance of the inventions is itself partly conditioned by the functioning of the economic system. For example, we may say that electricity did not become available sooner because it had to wait until the potentialities of steam power were exhausted by the economic system and until the attention of inventors and engineers was ready to be diverted to the problems of electricity. If this is so, there may be discontinuity in the *appearance* of inventions, but there is no necessary time lag between those major inventions as sources

of significant economic innovations. Thus, even for application
to a primary model of the Kondratieff cycle the assumption of
discontinuity of technical opportunities would have to be
closely scrutinized in the light of historical evidence.

The queries raised above should not be interpreted as denying the importance of entrepreneurial genius or the jerky character of economic evolution. They stem from a critical
consideration of one point only, the association between distribution of entrepreneurial ability and cyclical fluctuations in
the rate of innovation, an association that appears crucial in
Professor Schumpeter's business-cycle theory. Nor need it be
emphasized that the discussion above applies exclusively to
the first approximation, the primary model, and neglects completely the secondary factors. It is the former that Professor
Schumpeter stresses as providing the fundamental explanation of business cycles, and it is the former that contains his
specific contribution. The term "secondary factors" subsumes
the variety of forces treated in many other business-cycle
theories, and there is a tendency in Professor Schumpeter's
discussion to slight them, to consider them at best as influences
inferior to the factors cited in the first approximation.

III

We pass now to the four-phase model of a cycle conceived
in terms of departures from an equilibrium line, and the bearing of this model upon statistical analysis of time series. The
procedure preferred by Professor Schumpeter involves establishing points of inflection, first in the original series, then in
the line that passes through the first series of inflection points
and so on, successively decomposing the total series into several cyclical lines. Professor Schumpeter himself recognizes
the difficulties involved in the application of this procedure
(see page 211, vol. I). There is first the delicate problem of
smoothing the series so as to eliminate the effect of erratic
fluctuations on the second order differences used to establish

inflection points. A more serious difficulty arises because the assumption that the inflection points are in the neighborhood of equilibrium levels implies a specific pattern of cyclical movements; and there is no ground for expecting cyclical fluctuations in actual series to conform to this pattern.

For these reasons Professor Schumpeter does not recommend the method for general application and recognizes it only as a first approximation and a far from infallible guide. He presents applications of this method in his book to just two series: one used for purely illustrative purposes in chapter 5, a monthly series on revenue freight loadings for 1918-1930 (Chart III, page 218) and the other used for analytical purposes in chapter 8 (Chart IX, page 469), an annual series of wholesale prices in the United States from 1790 to 1930. For the rest, statistical analysis is confined to a graphic portrayal of the series, sometimes reduced to successive rates of percentage change, sometimes smoothed by a simple moving average, and in one case with a fitted trend curve and fitted cycles. The preponderant number of series are, however, left in their original form and the statistical analysis for almost all of them is in the form of verbal statements of quantitative import, based upon observation of the charts.

The difficulties encountered in the matter of inflection points and the paucity of formal statistical analysis in the treatise lead to a doubt that Professor Schumpeter's concept of equilibrium and of the four-phase model of business cycles are such as to permit of application to statistical analysis. This doubt is strengthened when it is considered that the concept calls for segregating movements of the equilibrium line caused by external factors and growth from movements caused by innovations. Hence the usual lines of secular trend, drawn so as to bisect the area of cyclical fluctuations, are not acceptable from the viewpoint of Professor Schumpeter's theoretical model. This model requires, as I see it, that the line underlying any given cycle should express at any given time only the level that can be maintained by the activity of the inert adaptive character not properly dignified by the term entrepreneurial. To segregate this level from the slant given to the line by the cumulation of innovations is indeed difficult.

By refusing to deal with secular trend lines based upon formal characteristics (irreversibility, smoothness, etc.) Professor Schumpeter sacrifices the possibility of basing the distinction between long-term movements and cyclical variations upon observable criteria. By refusing to accept peaks and troughs as guides in the determination of cycles he scorns the help provided by that statistical characteristic of cycles in time series. One cannot escape the impression that Professor Schumpeter's theoretical model in its present state cannot be linked directly and clearly with statistically observed realities; that the extreme paucity of statistical analysis in the treatise is an inevitable result of the type of theoretical model adopted; and that the great reliance upon historical outlines and qualitative discussion is a consequence of the difficulty of devising statistical procedures that would correspond to the theoretical model.

IV

The validity of the three-cycle schema, the last topic under discussion, hinges largely on the nature of the historical evidence and qualitative analysis. As already indicated, Professor Schumpeter does not claim for the Kondratieff-Juglar-Kitchin combination any necessary connection with his theoretical model. But he does present it as a schema called for by historical reality, as a classification fully justified by the way it describes successive business cycles since the last quarter of the eighteenth century in the three countries under observation. Yet, in spite of numerous references to this classification in the historical outlines, in spite of the emphatic way in which its validity is claimed in the treatise, there remain serious doubts that such validity has been demonstrated or could be demonstrated with the type of materials and analysis employed by Professor Schumpeter.

The cycle is essentially a quantitative concept. All its characteristics such as duration, amplitude, phases, etc., can be conceived only as measurable aspects, and can be properly measured only with the help of quantitative data. Furthermore, the distinction between cycles and irregular movements traceable to external factors can be made at all adequately only if the successive cycles are measured and averages are struck in which the influence of external factors can be reduced, if not eliminated. This does not mean that observation of cycles on the basis of qualitative information is neither possible nor valuable. For whatever quantities reflect cyclical changes, these changes result from discrete acts by individuals or non-personal units in the social system. Some of these discrete acts may be recorded singly and separately in historical records; of others a crude count or impression can be derived from contemporary qualitative reports. The study of such qualitative data in conjunction with statistics is indispensable for a close analysis of the latter. And the former without the assistance of the latter can often give a crude idea of the succession of cyclical phases and of the larger differences in amplitude between one cycle and another. But it is difficult to see how qualitative records can yield much beyond a suggestion of dates of peaks and troughs of a single type of cycle; how one could, on the basis of historical records alone, distinguish the dating and phases of several concurrently existing cycle types.

The question raised bears most upon the establishment of the Kondratieff cycles. To establish the existence of cycles of a given type requires first a demonstration that fluctuations of that approximate duration recur, with fair simultaneity, in the movements of various significant aspects of economic life (production and employment in various industries, prices of various groups of goods, interest rates, volumes of trade, flow of credit, etc.); and second, an indication of what external factors or peculiarities of the economic system proper account for such recurrent fluctuations. Unless the former basis is laid, the cycle type distinguished cannot be accepted as affecting

economic life at large—it may be specific to a limited part of
the country's economic system. Unless the second, theoretical,
basis is established there is no link that connects findings relating to empirical observations of a given type of cycles in a
given country over a given period of time with the broader
realm of already established knowledge.

Neither of these bases has ever been satisfactorily laid for
the Kondratieff cycles. Kondratieff's own statistical analysis
refers largely to price indexes, interest rates, or volumes of
activity in current prices—series necessarily dominated by the
price peaks of the Napoleonic wars, of the 1870's (not unconnected with the Civil War in this country), and of the World
War. The prevalence of such fifty-year cycles in volumes of
production, either total or for important branches of activity,
in employment, in physical volume of trade, has not been
demonstrated; nor has the presumed existence of these cycles
been reconciled with those of a duration from 18 to 25 years
established for a number of production series in this and other
countries. Nor has a satisfactory theory been advanced as to
why these 50-year swings should recur: the explanations tend
to emphasize external factors (inventions, wars, etc.) without
demonstrating their cyclical character in their tendency to recur as a result of an underlying mechanism or as effects of
another group of external factors of proven "cyclicity."

These doubts as to the validity of the Kondratieff cycles
are not dispelled by the evidence Professor Schumpeter submits. The part of his discussion that deals with qualitative,
historical evidence leaves unanswered two crucial questions.
The first refers to the particular aspect of activity that is considered as revealing the Kondratieff cycles and is thus observed to establish the dates. Such observation obviously cannot relate to economic activity at large, for qualitative data
on the course of general economic activity necessarily deal
with short-term changes and would not serve to differentiate
the underlying Kondratieffs from the much more clearly
marked shorter cyclical swings. Therefore, in order to set the
dates of Kondratieffs, one must choose some activity particu-

larly sensitive to these long swings. The natural choice would
be the economic innovations whose introduction forms the
substance of Kondratieff prosperities. But as Professor Schumpeter observes, such innovations usually make their appearance before the Kondratieff that is associated with them. Thus
steam railroads began to be constructed before the railroadiza-
tion Kondratieff (*i.e.*, before 1843); and electricity was well
known before the Kondratieff associated with it began in 1898.
One then tends to infer that a Kondratieff begins when the
underlying major innovation is being introduced on a large
scale and at a rapid rate. But does this mean that the prosperity of a Kondratieff is the period at which the introduction
of the innovation displays the maximum absolute or percentage rate of increase?[2] One searches in vain for a definite formulation of the criterion by which historical evidence is analyzed to distinguish the Kondratieff cycles from the Juglars
and used to establish the terminal and the four phase dates
for the former.

The second question raised by the discussion of the Kondratieffs in the light of historical evidence refers to the treatment of "accidental" external factors and of transient secondary
influences. As Professor Schumpeter himself recognizes, any
given cyclical turn, in any observable type of cycle, can be
attributed to one or several specific historical events, *i.e.*, to
some transient accidental circumstances in the neighborhood
of the turn. And yet it should be possible in the analysis to
distinguish between these accidental concomitants and the
underlying cyclical swings. As already indicated, this segrega-
tion is accomplished in statistical analysis by averaging or
similar devices. In the treatment of qualitative, historical evidence the task is more difficult. It might be facilitated by a
classification of various types of factors that would distinguish
in advance cyclical factors from others; but even then the con-

---

[2] This criterion would not fit experience in the United States, since the
percentage rate of growth in the additions to railroad mileage was at its
maximum before 1842; and the absolute rate of addition was at its
maximum long after 1860.

currence in historical reality of accidental and cyclical factors might necessitate what is essentially quantitative analysis. It is not clear how Professor Schumpeter deals with the problem. In some cases he recognizes an "accidental" disturbance that produces what appears to be a cyclical turn, but does not disregard this turn as conforming with his schema. In other cases he attributes the departure of reality from the hypothesis to accidental historical conditions (notably in explaining why prices continued to decline in the United States after 1842 when there was supposedly a Kondratieff prosperity). The opportunity in such treatment for personal judgment is perhaps inevitable in the use of qualitative data; but the unfortunate consequences for the effort to establish the validity of the Kondratieff cycles and their dates are not diminished thereby.

As to the statistical basis for the recognition of Kondratieff cycles, Professor Schumpeter's approach, for reasons already indicated, can yield little of value. The failure to follow articulate methods of time series analysis reduces the statistical methods to a mere recording of impressions of charts, impressions with which it is often difficult to agree. To quote but two instances. (1) In Charts XII and XIII (pp. 486 and 487) Professor Schumpeter presents data on pig iron consumption (annual) for the United States, the United Kingdom and Germany for the period roughly from 1857 to 1913; and comments that the lines reflect "all three cycles . . . very well" (p. 485). But I, for one, cannot detect any traces of Kondratieffs in the lines either for Germany or for the United Kingdom; and would record two long cycles in the American series, one from 1857 to 1875 and the other from 1875 to 1895, rather than a single Kondratieff swing. (2) Chart XLII presents a monthly index of industrial production for the United States from 1897 to 1935. Professor Schumpeter then comments that the movement during 1898-1912 shows a rate of increase lower than that from 1922 to 1929; and this is cited to support the existence of a Kondratieff prosperity (1898-1912), as contrasted with a subsequent Kondratieff recession that is assumed to terminate in 1925.[3] But a glance at the chart suggests to me that the line from 1898 to 1912 is appreciably steeper than the line that would characterize the post-war decade; and that any higher rate that might be shown by a line drawn from 1922 to 1929 would be due exclusively to the position of the terminal years in the shorter-term cycles. Whichever judgment of the charts is correct, disagreement is easily possible; and such ease is an eloquent testimony to the insufficiency of the crude statistical procedures followed in the treatise to provide a basis for establishing cycle types of so elusive a character as the Kondratieffs.

The Kitchins are too short and perhaps too mild to be discernible with the available qualitative historical evidence, especially for the years before 1919. Hence the distinction between the Juglars and the Kitchins is based in the treatise largely upon statistical evidence, *i.e.*, again largely upon the impression conveyed by the charts. The series used for the pre-war years are almost exclusively annual, and the comments refer to the existence of the Kitchins rather than to their dates. Only for the years since 1919 do the plenitude of quantitative and detailed data and the emphasis that Professor Schumpeter places upon a thorough discussion of changes during these recent two decades, lead him to date the Kitchins and use them together with the Kondratieffs and Juglars to explain the successive economic conjunctures in the three countries under his observation.

The evidence brought together in the two volumes, and still more other available measures of cyclical behavior, suggest with some plausibility the desirability of distinguishing more than one type of cycle, or recognizing in addition to the shortest unit of cyclical swing observable in the economic system others appreciably longer. But whether the distinction should be drawn in the specific form suggested by Professor Schum-

[3] To be sure, Professor Schumpeter deprecates the significance of this chart as evidence of Kondratieff phases; but the statistical evidence that he submits for Kondratieffs consists essentially of similar items, each of them qualified.

peter is still an unanswered question. Annual series provide too
crude a guide for establishing cycles as short as the Kitchins.
A mere observation of "notches" on the surface of Juglars, or
even of prominent short-term oscillations would not suffice:
either result could be produced by random variations, and
these short-term variations would have to be analyzed to demonstrate that they could not be due to mere chance. Hence
only monthly series could be used as statistical evidence of
Kitchins. But the series presented in the treatise cover too
short a period to provide sufficient basis for the generalization
that Kitchins existed in the past.[4] And no direct evidence
seems to be presented to confirm the generalization so explicitly made that it is possible to count three Kitchins for
every Juglar.

V

The critical evaluation above of what appear to be important elements in Professor Schumpeter's conclusions, viewed
as a systematic and tested exposition of business cycles, yields
disturbingly destructive results. The association between the
distribution of entrepreneurial ability and the cyclical character of economic activity needs further proof. The theoretical
model of the four-phase cycle about the equilibrium level does
not yield a serviceable statistical approach. The three-cycle
schema and the rather rigid relationship claimed to have been
established among the three groups of cycles cannot be considered, on the basis of the evidence submitted, even tolerably
valid; nor could such validity be established without a serviceable statistical procedure. The core of the difficulty seems to

---

[4] It is also to be noted that for recent years economic conditions in this
country dominated those of Europe to an extent much greater than before the war. It is also in this country that the cycle in general business
conditions was observed to be shorter than in England or Germany.
Hence an analysis, confined to only the recent decades, would run the
danger of overlooking the possible absence of Kitchins in England and
Germany during the nineteenth century.

lie in the failure to forge the necessary links between the primary factors and concepts (entrepreneur, innovation, equilibrium line) and the observable cyclical fluctuations in economic activity.

And yet this evaluation does injustice to the treatise, for it stresses the weaknesses of the discussion and overlooks almost completely its strength. Granted that the book does not present a fully articulated and tested business-cycle theory; that it does not actually demonstrate the intimate connection between economic evolution and business cycles; that no proper link is established between the theoretical model and statistical procedure; that historical evidence is not used in a fashion that limits sufficiently the area of personal judgment; or that the validity of three types of cycles is not established. Yet it is a cardinal merit of the treatise that it raises all these questions; that it emphasizes the importance of relating the study of business cycles to a study of the underlying long-term movements; that it calls for emphasis on the factors that determine the rate and tempo of entrepreneurial activity; that it demands a statistical procedure based upon a clearly formulated concept of the business cycle; and that it valiantly attempts to use historical evidence. In all these respects the volumes offer favorable contrast with many a book published in recent years on business cycles, whether of the type in which abstract reasoning is unsullied by contact with observable reality or of the opposite category in which mechanical dissection of statistical series is the sum total of the author's achievement.

Furthermore, both the summary and the critical discussion above necessarily fail to show the achievements of the treatise in providing illuminating interpretations of historical developments; incisive comments on the analysis of cyclical fluctuations in various aspects of economic activity; revealing references to an extraordinarily wide variety of publications in directly and indirectly related fields; thought-provoking judgments concerning the general course of capitalist evolution. It is difficult to convey the flavor of the book except by saying

that in many of its parts it reads like an intellectual diary, a
record of Professor Schumpeter's journey through the realm
of business cycles and capitalist evolution, a journal of his
encounters there with numerous hypotheses, diverse historical
facts, and statistical experiments. And Professor Schumpeter
is a widely experienced traveller, whose comments reveal in-
sight combined with a sense of reality; of wide background
against which to judge the intellectual constructs of men and
the vagaries of a changing social order.

Thus, whatever the shortcomings of the book as an exposition of a systematic and tested theory of business cycles, these
shortcomings are relative to a lofty conception of the requirements such theory should meet. It is the cognizance of these
requirements that makes the book valuable even to one who
may not be interested in the author's comments on the various
and sundry historical, statistical and theoretical matters. But
these comments are of high suggestive value and should, if
given circulation, prove effective stimuli for further theoretical, historical and statistical study of business cycles and economic evolution. It is my sincere hope that Professor Schumpeter's labor embodied in the treatise will be repaid by an
extensive utilization of it by students in the field, aware though
they may be of the tentative character of his conclusions and
of the personal element in some of his comments and evalua-
tions.

5

ECONOMIC TRENDS AND
BUSINESS CYCLES *

I

Business cycles characterize the short-term behavior of only some economic societies. To quote from Wesley C. Mitchell's writings: "Business cycles do not become a prominent feature of economic experience in any community until a large proportion of its members have begun to live by making and spending money incomes. . . . Further, there is evidence that business cycles are most pronounced in those industries which are dominated by full-fledged business enterprises . . ." (*Business Cycles: The Problem and Its Setting,* New York 1927, p. 182). And in the more recent writings business cycles are defined as "a type of fluctuation found in the aggregate economic activity of nations that organize their work mainly in *business enterprises*" (*Measuring Business Cycles,* New York 1946, p. 3, italics mine).

Viewed in their international aspects, economic trends affect the economic organizations of the several nations in different ways; and at any given time may delimit the area in the world in which business cycles can flourish. Hence in considering the effect of economic trends upon business cycles we must first examine the characteristics of economic organization of nations that constitute the milieu within which business cycles, as we understand them, are an expected and recognized aspect of short-term behavior.

* Delivered as one of a series of lectures in honor of Wesley C. Mitchell before the Graduate Economics Club of Columbia University, October 10, 1947.

These characteristics may be set forth as: (1) a high level of the technical arts (using the term 'technical' most broadly) associated with the industrial system; (2) the dominance of business enterprise as a unit of economic organization; (3) relatively free and peaceful state of economic relations among national units. The bearing of these characteristics may now be indicated.

1. That a high level of the technical arts, associated with the industrial system, is ordinarily taken as a characteristic of an economy subject to business cycles, has two implications. The level of technique assumed means that mankind controls various natural calamities to a point where *man-made* disturbances like business cycles can be felt and can constitute a serious problem. To use an extreme illustration—in the 11th through the 14th centuries, when medieval European communities suffered at frequent intervals from famines and epidemics and a calamity like the Black Death could wipe out half of a country's urban population in a year, there could be little question of cycles originating in the sphere of economic activity; nor could there be much long term calculation or planning of economic activity—of the type pursued by business and other enterprises in modern times. Confirmation of this statement will be found in Dr. Mitchell's discussion in *Business Cycles*, of Scott's annals of early disturbances in pre-industrial England and in his comments on the business annals for China for recent decades.

If the high level of technique, and the consequent freedom from natural calamities, is a *permissive* condition of business cycles as a man- or society-made phenomenon, it is also a positive condition: industrial technology is accompanied by large investment in durable capital, by associated connection between durable capital and long-term financing, and by a characteristic structure of the national product in its division between consumption and capital formation. The crucial part played by capital goods industries and long-term investment in generating cycles—unless restrained by some specially designed social policies—need not be expounded in detail here.

2. The second feature of economies that are the *habitat* of business cycles—the dominance of business enterprise—needs no protracted explanation. However, two aspects of this dominance should be clearly distinguished. The first is that it imposes a pattern of rational calculation and pecuniary motivation upon economic activity—freeing it from the qualifying influence of extra-market, extra-economic factors. The basic differences between the motives and criteria by which production, distribution and consumption are guided within the family, the state, or some nonprofit institutions, on the one hand, and profit seeking business enterprises, on the other, are marked. It is only to the extent that a large proportion of a country's economic activity is guided by the pecuniary calculus and a search for profits by business enterprises, that business cycles constitute an important feature of its behavior.

The second aspect of the dominance of business enterprise, perhaps more problematical in its bearing upon business cycles, is the extent to which it calls for a sufficient number and variety of units to result in effective competition, for independence of action of individual units (absence of collusion)—which in its accentuated form is what Karl Marx refers to as the anarchy of capitalist production. The significance of this point may be illustrated by the extreme example of a national economy in which there is a single, huge business enterprise. Of course, one might ask whether such an enterprise would not inevitably be the state, and hence not a pure business enterprise. Assume then that there are four or five such giants. Could business cycles occur under such conditions; and if they did, would they not be quite different from business cycles as we know them? It seems to me that business cycles are conditioned by the existence of a sufficiently large number of enterprises and of a wide area for their independent action in competitive conditions—although it is difficult to formulate the condition more specifically.

3. The final characteristic of economic society noted as a prerequisite for business cycles—relatively peaceful and free relations among nations—may also be viewed from two angles.

The first is that the absence of armed conflicts of shattering
proportions is similar to the absence of profound natural calamities which the controls of advanced technology bring
about. In Scott's annals for pre-industrial England, which Dr.
Mitchell quotes as a record of conditions in which business
cycles could not flourish, wars and war scares play a prominent
part. Clearly if industrial societies of the world are to be
plagued every twenty-five years or so by conflicts of the magnitude of the last two world wars, cycles may survive; but
they will be so dominated by preparation for, conduct of, and
recovery from wars, that the fluctuations will scarcely be *business* cycles in the ordinary sense of the word.

In addition to this permissive aspect of relatively peaceful,
and consequently free, relations among nations, there is the
positive aspect bearing upon business cycle theory and study.
The mechanism of such relations, in the complex interrelation
of money standards and flows, movements of commodities in
foreign trade, of population across the boundaries, of short-
and long-term funds, all play important parts in propagating
business cycles from one country to another and in accelerating or retarding their course within any given country. This
does not mean that were the industrial countries completely
isolated, business cycles could not originate and flourish in
them. But it may be claimed that the worldwide impact of
the phenomenon in question is an important element in the
attention directed toward them; and the existence of channels
by which they can be spread or stemmed, an important element in their explanation.

If, then, we accept as basis for further discussion the thesis
that business cycles are phenomena peculiar to countries that
have reached the level of an industrial economy, are dominated by business enterprise, and live in relatively peaceful
and free conditions of international intercourse, it may be
asked how the observable economic trends are affecting the
conditions in which business cycles can occur. Do these trends
indicate an extension or contraction of the area over which
business cycles can transpire or recur without so extreme a

modification of their pattern as to raise a question whether they belong to the same species?

Since I know of no single study that summarizes the basic trends in economic organization of nations for the last 150 to 200 years, I am forced to look at the evidence that is easily available and precipitate generalizations that are too blunt and that perforce overlook some important aspects. But the conclusions seem fairly clear.

The period witnessed the spread of the industrial system. Despite differences among nations, there was a marked extension of the advanced methods associated with the application of experimental science to problems of production—first clearly manifested in the agricultural and industrial revolutions in England, the former beginning in the early and the latter in the late 18th century. So far as the extension of the industrial system meant extension by society of defense against natural calamities and of an economic structure in which deferred consumption and large durable capital investments were important, this particular trend meant an extension over the world of the area in which business cycles could occur.

The picture with respect to the dominance of business enterprises is different. At first, the example of England in the economic sphere and the political revolution under the leadership of France meant not only emphasis upon the high social value of the individual business entrepreneur but also reduction in the activities of the state. The extension of the industrial revolution to the European continent after the Napoleonic wars and its somewhat later spread to the United States did mean a marked extension of the area dominated by business enterprise in a relatively free form and enjoying the advanced base of technical arts. To some extent the process continued after the first half of the 19th century. But beyond that date new elements entered the picture. The industrial system was still spreading, but it penetrated into countries in which, for one reason or another, free business enterprise was not as dominant as in the countries that had entered upon industrialization earlier. In Germany and Japan the survival of

authoritarian, largely feudal elements, was quite pronounced;
and while the shift toward the industrial system did represent
a more democratic political organization and a freer system
of business enterprise than had existed before, there is some
question whether 'dominance of business enterprise' had quite
the same meaning as in England, France, or the United States.
And, of course, there is the even more striking case of Russia,
where the relaxation of authoritarian elements in social structure
that accompanied the early phase of industrialization was succeeded by a highly authoritarian regime, in which a forced
draft of the industrialization process was accompanied by
dominance of a single party state.

Why was the spread of the industrial system from its original locus in England to other countries, after a time, accompanied, on an international, and in the case of Russia,
intra-national scale, by an increasing weight of the state and
of authoritarian elements in the social and economic structure?
Possibly, there is something about the aggressive character of
industrial capitalism that induces the *follower* countries, as
distinct from the *pioneer* countries, to use the engine of the
state to force an accelerated industrialization process by authoritarian means. Perhaps in some of these older countries
the combination of population, resources, and the survival of
strong elements inimical to the industrial system created a
situation in which industrialization was possible only with
such drastic rearrangements and breakage of the cake of historical custom as could be effected by a strong state alone,
ruthless in its endeavors and not too mindful of the welfare of
the existing population. The validity of such hypotheses is of
extreme importance for the prognosis of possible industrialization in the huge populated countries, such as India and China,
that have not yet entered the phase of industrialization to
any marked extent. All we need say in the present connection
is that, upon a view of the world at large, the areas in which
dominance of business enterprise has accompanied industrialization accounted for a diminishing proportion of all *industrialized* areas; and that partly because of this trend, partly

because of certain tendencies immanent in the development of business capitalism from within, even in the older industrial countries the dominance of business enterprise has begun to recede.

Nor do the changing relations *among* nations show a clear trend of extension throughout the world of conditions under which business cycles can flourish. The century that elapsed between the end of the Napoleonic wars and World War I, roughly dated from 1815 to 1914, was a peaceful era, with international economic flows—of commodities, men, and capital—relatively free, tariffs and the like notwithstanding. To this period belong the free trade policy of England, the huge free migration of people, and the large and relatively free wanderings of capital. But since 1880, and particularly from 1914 to the present, conditions have, on the whole, been markedly different. Two wars, catastrophic in their magnitude; a dislocation of the international network of trade, migration, and capital investment; an increasing degree of subjection of international flows to extra-economic motives—all are phenomena too familiar to need elaboration. While it is difficult to establish a prognosis for the future, the least that can be said is that factors indicative of a possible return to the peaceful and freer international conditions of the 19th century are conspicuous by their absence.

The picture that thus emerges from a broad look at the last century and a half is that although technical conditions have spread over increasingly wider areas where business cycles could emerge and run their course, social and international conditions have, at least since 1880 and particularly since 1914, tended to restrict the free operation of business enterprise; and have thus narrowed the relative proportion of the industrialized world in which business cycles could occur. Furthermore, this trend in social and international conditions may well persist; and we should expect that business cycles will affect a decreasing proportion of the world, or if present, will be drastically modified in their internal and external characteristics.

II

So far we have discussed economic trends in their international setting. Let us shift the focus to a single country, and consider the economic trends within it in their bearing upon domestic business cycles. Naturally, the country should be one in which business cycles can occur, i.e., one which throughout its observed history of the last one and a half to two centuries was marked by prevalence of the industrial system and dominance of business enterprise.

Our guiding thread is the view that business cycles are alterations in the rate of economic activity that characterize and affect simultaneously the major aspects of a nation's economy —production, prices, employment, income payments, profits, etc. In this synchronism of up and down movements in the various sectors of a national economy lies the crux of the business cycle problem. This suggests, by the way, that from the viewpoint of the problem involved, it is business cycles in economies characterized by sufficient diversification that are important. Where a country's economy is dominated by a single industry, the general cycle in the country's economic conditions reduces itself to a single industry cycle. Only in a diversified national economy does the question arise why, despite vast technical and institutional differences in conditions among various sectors, sufficiently synchronous movements arise to merit the title 'business cycles'.

This *unity in diversity* provides an important clue in consideration of the effects of intra-national economic trends upon business cycles. For the economic trends, so far as one can observe, differ in rate for the several sectors and aspects of the economy; and hence bring about marked shifts in the weights to be assigned to these sectors in their contribution to any nationwide phenomenon. Economic trends affect the specific long-term composition of that diversity which, in its synchronous short-term behavior, manifests the unity of movement that we call business cycles. To use a biological analogy, this aspect of economic growth, important in its effect on business cycles, is *differentiation.*

But another aspect of intra-national economic trends may also be important—viz., the very rate of sustained increase (or decline) in the magnitude of the nation as an economic unit. If for purposes of discussion, we accept total output or production (most broadly understood) as a measure of a nation's economic magnitude; and define a sustained change as one observable over a period of at least twenty-five years, we can define the rate of a nation's economic growth as the rate of sustained increase in its total output. This rate of economic growth is different for different nations and periods; and clearly variations or differences in it may affect characteristics of business cycles.

Two characteristics of business cycles we will deal with are: (a) duration—meaning the full span from the initial to terminal trough; (b) amplitude—meaning the decline in the rate of movement from the period of expansion to the subsequent period of contraction. How do the trends in a country's economy, i.e., the rate of sustained increase (or decline) and the shifting weight of the various sectors, affect the duration and amplitude of its business cycles?

I have no hope of giving a specific answer—partly because the studies made so far provide no tested answer, and partly because I am not sufficiently familiar with data and studies in the field. All that can be done here is to outline the channels by which the effects of economic trends, so stated, upon the characteristics of business cycles, so defined, can be traced —without telling what the results of such a tracing would show, or being sure that the outline suggested is the best tentative blueprint.

The effects of economic trends on the duration of business cycles may be explored under four heads: (1) shift in relative importance of various sectors, distinguished—for technical or other reasons—by different time spans of the *specific* cycles that characterize them; (2) shifts in productive and institutional conditions that cause secular trends in the span of spe-

cific cycles within each sector; (3) changes in the identity
and characteristics of the sectors which, partly because of
rapid growth, play a strategic and dynamic role in business
cycles; (4) changes in the rate of over-all growth.

1. The several sectors of a country's economy are subject
to cycles of different duration, largely because technical conditions or institutional factors may make for quicker or slower
response to either expansive or contractive stimuli. These differences are clearly observable in the production sector between, say, residential construction on the one hand, and textiles or hog production on the other. Similarly there are
marked differences in duration between inventory cycles in retail trade and replacement cycles in shipbuilding; or between
cycles in long- and short-term debt structures. In a sense, nationwide business cycles may be viewed as weighted totals of
specific cycles of the various sectors of the economy, with a
given pattern emerging because of preponderant weight of
processes with roughly equal time spans. But economic trends
may cause shifts in weights for the several sectors of the
economy characterized by different time spans of cyclical response, and such intersector shifts of weights affect the duration of nationwide business cycles. Offhand, it is impossible
to say in what direction such secular shifts are operating
—to extend or to shorten the duration of business cycles; and
it is possible that no distinct trend is thus imparted to the
duration of business cycles.

2. Within each sector, distinguished by different time spans
of cyclical response, there may be secular movements in the
time span itself—an effect of changes in either technical or
institutional conditions. To illustrate, if major technical
changes are made in residential construction (say through extensive prefabrication) and if the institutional conditions are
also affected by badly needed reforms in the regulation of construction activity, the duration of the specific cycle in residential construction may well exhibit a secular shortening.
If so, whatever secularly changing weight is to be assigned to
residential construction in the nationwide total output, would

have to be combined with a secular trend in the duration of specific cycles in construction. Here also it is hard to say what influence economic trends exercise on the duration of business cycles. Perhaps, on the whole, technical progress tends to reduce the time span in that it permits a prompter response to both expansion and contraction stimuli. On the other hand, many institutional factors move in the opposite direction, particularly those inherent in the shift from relatively free competition by a number of small units to a situation dominated by a few large concerns which do not necessarily respond promptly to urges to expand and, even more, to contract, particularly in the sphere of price adjustment.

3. The consideration above of the possible impact of inter- and intrasector secular shifts on the duration of business cycles emphasizes the quantitative weight of each sector, but pays no attention to the fact that such purely quantitative weights may not properly reflect the strategic importance of a sector as a business cycle *leader*. New industries, or new areas of investment, may influence business cycles disproportionately to their weight in terms of production, employment, and the like. To put it differently, the quantitative weight of a sector in some specific aspect of the country's economy, such as venture investment or speculation may be more important than another more orthodox measure of a sector's weight. For example, from about 1835 to the 1870's railroad construction appeared to be a strategic industry in business cycles in this country, in England, and in several European countries. The weight of this industry in total output, employment, and the like may have been quite small; and I am not sure that even its share in total net capital formation was overwhelming. But it was an activity in which venture capital and speculative endeavor were concentrated; and it was watched by the business community as an important indicator of the state of economic conditions. At other times, other industries may have played the role of the leader in economic growth and in cyclical expansions, e.g., cotton textiles, steam, and iron earlier; electricity and electric utilities later; or automobiles and ra-

dios in more recent times. Each of these industries has a production time span, and hence a cycle time span of its own; and it tends to put its impress upon business cycles. The 10-year cycles marked by the crises of 1837, 1847, 1857, and 1866 are commonly associated with the railroads; and replacement of railroad construction by another industrial leader, say automobiles, with a shorter production span, may well be an important factor in the change in the duration of business cycles. But here again, since there is no basis for a definite trend in the succession of leader industries, no generalization as to the trend in the duration of business cycles associated with this factor can be made.

4. We come finally to the question whether the rate of overall economic growth affects the duration of business cycles. The question has meaning to the extent that we envisage the business cycle processes as having momenta of their own; and the conditions reflected in the rate of growth as exogenous factors that can either retard or accelerate the cyclical processes. One may first assume that a rapid rate of economic growth would tend to prolong periods of cyclical expansion and shorten periods of cyclical contraction. A sustained secular decline would have a reverse effect. A change in the rate of economic growth would have similar consequences; and in fact if the rate of over-all growth in a country tends to recede, other conditions being equal, the periods of cyclical contraction would tend to be somewhat longer than they would be otherwise. But the periods of cyclical expansion would be shorter than before, and the effect on the length of the full cycle is not determinable from such general considerations. However, since public attention is ordinarily focussed on the contraction or depression phase, and tends to take the expansion phases as the expected normal, prolongation of depressions is generally understood to be an aggravation of the business cycle problem. All recent discussion about economic maturity is very much colored by the fear that economic growth factors have become less effective in pulling the economy out of its depression tail spins.

A somewhat more elusive connection may be suggested. In a business economy, with no regulation of economic growth, the latter may be accompanied by disparate movements in the several sectors—in which the more rapidly growing ones quickly reach what is temporarily a disproportionate weight in the economy. The higher the rate of over-all growth, the more quickly such secular disequilibria are reached—to be corrected by a cyclical contraction, which in turn may be short because of the lifting power of the large secular potential. There may thus be some basis for associating high rates of over-all secular change with short durations of business cycles; and low rates with long durations.

The scheme above by which the effects of intranational economic trends on the duration of business cycles were traced may be applied to *amplitude*. Here also we distinguish various sectors in the economy, by the sensitiveness of their response to business cycles as reflected in amplitude; then study *inter*-sector shifts in weights and secular shifts in the amplitude of cyclical response *within* each sector. Here also the succession of different industries or sectors in the role of dynamic bellwether may mean, given differences in amplitude of response, changes in the amplitude of business cycles. Finally, changes in the rate of over-all growth may exercise some effect upon the differential rates of movement during business cycles —with a suggestion, although none too clear, of wide amplitudes of cyclical change per year being associated with high rates of secular growth.

While the application of the scheme to changes in the amplitude of business cycles requires no further discussion, one additional comment might be made. In the case of amplitude, there is some suggestion of compensatory movements among trends in their effects upon business cycles—in that a secular decline in the sensitiveness of cyclical response in one aspect of economic activity is likely to be compensated by a secular rise in the sensitiveness of cyclical response in another related aspect of economic activity. To illustrate: with the shift from vigorous competition among a large number of relatively small

enterprises to the domination of some industries by a few large
enterprises, there may have been a secular decline in the
cyclical sensitiveness of prices. But for this very reason there
may have been an increased sensitiveness of cyclical response
in production and employment. The failure to raise prices
during expansion removed at least one brake upon expansion
of production and employment; the failure to cut prices during contraction (either by surviving enterprises or via failures
and reorganization) may have removed a brake upon contraction in production and employment. The shift in popular concern aroused by business cycles from one about solvency and
the fate of business enterprises to one about employment and
the fate of employee groups is perhaps associated with the
trends just stated. Another plausible hypothesis is that a secular decline in the sensitiveness of foreign trade (due, e.g., to
state intervention and control) may cause a secular rise in the
sensitiveness of domestic trade—particularly in a country in
which business cycles tend to have a greater amplitude and a
different timing from that characterizing the totality of countries with which it trades. Indeed, one is tempted to entertain
the theory that under given conditions of business organization
and productive technology, there is a constant business cycle
potential, an *élan cyclique;* and that, if secular trends constrict
its manifestations in one aspect of economic activity, it will
emerge all the more strongly in a compensatory movement
elsewhere. However, I would not press too far this thesis 'of
cyclical nature being driven out of the door and coming back
through the window.'

A few more comments on the schemata just suggested. First,
discussion has been in terms of effects of intranational economic trends upon only two characteristics of business cycles:
duration and amplitude (differential movement between expansion and contraction, per time unit). The same procedure
can be applied to any quantitative characteristic of business
cycles—duration of expansion and contraction separately;
total amplitude rather than rate of change per time unit; or
any other aspect of the cycle pattern.

Second, the first two points of the scheme, the approach via intersector shifts and intrasector trends, implies an additive concept to business cycles—views the latter as movements in a comprehensive total. But we need not interpret this implication narrowly, in the sense that the business cycles for a country are fluctuations in a *single* comprehensive total, such as national income. We can retain the proper view of business cycles as roughly synchronous movements of different aspects of a national economy with a variety of sub-components; but treat each of the aspects as an additive total. E.g., if we conceive the business cycle as a movement in total production, general price level, total volume of trade, etc., each of these can be treated as the result of the simple addition involved in the approach via inter and intrapart shifts. Or if over-all production is too generalized a total and we wish to distinguish mining, manufacturing, etc., each of the latter can be viewed as a composite of inter and intra-trends, and then the various branches of output combined by the same procedure. In other words, nothing in the approach prevents us from driving its shafts as far down into the diversified economy as we wish and as data permit, and then by addition at successive levels, arriving at as single and as comprehensive a total as we may desire.

Third, though the approach suggested may have considerable potentialities in application to various cyclical characteristics and at various levels of generality or specificity, it is nevertheless obviously limited. Clearly, the historical succession of business cycles in any country can not be fully explained by viewing their changing characteristics merely as effects of intranational economic trends along the four channels suggested above. Too many factors that may cause changes in the characteristics of successive cycles are missing. Without any attempt at a comprehensive listing, one can easily point out several of them. First, the very timing of specific cycles in various sectors, i.e., the extent to which they tend to coincide or diverge, has not been considered at all. Second, certain types of disturbance lying in the international or domestic spheres—such as foreign and civil wars—are obviously important factors not covered under intranational economic trends. Finally, there is the multitude of other irregular events in the stream of history, not classifiable under economic trends or major conflicts, that can clearly produce differences in characteristics of business cycles as we study their historical succession in any country.

But it is not the intention to provide here a scheme for a complete explanation of the historical diversity of business cycles. I am concerned only with indicating how economic trends in the structure and magnitude of a nation's economy tend to affect the characteristics of its business cycles. The main purpose of such an attempt is to suggest that the basic aim of business cycle study—the establishment both of invariant characteristics and of the limits of invariance—cannot be successfully attained without direct consideration of these economic trends and measurement of their effects. If such effects exist, and if trends in the structure and in the rate of growth of a national economy are marked—even over the relatively brief historical period during which business cycles have had time to manifest themselves—then clearly reliable generalizations concerning business cycles can be derived only by taking account of the changing secular framework within which they occur.

III

There is no need to summarize the discussion, which is but an articulation of a simple idea. The latter is clearly suggested by the definition of business cycles, used by Dr. Mitchell, which links them with the dominance of business enterprise and emphasizes them as movements in the aggregate economic activity of a nation. The first attribute of this definition prompts a question as to the effect of international economic trends upon the area in which business enterprise is dominant; the second as to the effect of intranational economic trends upon the stability of business cycle characteristics. And the conclusion of our brief consideration is simply a need for greater awareness and for a more direct account of economic trends in their impact upon business cycles.

But from these simple thoughts conclusions follow for emphasis in economic study, conclusions that are not less important for being so obvious and trite. The first is, of course, the need to revive the study of economic trends, and do for that aspect of economic change what Dr. Mitchell has done for the shorter-term fluctuations in his 1913 volume on business cycles and in subsequent writings. This corpus of economic study must be rescued from the neglect into which it has fallen since the days of the classical school and Karl Marx, and the problem be given the attention it deserves. It is high time that the field be cleared of the debris of discredited theories; and of a tangled growth of semijournalistic approaches which see the 'new wave' in what may easily prove to be extremely transitory aberrations of human history. It is high time that we show clearly that the various theories are merely hypotheses many of which need reformulation before they can be tested; assemble the fundamental factual basis for study; and examine clearly the theories, concepts, and tools for empirical study to make them useful in a dispassionate consideration of a well-defined realm of observable experience. The task is far from simple and in the process we may well have to abandon the snug and familiar shelter of traditional economics. But it is difficult to see how the challenge can be evaded, except at the danger of having all study of economic change lose validity, and of our remaining exposed to the variable winds of fashionable doctrines usually grounded in the limited experience of a country or two over a short stretch of history.

But there are also obvious consequences to the study of business cycles proper. The first is that the rapidly changing secular milieu of business cycles, with its effects upon their characteristics along the lines suggested or other lines, makes indispensable a clear definition of the boundaries of empirical data that are being interpreted in any study. It is a most baffling feature of many theoretical writings in the field, of

many elaborate explanations of the causes of business cycles—
especially those that employ recorded factual materials spar-
ingly—that the authors do not specify the segments of historical reality to which their theories are assumed to apply. When
Hawtrey and Keynes advance hypotheses for the explanation
of economic cycles, it is not clear from their writings what
nations and what historical periods they have in mind. Are
their theories supposed to explain cycles in England and in this
country alone, over the period, say, since 1800? Or are they
also assumed to explain business cycles in Japan and India;
or the kind of cycle that may be associated with the South
Sea bubble (1720) or with the Tulip Mania (1634-37)? I
would be inclined to suspect that in many such theoretical
expositions the writer almost unconsciously uses the relatively
recent experience in one or two countries with which he happens to be most familiar; that, to illustrate, when Hawtrey
stressed the strategic importance of wholesalers in the business
cycle, he may well have had in mind British experience during
the late 19th and early 20th centuries when wholesale foreign
trade firms played an important role in the British economy.
This specific suggestion may well be wrong, but I am using it to
stress the importance of asking what body of empirical evidence
a business cycle theory that does not specify the area of historical
experience is trying to organize and illuminate.

Second, the consideration of international economic trends,
along the lines discussed, calls for a possible extension of the
concept of economic cycles, in which, in addition to business
cycles proper, we may wish to distinguish other types of cycles
—associated with economies in which the business enterprise is
not dominant or in which external disturbing factors, such as
major wars, are important. Perhaps we should not use the term
'cycles' in this connection, but talk of short-term changes of a
less regular character. Whatever the semantic proprieties,
there is surely need for greater attention to short-term fluctuations in countries not characterized by the combination of
industrial economy, free business enterprise, and peaceful international relations. It is my impression that business cycle

study is concentrated on the experience of England and this country, with somewhat less emphasis on that of Germany and France, and for these countries chiefly for the limited historical periods in which the combination of internal and external characteristics of economic organization was that noted. The strategic importance of extending study to the late mercantilist period or to countries in which some of these elements are missing is clear. I am not sure, e.g., that a close examination of experience in a rigidly planned economy, such as Russia, would not reveal some cycles of its own—which, being those of cumulative error and of subsequent correction, bear some family resemblance to business cycles as we know them in countries of free capitalist enterprise.

Third, the consideration of intranational economic trends calls also for intensification of business cycle study in directions beyond the establishment of a relatively invariant, typical pattern of the rhythm in economic activity. It calls for a direct examination of the specific cycles in the different sectors of the economy that accompany the different historical periods and of the changing importance of the sectors in the country's economic system. The task is not easy, if only because economic trends are rapid movements that limit the number of cycle units which can be found in any single secular phase. But the intensification of analysis in this direction is obviously indispensable, at least as a safeguard against unqualified use of typical or average measures derived from periods marked by pronounced and rapid secular shifts.

Above all, the observations above suggest extreme caution in any economic analysis that attempts to establish invariant functions by means of historical data, that lifts out of the changing historical reality some empirical constants to fit into rigidly defined theoretical schemes, and that applies what is essentially the logic of controlled experiment to what is basically uncontrolled reality. The use of econometric methods with their probabilistic implications and claims to the establishment of invariances on the basis of a relatively short span of historical experience is subject to critical and careful scrutiny to see whether short-term relations have not been mistaken for long-term, and whether the formal criteria devised for solving sets of simultaneous equations are in fact a good substitute for the type of experimental controls used in other sciences to eliminate all nonrandom factors and limit variance to random sources alone.

There is little new in these remarks. Almost everything that has been said is found explicitly or implicitly in Dr. Mitchell's writings, for the simple reason that his approach to business cycles forces awareness of the secular milieu within which these cycles occur. The only new element in the discussion is perhaps the emphasis—a result partly of the accumulated experience of recent years in which economic trends have become more spectacular than they were previously; partly of the increased supply of data in which national aggregates have become more accessible and have suggested, more directly than it was possible heretofore, the tracing of interpart and intrapart trends.

But even this emphasis, which does not deny the utility of formalistic abstractions and of mechanistic analogies—provided that one is aware of their limitations—is in direct continuation of the intellectual tradition of which Dr. Mitchell is so notable a representative. This tradition of distrust of formalism, of recognition of complexity of historical reality, of awareness of limitations of the human mind unchecked by objectively recorded data, can still make an enormous contribution to our knowledge, and possibly eventually even improvement, of human society.

6

NATIONAL INCOME AND
INDUSTRIAL STRUCTURE *

I

Industries are ordinarily differentiated by the raw materials they use, their productive processes, and the finished products they turn out. The extent to which the raw materials are organic, mineral, or synthetic; domestic or foreign; perishable or durable, puts a stamp upon the economics and sociology of an industry. That the productive process lends itself to large scale machine operation or requires the personal effort of skilled craftsmen; can be handled by private enterprise or must be entrusted to public agencies; does or does not require large, capital investment—are also factors determining the economic and social patterns by which an industry is guided. Finally, the characteristics of the finished product—the type of want it satisfies, its dependence upon foreign or domestic purchasers, the extent to which its sale can be left to private markets or must be regulated by public agencies, the manner in which demand responds to fluctuations in the purchasing power of buyers—may serve to distinguish one industry from another, despite common raw materials and similar although not identical production processes. A country's industrial structure may be defined as the relative distribution of its resources and total output among the several industries differentiated in the manner just suggested.

However, in considering the bearing of the industrial struc-

* Reprinted by permission from *Proceedings of the International Statistical Conferences 1947*, vol. V, Calcutta, 1951, pp. 205-239. A brief abstract appeared in *Econometrica*, January 1948, pp. 86-90.

ture upon the measurement of a nation's total output, i.e., its national income or product, differences among industries must be viewed from a plane somewhat broader than the purely technical one of materials, processes, and products. That one industry consumes an organic and another a mineral material does not, in and of itself, raise questions bearing upon the measurement of the two industries in estimating national income. Important questions arise only when the purely technical characteristics spell major differences in the nature of the economic institutions under whose aegis the industry functions. To illustrate: if because of the characteristics of its material, processes, and product, one industry is carried on as an integral part of the family economy, largely self-subsistent and relying to only a limited extent upon the markets, while because of the technical conditions of production, another industry is carried on by business enterprises organized with exclusive orientation to markets, questions arise as to how the net products of the two industries are to be measured so that their contributions to national income can be compared? Similarly, it is only to the extent that technical differences between two industries compel one to be conducted under government auspices and another under free enterprise that important problems arise in measuring the two industries in national income; or in defining national income for two countries differing in their industrial structure with respect to the relative importance of business and government.

Thus, industrial structure has a bearing upon the concept of national income so far as differences among industries are viewed as differences in the basic pattern of social and economic institutions under whose aegis the industries are carried on. Viewed in this light, three basic contrasts in industrial structure may be suggested. The first, between self-subsistent and market-oriented structures, is largely identical with the widespread distinction between industrialized and non-industrialized countries. From the viewpoint of conceptual problems, the difference between industrial and underdeveloped countries lies in the fact that major portions of the productive activity of the latter are likely to take place within the family and the community, not in business enterprises working for the market. National income is not difficult to define for a country that is predominantly agricultural, but in which agriculture is organized on a business basis (e.g., New Zealand). But for a country like China or India, whose major emphasis is also on agriculture but in which a great deal of agriculture (and related processes) is carried on within the family and rural community, it is difficult to define and approximate national income in a way comparable with that for industrialized or market bound economies. The second basic contrast—between domestically oriented industrial structures and those heavily dependent upon foreign economies—also gives rise to problems in defining national income, problems residing largely in a proper delimitation of the nation as a unit of measurement.[1] The third contrast—between privately and publicly organized industrial structures—creates obvious problems of comparison.

This paper is confined to national income problems involved in measurement for countries whose industrial structures exhibit the first type of difference—that between a relatively self-subsistent family or communal economy and one operated primarily by enterprises oriented to the market place.

[1] An interesting recent illustration of this problem is provided by the estimate of income for Northern Rhodesia (Phyllis Deane, "Measuring National Income in Colonial Territories," *Studies in Income and Wealth, Vol. Eight,* National Bureau of Economic Research, 1946, pp. 147-74). National income estimated as the yield of local productive factors entering the income of residents amounted, in illustrative figures, to about £7½ million; but if income of foreign firms operating in the territory and services rendered abroad by the colony's residents are included, the total is £13.0 million—almost double. How the national income of Rhodesia is defined is obviously of great importance to the resulting total—a situation that might be true of any colonial territory that is small (with respect to population or total output) relative to its "mother" country.

II

Problems in national income estimation for industrial and pre-industrial economies [2] can be appraised properly only if we seek in national income some measure of the *real* net volume of goods produced, undistorted by duplication and unaffected by purely monetary differences in price levels. If we accept the formal accounting practices followed in the several economies and do not concern ourselves with what in fact happens under the money surface of economic circulation, we avoid many of the problems involved. The results, however, will be of limited use, since at most they give us the volume of pecuniary transactions, corrected for some types of duplication. They will fall far short of what is ordinarily wanted, viz., a comparison of the real, unduplicated volume of commodities and services yielded by the productive systems of the two countries.

The concept of national income we, therefore, adopt is the net output of commodities and services flowing during the year from the country's productive system into the hands of ultimate consumers or into net additions to the country's stock of capital goods. National income, thus defined, must be measured for two countries so that, despite differences in industrial structure, the real net output of commodities and services can be fairly compared.

When, with this definition in mind, we inspect current estimates for countries differing in industrial structure, we are forcibly struck by the large disparity in per capita real income. Colin Clark's compilation, *Conditions of Economic*

[2] These terms are used below to denote, on the one hand, an economy dominated by business enterprises, using advanced industrial techniques and ordinarily with a large proportion of its population in large cities; and, on the other hand, an economy in which a large part of production is within the family and rural community, a minor share of resources is devoted to advanced industrial production, and a minor part of its population live in cities.

Progress (London, 1940), illustrates the point. For 1925-34 income is measured in international units, defined "as the amount of goods and services which one dollar would purchase in the United States of America over the average of the period 1925-1934" (pp. 39-41). In these units the picture is (pp. 54-7):

> Per capita income for four countries designated by Clark as Great Powers (United States of America, Great Britain, Germany and Austria, France) is 408
> Per capita income for pre-industrial countries (China; British India; Dutch Indies; Africa, excepting Algeria, Egypt, South Africa, Morocco, Tunis; Asia, excepting China, India, Japan, Palestine, Turkey, Syria, Cyprus; and Oceania, excepting Australia, New Zealand, Hawaii, and Guam) is 43½

The former category includes over 290 million people or somewhat less than 15 percent of the world's population as estimated by Clark. The latter comprises over 1,100 million, or well over one-half of the world's population. An even more extreme contrast is that between the United States and China. For the former per capita income is about 500 international units (see pp. 54 and 56); for the latter, about 40 (see p. 46).

A ratio of some 10 or 12 to 1 between the per capita product of the most advanced industrial country and that of countries well behind in industrial development sounds plausible. Anyone who has seen, smelled, and touched the tangible industrial power of the United States and compared it with the physical apparatus of a pre-industrial country may legitimately feel that the ratio should be much greater. But if one is not too misled by purely visual or sensual contrasts and considers the figures more closely, elements emerge that justify incredulity or at least searching questions.

First, in following his definition of international units Clark attempted to raise the estimates for pre-industrial countries for several elements missing in the figures ordinarily derived. Thus, for both China and India, food output (and consumption) was estimated not at producers' prices in the country but at retail prices in an industrial economy like Great Britain; and at least for India substantial corrections for differences in prices paid for other types of productive service, between India and Great Britain, were made. In other words, the figures are literally what they are intended to express—the bundles of commodities and services that could be purchased in the United States during 1925-34 with 40 odd dollars.[3]

Second, with respect to economic conditions during the decade, the comparison favors the pre-industrial countries. One of the most severe industrial depressions on record obviously affected industrial much more than the pre-industrial countries and was reflected most sensitively in the more precise national income estimates for the former. The figures for the pre-industrial countries can scarcely be said to reflect transitorily unfavorable economic conditions.

Third, and most important, an average income, particularly the arithmetic mean, substantially exceeds the incomes of most individuals, since the customary size distributions are usually skewed to the right. Furthermore, what we know about the internal structure of size distributions suggests that while there is some mobility, the majority of units in any size group tend to remain in that group for several years. This means, in terms of Clark's figures, that: (a) more than half the population of pre-industrial countries receive a per capita income less than 40 odd international units; (b) of this half a substantial proportion, say two-thirds (or one-third of the world total) are in the income brackets well below 40 international units per year for a substantial period.[4]

[3] Clark's adjustment brings China's per capita income close to that shown by the recent, more detailed estimate by Mr. Ta Chung Liu in *China's National Income, 1931-1936* (Brookings Institution, 1946). Mr. Liu's figure, adjusted for comparability with the United States, yields a per capita income of $37, close to Clark's figure of $40 in international units.
[4] The discussion is in terms of income produced per capita. While savings are quite limited in pre-industrial countries, some proportion of national income is ordinarily saved. The arguments in the text could be applied to the distribution of income consumed with the arithmetic mean say

Now, if we ask, could people live in the United States during 1925-34 for several years on an income substantially below $40 per capita, the answer would be 'yes,' if they were sufficiently wealthy to have lots of possessions to sell, sufficiently lucky to have rich relations, or sufficiently bold to rob other people. The one-third to one-half of the pre-industrial population of the world would scarcely be in that position; and if we assume that all they have produced and could consume per capita was less than 40 international units for several years, the conclusion would be that all would be dead by now. One is thus forced to conclude: (a) either that the estimates, even after the customary adjustments for comparability with industrial countries, are still deficient in omitting many goods produced in pre-industrial countries; or (b) in fact the whole complex of goods produced and consumed is so different that we cannot establish any equivalence of the type represented by Mr. Clark's international units. We shall see from subsequent discussion that neither suspicion is unjustified.[5]

The form in which the question was raised—how it is possible for a large proportion of the population in pre-industrial countries to survive on an income that produced, for several years, less than the equivalent of $40 per year—obviously reflects my bias as a member of an industrial society. Personal experience and observation tell me that such an annual product is well below the starvation level. But were I a member of a pre-industrial society I might well have asked how it is pos-

---

about 5 percent lower than mean per capita income. However, the distribution of income consumed is less unequal than that of income received or produced.

[5] T. C. Liu argues for the plausibility of a $37 per capita consumption for China by referring to the data for 1935-36 for the United States, according to which small percentages (5 to 6) of farm families in some regions had a family income of less than $250. But this is a comparison of *average* values with the extreme of an income size distribution and overlooks the fact that this extreme is composed largely of families that may have sustained entrepreneurial losses in this single year, not of families that are at this level for any length of time.

sible for the majority of the population in the United States to consume as much as $500 dollars per year, or whatever its equivalent would be in international units of rupees or yuans. Especially, on being told that of this huge income less than 10 percent is saved for net additions to capital stock, I might well ask how the population manages to consume so much— given the limited amount of food one can eat, clothes one can wear, or houses one can inhabit. And a suspicion similar to that voiced above could be entertained, namely, that these income figures for industrial countries must include many categories of items that are *not* included in income as ordinarily conceived in pre-industrial countries; and that the whole pattern of consumption and living in industrial countries is so different as to explain the ease with which these huge quantities of goods are produced and especially consumed.

Let me turn now to a more direct exploration, first of the categories that may be omitted from the national income figures for pre-industrial countries but included in those for industrial countries; second, of problems involved in the basic differences in consumption and production levels in the two types of country.

III

In a decentralized, agricultural, self-subsistence economy many productive activities take place within the family or the local community without finding overt expression on the market. The range of such non-market activities is extremely wide, extending from the production of primary food and other materials, through their fabrication, to the provision of all kinds of services—personal care, household operation, recreation, education, religion. Short of an intensive study of the households and of the agricultural communities for a year or longer, it is extremely difficult even to identify the contents of this productive performance outside the market sphere; and after its contents have been ascertained, it is even more difficult to assign values that would put these productive activities

on a basis comparable with their counterparts in an industrialized market-bound economy.

One is, therefore, not surprised to find that in the estimates
for pre-industrial countries the statistical allowances ordinarily
made to cover the value of such hidden non-market services
are far from adequate. For example, in the case of India, Colin
Clark allows for the retail value (at the English price level)
of wheat and other grains, using flour prices for conversion
(*op. cit.*, p. 43). This means that the only domestic manufacturing of wheat and other grains allowed for is its milling into
flour. But what about further fabrication carried on in the
domestic economy into final consumable goods? Likewise, in
the estimates of untraded goods and services for Northern
Rhodesia, Miss Deane includes "corn as meal, ground nuts
after being shelled, and so on" (*loc. cit.*, p. 155), but does not
allow for the services involved in further conversion, cooking,
baking, etc. Even in the case of China, the excellent field
studies of J. L. Buck, which provide many of the basic figures
for pre-war national income estimates, do not include, and de-
signedly so, all the productive activities carried on within the
farm household. And in dealing with India's estimate, Mr.
Clark excludes the services of women on farms in order "to
obtain comparability with the figures of other countries" (p.
42).

While freely admitting the difficulty of including *all* the extra-market productive activities of a pre-industrial economy,
I am inclined to argue that once a comparison between it and
an industrial country is attempted, there is little justification
in accepting the conventional rules of national income accounting in industrial countries. In estimating income for the United
States, we exclude the services of women on farms, as we do
the services of urban housewives, partly because there is no
good basis for valuing them, partly because they are governed
by rules different from those guiding business enterprises, and
partly because we assume that the omission is not too large
as compared with what is included. But for a pre-industrial
country the latter assumption is patently invalid; the accept-

ance of primacy of business enterprise is out of the question; and if national income is to be merely a measure of goods exchanged for money, an estimate had better not be attempted for pre-industrial countries at all.

Clearly the apparent consistency of applying the rules of national income accounting in industrial countries to those in a pre-industrial economy is no consistency at all. For in scrutinizing the contents of the net output of industrial countries we find a surprising variety and volume of commodities and services that represent nothing but professional, i.e., business pursuit of productive activities for which there is a clear counterpart within the family and community life of pre-industrial economies. The recent valuable publication of the United States Department of Commerce, *National Income* (supplement to *Survey of Current Business,* July 1947) provides a wealth of data to illustrate the point. Table 30, pp. 41-43, gives details of the finished commodities and services purchased by consumers—a total that constitutes the overwhelming proportion of national income (as defined by the Department of Commerce) in any except the war years. Each commodity category, except those that relate to such products of industrial civilization *par excellence* as automobiles and radios, represents activities for which there is a clear parallel within the family and community life of pre-industrial societies. Manufactured foods and tobacco, clothing, shoes, furniture—all commodities that are common to both industrial and pre-industrial economies—have market values in the former that embody a great deal of family work in the latter. And the same is true of various services. Thus, according to the Department of Commerce estimates, consumers spent over half a billion dollars on cemeteries and funerals in 1929; and while these functions are presumably performed satisfactorily in India and China, I cannot find any allowance for them in the estimates. The American consumers spent close to one billion dollars on life insurance in 1929. What about the value of such insurance provided by the family system of China, where the family comes to the succor of a member who may have been afflicted by one of the bad turns of fortune for which life insurance is supposed to compensate in industrial societies?

But let us grant that a pre-industrial country, in adapting its resources and skills to needs, manages to develop, within the family or the community, many productive activities that are taken over, if in modified form, by market-bound business enterprises of an industrial society. What can one practicably do to provide for a fair inclusion of these non-market activities, or in some other way attain proper comparability of measurement between the two types of economy?

That one should try, by intensive field study, to get an inclusive picture of non-market productive activities in pre-industrial society is good advice, too obvious to be stressed. It is, however, a long run measure likely to yield results but slowly—given the difficulties of proper study of pre-industrial economies and the eventual problems of assigning some magnitudes to the activities, once they have been identified. When and if such studies accumulate for any country to a point of providing an adequate basis for inclusive treatment, the way will be open to adjust for at least the major omissions in current estimates. Even with perforce arbitrary valuations, the inclusion of these extra-market activities will result in a smaller error than is inherent in the current estimates for pre-industrial countries which tend to omit them almost completely, with the apparently single exception of foods (in raw or semi-crude form) retained for consumption.

While waiting for such intensive studies, we might consider short-term expedients. As a tentative suggestion, advanced for discussion rather than as a tested recommendation, I would like to make two points. The first concerns activities closely connected with commodities whose market value in industrial societies enters the value of the finished goods flowing to ultimate consumers. In the case of pre-industrial societies primary and semi-finished commodities flowing into ultimate consumption should be given the prices in industrial societies of the finished, fully manufactured products they enter, not of their exact crude or semi-finished counterparts. The second point concerns services rendered directly to consumers, not embodied in new commodities; of these services in an industrial society, specific magnitudes would be included only for those categories that represent definitely much greater contributions to consumers' welfare in industrial than in pre-industrial society or vice versa, and for all those in which differences in relative supply are at all dubious a proportionate relation to other services would be assumed. Let me try to clarify each suggestion.

The first means that, e.g., the amount of wheat produced and retained for domestic consumption in a pre-industrial country should be valued at the retail prices in industrial countries, not of wheat or of flour, but of the fully manufactured foodstuffs of which wheat is the component; and likewise with corn, rice, cotton, wool, hides, etc. This suggestion is practicable to the extent that whatever scanty statistics are available for pre-industrial countries usually cover the production of primary and semi-finished commodities, and ordinarily their exports and imports; consequently, the flow into domestic consumption can be estimated. Also, for at least some industrial countries, e.g., the United States, it is possible to calculate the total spread between the value of primary materials at the producer's door and the value of the finished products they enter, at the cost to ultimate consumers. But while practicable, is such treatment justifiable?

It obviously assumes that the relative weight of fabrication and treatment that intervenes between the material in its crude form and the product in its most finished form (that is, in the form in which it flows to the household in the *industrial* society) is the same for the two economies. Yet one might argue that, by and large, the relative extent of such fabrication and treatment is greater in industrial than in pre-industrial societies. For example, the way in which primary foods are treated, packaged, etc. before they are sold to an urban family in Chicago represents a much more extensive fabrication of wheat than the operations performed on wheat on a North China farm before the Chinese housewife proceeds to do with it whatever the Chicago housewife does with the wheat product she buys. However, a large part of such treatment in industrial society is merely an offset to the disadvantages of the centralization of production. Food products must be treated, packaged, etc. because they are produced thousands of miles from where they are consumed; and in a pre-industrial society the efficiency of production is much greater in respect of reducing the distance between producer and consumer—a point to be discussed further below. Above all, we assume that once the products are eventually consumed by the individuals and households of a pre-industrial economy they must have attained the same satisfactory state of 'finishedness' as the final products of an industrial economy.

At any rate, the acceptance of the suggestion advanced here, and it is advanced only as a tentative expedient, must be decided by weighing the error involved in following it against the error attached to estimates that fail to follow it. The error attached in not following the suggestion is twofold: (1) included in national income for industrial countries is an element of commodity production that is gross, rather than net, being merely an offset to the disadvantages of the concentration of manufacturing in centers distant from the centers of raw materials and of consumption; (2) omitted from national income for pre-industrial countries are many productive activities concerned with commodities, which, being carried on to a great extent by market-bound enterprises, are included in national income for industrial countries. The error implicit in following the suggestion would be to exaggerate the national income of pre-industrial countries to the extent that *productive* treatment of commodities in the latter is relatively less than in industrial countries. Of the two errors, that involved in following the suggestion seems much smaller than that in not following it; and we urge an attempt to apply and test it as a practical expedient.

The second suggestion refers to services not embodied in new commodities. Of these there are definite categories of which we can be sure that the relative, per capita supply, is of greater economic magnitude in industrial than in pre-industrial societies, and vice versa. For example, the supply of qualified medical or educational services is definitely greater in industrial than in non-industrial societies, in the sense that the tangible benefit to consumers, measured by any standard, is greater in the former than in the latter. But can we say the same of religious services, or of such services as are provided by funerals, recreation activities, or barber shops and beauty parlors? Many of these are provided within the family or community in pre-industrial societies, while they are sold on the market in industrial societies. They are therefore likely to be included in national income estimates for the latter, and omitted, in good part, from the estimates for the former. There is no basis for assuming that the per capita supply differs among the two types of economy; and there are great difficulties in establishing any comparability between these types of activity in countries that differ greatly in their social organizations and patterns of life.

With respect to this category, which for convenience can be described as culture-myth services, one of two practical expedients may be adopted. The first would be to omit them from national income estimates for both types of country, thereby reducing the totals for industrial countries relatively more than the ordinary estimates for pre-industrial countries. The second would be to assume that the supply of such services in pre-industrial countries is in the same proportion to all other consumer services as it is in industrial countries—an assumption that perhaps results in too moderate an adjustment. The advantage of the second expedient is that, unlike the first, it permits us to leave the comparison between the two types of country on as inclusive a basis as is permitted by national income estimates for industrial countries.[6]

[6] Throughout we face the choice between "inflating" national income totals for pre-industrial countries to make them as comprehensive and as "gross" as the estimates for industrial countries; and "deflating" national income totals for industrial countries to make them as restricted and as "net" as the ordinary estimates for pre-industrial countries. The usual

IV

We have discussed so far extra-market productive activities, a substantial part of which is likely to be omitted from national income estimates for pre-industrial countries while they are more fully included in those for industrial countries. We are now ready to consider several categories, still within the area of the flow of goods to ultimate consumers, that are fully represented in estimates for industrial countries and yet are costs rather than final products, in the sense that they serve merely to offset some of the disadvantages of industrial organization.

The first category was suggested in the discussion above of the degree of fabrication of consumer commodities in industrial societies. A characteristic feature of the latter is that production tends to be concentrated in relatively large units, at some distance from the consumers who ultimately use the finished products. Thus, from the completion of commodities by producers to the time they reach the hands of consumers there is a long chain of transportation and distribution; just as there may be a long chain of transportation and distribution between the origin of the raw material with primary producers and its use in the manufacturing or construction establishment. This can be clearly visualized by assuming in an industrial society a single shoe factory which, with the help of railroads and a whole network of trade, assembles raw hides

---

choice in the national income literature, and followed in the illustrative calculation in the Appendix, is to "grossify"—bring the estimates for pre-industrial countries *up* to the level of comprehensiveness and grossness of those for industrial countries. A more desirable but more difficult solution would be to raise the estimates for pre-industrial countries only for such elements of real productive activity as tend to escape measurement and to reduce the estimates for industrial countries (and to a lesser extent those for pre-industrial countries) by omitting such elements as are not net, i.e., represent merely offsets to the disadvantages of industrialized urban societies.

from many livestock farms; then, with the help of transportation, trade, advertising, etc. manages to place the finished
shoes at the disposal of the individuals and families that wear
them. A hypothetical situation in an idealized self-subsistence
economy is in sharp contrast: a handicraftsman residing in
each village gets hides from the local farmers, converts them
into shoes, and sells or barters them to local inhabitants—all
without recourse to transportation, trade, advertising, etc. If
the number of shoes and their quality are exactly the same,
net product in the sense of the real flow to ultimate consumers
is identical in the two situations. Yet in one, production, in
the narrow sense of converting hides into shoes, accounts for
merely a small part of the finished goods, whereas in the others
it accounts for practically all of it. The transportation and
distribution activities in an industrial society can thus be
clearly seen as offsets to the disadvantages of large scale, machine manufacturing which, needless to say, are more than out-
weighed by its economies.

This problem is disposed of in current estimates for pre-
industrial societies either by taking the finished consumer
products at the *retail* prices of industrial societies, thereby allowing for the inclusion of all these transportation and distribution services (as Colin Clark does in the case of India or
China); or by making a special adjustment for differences in
the marketing structure of agricultural production (as T. C.
Liu does for China). These are perfectly legitimate adjustments, and I have only a few comments.

First, the adjustments just described are *part* of the one suggested in the preceding section, in which not the finished
product but the crude materials of pre-industrial societies are
to be valued at the retail prices of the corresponding finished
products of industrial societies. If the suggestion is accepted,
the adjustments of the type made by Clark and Liu are automatically included. Second, even with the latter adjustments,
revaluing to the price levels of industrial society involves
'grossifying' the output of pre-industrial societies, to bring it
on a par with the output of industrial countries. As already

suggested, it would be just as valid to 'nettify' the output of industrial societies to bring them on a par with pre-industrial societies, by omitting from national income all services embodied in the value of commodities that represent the extra transportation and handling. Third, while the adjustments discussed here are on the surface merely for differences in price levels, they are in fact an application of the basic definition of national income: only when the latter is defined as the real flow of goods to ultimate consumers and of net additions to capital stock, does the need for the adjustments become apparent.

But there are several other categories of productive activity in industrial societies whose value does not enter the retail prices of consumers' finished commodities, and yet they are merely offsets to costs imposed by the organization of production. Such activities ordinarily enter income estimates for industrial countries in the form of direct services to consumers (rather than as the cost of consumer commodities); and in some national income concepts in the form of the purchase of commodities and services by the government (e.g., in the Department of Commerce national income total for the United States). Yet such activities are either absent from or present to only a limited extent in pre-industrial societies because their industrial structures impose no costs that have to be offset. And clearly the adjustment just discussed, in converting consumers' commodities to retail prices prevalent in industrial countries, does not dispose of the lack of comparability thus arising.

Three categories of such activities come readily to mind. The first is suggested by the fact that in industrial countries the dominant modes of production impose an urban pattern of living, which brings in its wake numerous services whose major purpose is to offset the disadvantages. A clear case is the transportation of employees to and from work—an activity that can hardly be said to constitute direct welfare to ultimate consumers and is merely an offset to the inconvenience that large scale industrial production imposes upon the active participants in it. But what about the extra costs involved in providing urban consumers with the appurtenances of living? The costs are heavy exactly because the concentration of large numbers in limited areas raises geometrically the discomfort and the costs of offsetting it. For example, the Department of Commerce sets for 1929 the cost of space rent for urban and rural nonfarm dwellers at $10.3 billion, which for a nonfarm population of 101 million works out to about $100 per capita. For farm houses the total is $829 million, which for a farm population of 30 million, works out to about $27 per capita. Yet surely the real values of the two are scarcely in the ratio of 4 to 1. The costs of urban housing may well be high because of the technical problems created by dense aggregations of people.

The second category represents costs of participation in the complicated technical, monetary civilization of industrial countries. Payments to banks, employment agencies, unions, brokerage houses, etc. including such matters as technical education, are payments not for final goods flowing to ultimate consumers, but libations of oil on the machinery of industrial society—activities intended to eliminate friction in the productive system, not net contributions to ultimate consumption. And while identical or similar activities exist even in pre-industrial societies, particularly those in which the money economy has begun to spread, one might reasonably argue that their magnitude is much greater in the more complex industrial countries which make claims upon their members for a finer adjustment to the dictates of the market system.

The third category is represented by governmental activities. In any society the major part of governmental activity is devoted to preserving and strengthening the fabric of social organization, and only to a limited extent to the provision of final services to ultimate consumers. The legislative, judicial, administrative, police, and military functions of the state are designed to keep society operating along accepted patterns, to create the conditions under which the economy can function, not directly to provide goods to ultimate consumers. The major yield of governmental activity is therefore indirect rather than direct goods, costs rather than net returns. Yet if we accept the concept at present followed by the Department of Commerce in this country (and the official estimates of Great Britain and Canada), the full magnitude of governmental outlay on commodities and services appears as part of the net output of society, of national income or product. It is quite likely that the necessary costs, which most of such activities represent, are absolutely and relatively much smaller in a pre-industrial than in an industrial society; consequently, their full inclusion in national income introduces a greater element of grossness in the estimates for industrial countries.

In considering how to deal with the three categories of activities just noted, which may be interpreted largely as offsets to friction in the organization of economic society rather than as direct elements in net output, we are confronted with difficulties. The first is that activities of the three types described occur even in pre-industrial societies: in most of the latter, cities, a monetary and credit economy, and a central government are far from unknown. Hence if we are to omit some of these activities from the national income of industrial countries, we should be in a position to do likewise for pre-industrial societies. A more important difficulty is that in many activities the elements of net contribution and offsets to costs are interwoven, and can be disentangled only by intensive analysis. How much of the high price of urban housing is the high cost of offsetting discomforts of living in a densely settled community, and how much represents greater facilities and comforts? How much of the huge outlay on passenger automobiles in this country is an offset to the disadvantages of urban living and how much a net contribution to welfare? What proportion of the cost of the telephone, telegraph, etc. is an offset to the obligations imposed by participation in a highly developed society, and how much a net contribution to the satisfaction of ultimate consumers *qua* consumers?

In the face of these difficulties it is not easy to indicate steps in the direction of attempting closer comparability. Yet three suggestions seem to be in order. First, such activities as beyond any doubt represent payments by consumers for services that are nothing but occupational facilities should be excluded from the estimates for both types of country. Clear examples are commutation to and from work and payments to unions and employment agencies; but one might add almost the entire gamut of what the Department of Commerce classifies as business services in its estimate of consumers' outlay (bank fees, brokerage fees, etc.). Second, where in industrial societies the costs of consumer services are inflated by the difficulties of urban life, some revaluation of these services by comparing their costs in rural communities is in order. The magnitudes involved, especially in such an item as cash and imputed rent on housing, are quite large. Finally, it seems indispensable to include in national income only such governmental activities as can be classified as direct services to ultimate consumers. This most important and inescapable step is urged here in full cognizance of the statistical difficulties, which are great. But if national income figures are to retain any meaning as measures of the real flow of goods to ultimate consumers or to stock of capital, the huge duplication piled up by considering all governmental activity as a final product must be removed. Such a step is important and necessary even for intra-country comparisons over time; it is equally if not more important for comparisons between industrial and pre-industrial societies.

These three suggestions are a maximum program: their proper application requires information on and a functional analysis of the service sector of consumers' outlay and of governmental activities that are probably beyond the present supply of data and the present state of knowledge of the real contents of national product even for advanced industrial countries. As a more practical, if theoretically less satisfactory expedient, we may consider adjusting the national income of pre-industrial societies—as currently measured—for the elements of grossness that are present to a larger relative extent in the estimates for industrial societies. Thus, instead of excluding the service components of consumers' outlay that represent pure costs, revaluing inflated urban services, and reducing governmental activities to direct services to consumers, we can inflate the corresponding elements in the national incomes of pre-industrial countries to achieve a comparable level of grossness. This is, in fact, the expedient adopted in the illustrative comparison of the national products of the United States and China in the Appendix. It has the advantage of being consistent with the application, to the commodity part of national product, of the raising ratio of finished products to crude materials derivable from the standard estimates of national income for industrial countries. But it is a temporary expedient; eventually it will be preferable to follow the suggestions in their original form, and to exclude from estimates for both industrial and pre-industrial countries such gross elements as occupational expenses of ultimate consumers, inflated costs of urban living and intermediate product of governmental activities.

V

From the consumers' outlay component of national income, we turn to the treatment of capital formation.

a) Some of the elements omitted from national income estimates for pre-industrial countries and of grossness in the estimates for industrial countries characterize also the estimates of capital formation or investment. Thus a great deal of capital formation within pre-industrial economies takes place outside the market and is not likely to be recorded (e.g., individual farmers' activities on improving the soil and communal construction activities). These are not likely to be covered fully in the estimates. Yet their relative share of total capital formation is likely to be larger in pre-industrial than in industrial economies.

Similarly, pre-industrial countries are likely to be characterized by a shorter distance between the producer and the user of capital goods, (unless the goods are produced abroad). For an industrial economy labor is more extremely divided. Whatever we have said about consumer goods, in terms of the illustration of shoes, could be repeated in an illustration in terms of plows or farm carts. Here also, an advanced industrial organization may mean a considerable amount of extra fabrication, transportation, and trade that are not necessary in the simpler, decentralized structure of a pre-industrial economy.

However, quantitatively, such elements of both omission and grossness as tend to inflate the difference between totals for industrial and pre-industrial countries are likely to be relatively smaller for capital formation than for consumers' outlay. First, the real volume of *all* capital formation, whether market bound or not, is likely to be exceedingly small in pre-industrial countries living, as they do, close to the margin of subsistence. Second, in the case of capital formation, i.e., construction, machinery, and equipment, the relation between producer and consumer tends to be fairly close even in an industrial society. At any rate, it appears to involve less of the cross-hauling, elaborate distribution, and advertising that tend to bring such large elements of grossness into the cost of consumers' commodities to ultimate consumers. And satisfactory use of at least industrial equipment and construction is not as subject to the inflation of costs by the difficulties of urban living as is true of the use of consumers' goods proper. These statements are particularly applicable to net capital formation, i.e., if we exclude, for the purposes of the present analysis, the intermediate product of governmental activity. We thus deal only with net additions to the stock of capital goods, not with such gross volume as would include the contribuion of governmental activity to the preservation and regulation of the society at large or of the economic system in particular.

b) What about such capital goods as serve only activities which, in the analysis of consumers' outlay, we characterized as representing offsets rather than net contributions to the flow of goods to ultimate consumers? If services of street cars and commuting trains are not contributions to the satisfaction of wants of consumers *qua* consumers, and, therefore, should be excluded from national product (the latter conceived as the sum of the flow of goods to consumers and capital formation), should we exclude from capital formation the additions to the stocks of street cars or of street railway trackage? Clearly, if the answer is 'yes,' a large proportion of capital formation in an industrial country will be omitted.

The answer, however, is 'no.' The addition to capital stock is part of national product properly defined, regardless whether the capital good in question will itself directly yield services to ultimate consumers in the future, or, while not in itself capable of yielding such services, is still useful in keeping society going and thus avoiding future outlays. We consider a new blast furnace an addition to capital and a proper part of capital formation, even though the furnace in and of itself can not turn out final consumer goods. It will assist indirectly in turning them out and in its absence, a potential increase in the supply of finished products would be impossible without an additional outlay of resources. What is true of a blast furnace is true also of a street car, or of a battleship.

There is no inconsistency in excluding the *direct* services of capital goods from annual estimates of the flow of finished goods to ultimate consumers, and in including the tools that yield these services in capital formation. In measuring the flow of goods to consumers we are not justified in including goods that are wanted by consumers not as consumers but as producers. In measuring capital formation we are in fact estimating the future contribution—direct and indirect—of the goods in question to the ultimate satisfaction of consumers' wants. And so far as in the technology of the economic system street cars are a useful and indispensable tool, we include them in capital formation.

VI

The last major problem of comparability, differences in the patterns of production in industrial and pre-industrial economies, is reduced by the suggestions advanced in the analysis above, especially by the omission of some commodities and services that in industrial society serve exclusively to offset disadvantages imposed by the productive system. But even with this and related suggestions pushed as far as possible, there will still be marked differences in the composition of the goods that constitute the national product of the two types of society.

The exact meaning of this difference for the problem of proper statistical measurement must be clearly seen. Assume that for all the goods that are in the comparison between two countries, A and B, prices can be established for each in both countries, even though some of the goods may not be produced or consumed in one. It would then be possible to estimate the total product of country A in prices of country B, and the total product of country B in prices of country A. Though all problems would not be solved thereby, the assumption serves to illuminate two points important in the analysis. First, the analysis can best be handled by dividing it into two parts: one is the difficulty or impossibility of securing prices in country B (A) for such goods as are produced only in country A (B); the second remains even if prices in both countries could be secured for all goods in the comparison. The second point is that the difference in the goods patterns can be discussed only in connection with the relative price patterns of the two countries.

The difficulty created by the fact that for goods produced only in pre-industrial countries it is often impossible to get a price in an industrial country (and vice versa) cannot in fact be resolved, short of a close analysis of the function of the good in question, finding a functional counterpart in the other country, and then finding a price for it by analogy. While in certain classes of goods—how could one find the functional counterpart in the United States of say shark-fin soup or of the services of a Chinese fortune-teller?—this may seem a counsel of despair, for simpler types of goods the task is not impossible (e.g., for certain classes of food or clothing). But it is important to remember that the comparability to be established, the counterpart to be found, is not that of scientifically established physiological or medical service—but of position in the economic scale. At the present stage of our knowledge of industrial and pre-industrial societies, it is difficult to extend the range of price comparisons; and we have to accept the fact that prices will be found only for such goods as are used in both types of country. This means that in practice price comparisons are established for only such goods as are common to both types of economy; and that the ratios are applied to the over-all totals with the implicit assumption that the price relations for the goods omitted are the same as those for the goods covered.

This resolution, by assumption, may be the only practicable one. But it brings into comparisons of national income for industrial and pre-industrial economies a potentially large bias. Comparable prices in general can be found only for goods whose qualitative characteristics are easily recognized and compared—commodities rather than services; simple crude materials rather than complex fabricated articles. And as between two countries comparable prices are most easily established for crude commodities that move freely in international trade, not between commodities, no matter how crude, that are peculiar to one country alone. But commodities that move in international trade are likely to show relatively narrow price differentials: were the differentials wide, foreign trade would tend to reduce them. Consequently, the selectivity of price comparisons, in their emphasis upon crude commodities with international markets, has an important bias—*understating* the price differentials between the two countries. How considerable the understatement is depends upon the factors that produce the price differentials. When one country is industrial and the other pre-industrial, the understatement can be large indeed.[7]

[7] See some observations in this connection in the Appendix. The examples given there could, I suspect, be easily multiplied by anyone who would take the trouble to compare prices first for internationally traded crude commodities, and then for non-exportable (or non-importable) types of commodity and service.

This observation applies to price comparisons for identical goods, at identical levels of fabrication and circulation. The bias is, therefore, over and above any of the other elements of disparity already discussed. Hence, it is not disposed of by the adjustments suggested, and cannot be mitigated except by extending the range of goods for which comparable prices can be found. Such extension, as already indicated, can be made only by dint of further analysis of the two types of society, and by a search for more common denominators than are evident on the surface. This is only one more argument for more intensive study, particularly of pre-industrial societies.

If we assume that prices can be found for all goods in both countries, the national product of country A can be valued in prices of country B and compared with national income of B; and the national product of country B can be valued in prices of country A and compared with the national income of A. Differences in the patterns of goods of the two countries then cease to make comparison impossible. But they introduce an entirely different type of difficulty, viz., they give two measures of what is essentially one difference: for the ratio of national income of A to B, when measured in prices of A, may be different from the ratio of national income of A to B, when measured in prices of B.

It need not be labored here that the two ratios would differ only if the relative quantities of goods in the two countries differed. Were the goods structure of national product, i.e., its percentage distribution among the various goods (including those with zero weight, i.e., absent) exactly identical, then no matter how the price structure (i.e., relative prices of goods) differed, the ratios would be the same in the two indexes. Similarly, were the goods composition of the national product of two countries different, but the price structures identical, the two ratios would be the same. In fact, in comparisons of industrial with pre-industrial countries, both the goods and the price structures are likely to differ materially; and as a result the ratio of the national products of the two types of country will differ as we weight the quantities by prices of the industrial or of the non-industrial economy.

Thus, given differences in price structure, those in the goods composition of the national products inevitably result in a lack of determinateness of the difference between the national products of the countries. Only the upper and lower limits are set—the ratios of the two national products weighted first by the price system of one country, then by the price system of the other. At present, we do not know how far apart the limits are; but further studies in the field would be well worth while.

One can do no more than suggest the direction of the bias involved in using as base the price system of one or the other type of country. In general, relative price and quantity differentials tend to be correlated negatively: if a good x is priced much more highly than good y in one country, other conditions being equal, the quantities of x produced and consumed will be in a smaller ratio to the quantities of y in that country. In other words, there is some adaptation of the goods structure of a country to the relative price structure. This means that when we value the quantities produced in a pre-industrial country in prices of the industrial country, we tend to assign too high a set of price differentials to goods with relatively large quantity weights, and too low a set of price differentials to goods with small quantity weights. This tends to impart an *upward* bias to the national income totals of pre-industrial countries; and since they are in general much lower than the totals for industrial countries, the ratio between the two tends to be reduced. Per contra, when we revalue the national product of an industrial country in the prices of a pre-industrial country, we impart an upward bias to the national income total of the former and thus tend to magnify the ratio between it and the national income of the latter.

Consequently, the common practice in current national income literature of revaluing the national product of pre-industrial countries in prices of industrial countries tends to impart an upward bias to the former and to reduce the disparity.[8]

[8] The discussion is in terms of the price *structure*, i.e., of relative price differentials among identical goods, not in absolute price levels. Prices of identical goods are in general much higher in industrial than in pre-industrial economies, higher than the official conversion rates of currencies in-

In this sense, the bias is in the right direction in that it serves to reduce the downward bias implicit in confining the comparison of price *levels* to internationally traded crude commodities. But with limited coverage of the price comparison, the differences in the price *structures* of the two countries are also underestimated; so that the upward bias due to using the price structure of the industrial economy as a base is minimized. One may, therefore, reasonably argue that in current practice, the downward bias in the evaluation of national product for pre-industrial countries due to the limited coverage of price comparisons, is much greater than the upward bias resulting from using the price structure of the industrial country as the base.

The range between the limits within which the ratio of the national products of the two types of country falls is likely to be increased as the variety of goods for which price comparisons can be made widens. In other words, as the difficulties of proper comparison between the national products of industrial and pre-industrial countries, due to lack of comparable prices, are overcome, the second type of difficulty—associated with differences in price structure—is likely to become more prominent. This is as it should be: as our knowledge of both types of economy becomes more adequate, the problem of establishing unequivocal quantitative comparability should become more complex. As such knowledge accumulates, it will be seen that, by accepting the valuations implicit in the price system, we are in fact accepting two yardsticks which, each applied separately, naturally produce different results. The eventual solution would obviously lie in devising a single yardstick that could then be applied to both types of economies—

---

dicate (with the exception of the highly complex products of industrial civilization). The adjustment for the *level* of prices, therefore, almost uniformly reduces the spread between the national products for the two types of country when measured in official currencies and converted by means of official exchange rates. It is the effect of the price *structure* that is different as we take the price system of the industrial or of the pre-industrial economy as the base.

a yardstick that would perhaps lie outside the different economic and social institutions and be grounded in experimental science (of nutrition, warmth, health, shelter, etc.).

This consideration brings us beyond the plane of intellectual discourse on which national income estimates at present rest. But it is not irrelevant that the ease with which national income comparisons, among countries with differing industrial and social structures are currently made, may largely be due to the shallowness of our knowledge and to our willingness to stay on the surface of social phenomena. As knowledge increases, it may be more rather than less difficult to make effective comparisons within the present frame of reference.

VII

In applying the above suggestions to an illustrative comparison of the national incomes of China and the United States (see the Appendix), we followed the path of least resistance. Rather than employ selective reduction and inflation, we raised the estimates for China to compensate for both possible omissions in them and the elements of grossness that are peculiar to the estimates for the United States. The purpose of this calculation is not to provide conclusive or even semi-conclusive results, but to test the feasibility of the suggestions and to get some idea of the size of the adjustments involved.

In this comparison, which uses Mr. Liu's gross national product estimates for China for 1931-36, the adjustments applied to secure greater comparability with the United States figures, yield a per capita product for China of $69 (U. S.); and a per capita consumption of $62½ (U. S.). The latter figure can be compared with that established by Mr. Liu of $37 (U. S.) per capita after his adjustments for differences in price levels, in the marketing structure of agriculture, in the supply of unpaid domestic services, and in the ratio of consumption to gross national product. While the application of the adjustments suggested here raises the per capita figures almost 80 percent, the calculation in the Appendix still takes no account of the downward bias implicit in the price comparison (we accepted Mr. Liu's estimate for this item) ; or of other sources of lack of comparability that might raise the figure for China even higher. Taking these points into consideration could easily bring per capita consumption in China to over $75 (U. S.) or twice Mr. Liu's adjusted figure. The experimental calculation yields, therefore, two significant conclusions: first, the adjustments suggested above are feasible and can be applied even with the present limited supply of data; second, the adjustments are sufficiently big to affect markedly comparisons between industrial and pre-industrial countries, and change materially the results of comparisons that have been made in the last two decades.

While the discussion, and the calculation, have so far been in terms of national product totals alone, the points raised are relevant to every important type of distribution. Thus, the usual industrial allocation of national income is affected by the fact that many extra-market activities in a pre-industrial economy elude measurement: these activities are in the nature of either manufacturing (or construction) or the provision of personal and other services. So far as they are omitted, and to an extent presumably greater than similar activities in agriculture, the industrial distribution of national income for a pre-industrial economy would show too large a share for agriculture and too small a share for other industries. The over-inclusion of certain activities in national incomes for industrial countries would exaggerate the shares of some industries, e.g., transportation, distribution, housing.

The distribution of income by size is also modified. Even pre-industrial countries have upper income groups that tend to be heavily concentrated in cities. In a national product estimate that follows closely the conventional rules of industrial countries, the incomes of urban population are likely to be more completely covered than the incomes of rural; which means that there is more complete coverage of upper than of lower income brackets. Any more inclusive treatment of extra-market activities in pre-industrial economies or adjustments for the elements of grossness in the estimates for industrial countries, are likely to shift the income distribution by size in favor of the groups at the lower end, thereby reducing the inequality of the income distribution as shown in unadjusted or incompletely adjusted distributions.

The effect on the percentage allocation of national product between the flow of goods to consumers and capital formation is somewhat different. As suggested above the elements of omission and grossness that affect comparability may well be relatively small for such items of capital formation as industrial construction or industrial machinery and equipment. If so, the adjustments advocated here, when applied in a specific rather than a crude wholesale fashion, may raise the flow of goods to consumers sector of national income of pre-industrial countries by a greater relative proportion than they would capital formation. Thus while the absolute magnitude of capital formation in pre-industrial countries and its ratio to capital formation in industrial countries may be raised, the ratio to the flow of goods to consumers within pre-industrial countries may well be lowered.

This suggestion applies to the real volume of capital formation or investment. A somewhat related point concerns the distinction between outlay and savings. In all countries, even advanced industrial, some categories of consumers' outlay include elements of savings in the sense that purchase is guided, at least secondarily, by the utility of the good as a storage of value (luxuries that tend to have stable values). In pre-industrial countries, with the prevailing limits for safe productive investment, such purchases of consumer goods, which in fact represent hidden savings, may well loom much larger, relative to total consumers' outlay, than they would in an industrial country. So far as they do, the volume of savings exceeds the volume of domestically financed productive investment or capital formation.[9]

[9] This is of importance for the analysis of the savings-potential of pre-industrial countries in connection with plans for industrialization. Conditions of political security and extension of productive investment opportunities are involved in any effective industrialization, hence the savings

These brief comments suffice to indicate that the attempt to introduce greater comparability between the national product totals of pre-industrial and industrial countries affects also the comparisons of internal distributions by industrial source, by size classes, or by type of use. This is natural since closer analysis of the contents of the national products for the two types of country reveals differences that have to be recognized in a proper comparison, differences that have a differing impact upon the industrial, size, and use classifications, traditional in industrial countries and often applied without modification to pre-industrial economies.

VIII

In conclusion, I would like to stress what it is that we are *not* trying to measure by means of national income estimates, and indicate why. Such comments may prevent misunderstanding as well as suggest lines of exploration other than those stressed here.

National income, as we conceive it, measures the flow from the productive system, but not the inclusive consumption totals for the economy. There is a significant difference between the flow of goods to consumers and what Joseph S. Davis calls the consumption level.[10] The latter includes, in addition to the current flow of goods from the productive system, the yield of goods owned by the consumers; and excludes from the current flow to consumers goods they do not actually consume during the period. With the much greater stock of goods in the

---

potential is suggested not only by the past flow of savings into productive investment but also by such elements of consumers' outlay as would become unnecessary with the progress of industrialization. The latter comprise the purchases of luxuries intended largely as a storage of value; and expenditures closely connected with traditional pre-industrial culture (funerals, feasts, religious observances, etc.) whose practice is likely to be greatly reduced by the secularizing influence of industrialization.

[10] See his presidential address, "Standards and Content of Living," *American Economic Review*, March 1945, pp. 1-15.

hands of individuals and households, the consumption levels per capita in an industrial economy may well show a greater relative excess over per capita consumption levels in a pre-industrial economy than might be revealed by a comparison of the flow of goods per capita—no matter how fully the latter is covered.

Nor are we trying to use national income estimates to measure what Professor Davis calls the level or plane of living, which includes, in addition to consumption, working conditions, cushions against major and minor shocks, freedoms of various kinds, and other spiritual constituents of social life. These ingredients of living are extremely important in spelling happiness and unhappiness; and it is easy to conceive of situations where the consumption level rises yet the plane or level of living declines; e.g., when the rise is attained by sacrifices of working conditions or of freedoms of a kind highly prized by the population.

Finally, we have not tried to push the analysis of national income estimates in the direction already mentioned, viz., of gauging the degree of satisfaction of wants ascertainable by experimental and scientific methods and in disregard of purely economic valuation imposed by society. Thus, we accept the valuation of foods as provided by the markets, attempting only to make both terms of the comparison (i.e., in an industrial and pre-industrial country) equally inclusive, and employing, for identical goods, the same prices. We are not trying to convert the foods into vitamin equivalents and thus translate physical quantities into vitamin content, completely bypassing the market valuation. Nor are we trying to do the same for clothing, fuel, shelter, and the like.

The refusal to extend discussion in these directions—of fuller coverage of consumption levels, of levels of living, and of experimentally established functional equivalents—is not due to the possibly low yield of such explorations. On the contrary, they promise results of great value. They might explain, more satisfactorily than can be done otherwise, the basic differences between industrial and pre-industrial economies, and the conditions on which of the latter can be industrialized. As already suggested, they might provide a more effective basis for comparisons and help overcome the difficulties imposed by differences in the goods composition of national product. Studies of nutrition indicate unmistakably that pre-industrial economies manage to obtain the basic vitamin supply at much lower economic costs, and hence at much lower prices, than a price comparison of *identical commodities* would indicate.

That we have paid little attention to these aspects of the comparison is due largely to a feeling that study has not advanced sufficiently to permit abandonment of the more traditional approach, *via* the customary definitions of national income or product. At any rate, I did not feel competent to discuss the problems that would emerge in any direct consideration of consumption levels, planes of living, and functional equivalents. It does seem to me, however, that as customary national income estimates and analysis are extended; and as their coverage includes more and more countries that differ markedly in their industrial structure and form of social organization, investigators interested in quantitative comparisons will have to take greater cognizance of the aspects of economic and social life that do not now enter national income measurement; and that national income concepts will have to be either modified or partly abandoned, in favor of more inclusive measures, less dependent upon the appraisals of the market system.

We can view national income comparisons among countries in the light of an entirely different set of basic criteria. Rather than concern ourselves with national product as a flow of goods to consumers present and future, we can view it as a measure of a nation's power—defined broadly as power to impose upon the rest of the world conditions which, for one reason or another, are considered favorable to the given nation. Whether we further specify such power to consist of the ability to provide security, or to expand the area of sovereignty, both the concept and comparison of income between industrial and pre-industrial countries will differ widely from those used in the analysis above. Many elements of the industrial economy we considered gross because they represented an offset to extra costs of urban civilization are not gross from the viewpoint of national power; for in armed conflict, the crucial weapon in the exercise of such power, many appurtenances of urban civilization can be temporarily sacrificed and the resources used for them diverted into other channels. Many elements of pre-industrial economy whose inclusion in national product we urged because they contributed to the flow of goods to consumers should perhaps be excluded from national income as a measure of national power because these decentralized extra-market activities cannot be effectively mobilized or controlled by the state in case of an armed conflict (even though they may be immensely useful in passive defense). Indeed, for many aspects of national income as a measure of national power, the relative disparity between industrial and pre-industrial countries is very much greater than the customary estimates of national income indicate, even before the adjustments suggested above.

We did not touch upon this line of approach for two reasons: its application to income measurement has not reached a point where its potentialities and problems are clear, and it differs so sharply from the customary approach that to include both within the bounds of a single paper would be impossible. But it seemed important at least to mention the approach, to invite attention to its implications and to suggest that the ordinary impressions of the vast relative difference between the economic performance of industrial and pre-industrial societies may well be colored by vague thoughts concerning differences in national power, rather than in supplying goods for the satisfaction of consumer wants.

These comments on the potentialities of explorations in the direction of a better analysis of the contents of living or of relevance to national power should not be interpreted as minimizing the importance and usefulness of national income analysis on the more orthodox level discussed here. Granted that from the viewpoint of contents of living (or national power)

national income, as ordinarily measured, stops half-way. It is
a compromise in the sense that it accepts the valuation of the
market place, with some adjustments, but without probing too
deeply beneath the surface of economic phenomena; and if
a national income estimate for one country is a compromise, a
comparison for an industrial and pre-industrial country is a
compromise of compromises. Nevertheless it is an enormously
useful device for measuring, if proximately, the magnitudes of
performance of the economies, and providing a quantitative
framework within which the weight of significant sectors can
be gauged. Nor does the realization that we deal with compromises free us from the necessity of looking closely and as-
suring ourselves that on the level of comparison accepted, the
scope and basis of valuation are as truly comparable as they
can be made. The major burden of this paper is that there is
room for improvement even in such proximate measures as
currently defined national income totals, improvement for purposes of comparing the totals and their components for industrial and pre-industrial countries. These opportunities for improvement can and must be pursued, before analysis can be
extended in any direction that transcends or differs materially
from the level of current national income estimates.

APPENDIX

Illustrative Calculation of the National Products of the United States and China on Comparable Bases

I GENERAL PLAN

We chose the United States and China largely because
recent estimates for both are available, and particularly detailed ones for the former. The two main sources are: for the
United States—the supplement to the July 1947 *Survey of Current Business* (referred to below as *DCS*) and Ta-Chung Liu's
China's National Income, 1931-36 (Brookings Institution,
1946).

The general plan of the analysis is as follows. For the United States, gross national product is divided into: (a) commodities; (b) services not embodied in new commodities. For the former we calculate the over-all ratio of the final cost of finished commodities to the value of raw materials consumed, at producers' prices. Among services not embodied in new commodities we segregate groups taken as comparable with the measurable service performance in a pre-industrial economy like China. For these several groups, whose magnitudes are approximated in the United States estimates, we assume reduction ratios reflecting the extent to which such services in a pre-industrial economy are either carried on within the family and community or to which they are superfluous, being in fact but offsets to the disadvantages peculiar to a highly developed industrial society.

The two ratios derived for the United States—of finished commodities to raw materials; and of the gross volume of services to a net volume representing comparable net coverage in a pre-industrial economy—are available for application to the data for China. Neither ratio allows, however, for differences in the price level between the United States and China for *identical* raw materials or *identical* services.

Our treatment of the data for China consists, therefore, of: (a) adjusting the raw material flow for differences in prices; (b) raising the latter by a ratio of finished products to raw materials; (c) adjusting comparable services not embodied in new commodities for differences in prices; (d) raising the result under (c) by a ratio of gross to net services.

2 ALLOCATING UNITED STATES NATIONAL PRODUCT BETWEEN COMMODITIES AND SERVICES

For 1931-36, the gross national product of the United States is estimated to be $68.26 billion per year (*DCS*, Table 2, p. 19). Of this total, net foreign investment, averaging $131 million, is not easily allocable between commodities and services; we therefore omit it, reducing national product to $68.13 billion per year.

Commodities account for by far the major part. The commodity sector comprises (annual average for 1931-36) : durable and non-durable products flowing to ultimate consumers— $31.98 billion (see *DCS*, Table 2, p. 19) ; gross private domestic investment—$4.14 billion (*ibid.*) ; and the commodities purchased by government. The latter can be approximately set at the amount governments purchase from business enterprises : these may include some services but probably relatively few. Government purchases from business enterprises are estimated to be at $3.75 billion per year (see *DCS*, Table 9, p. 23). Thus the commodity total, per year, for 1931-36 is $39.9 billion. The service total comprises the service sector of consumers' outlay, averaging for 1931-6 $22.64 billion (*ibid.*, Table 2, p. 19) ; and payments by governments for services of employees—$5.45 (*ibid.*, Table 9, p. 23)—a total of $28.1 billion.

3 CALCULATION OF THE RATIO OF FINISHED COMMODITIES TO RAW MATERIALS

The raw materials that flow into finished commodities are the products of agriculture and mining. Their basic components for 1931-36 are, therefore, approximated by taking the gross income for these two industries (i.e., gross sales and products retained, adjusted for intra-industry duplication alone). The annual averages involved are $8.3 and $2.3 billion, or a total of $10.6 billion (see Simon Kuznets, *National Income and Its Composition*, National Bureau of Economic Research, 1941, pp. 543 and 551).

However, some of these raw materials may go into exports and not become embodied in finished products purchased by consumers, by government, or by business enterprises (for capital formation) ; and, *per contra*, some of the finished commodities may be from imported materials. We must, therefore, adjust the total just derived for imports and exports. Imports of raw materials, raw foods, and semi-finished manufactures averaged for 1931-36 $1.16 billion (see *Statistical Abstract of the United States, 1944-45*, 1946, pp. 532-3) ; exports, $0.99

billion (*ibid.*), the latter amount to be scaled down 10 percent to the level of producers' prices. The net balance of imports over exports is therefore $0.27 billion ($1.16-0.89). Hence, the crude materials total, which forms the denominator of the fraction we are trying to estimate, is, for 1931-36, $10.9 billion per year ($10.6 + 0.3).

The numerator is the commodity total of $39.9 billion, derived above, also to be adjusted for imports and exports. Exports of manufactured foods and finished manufactures in 1931-36 averaged $1.07 billion, a total that need not be scaled down for transportation and distribution charges since the latter are part of the spread we are attempting to calculate. Imports of finished products averaged $0.67 billion (*Statistical Abstract, 1944-45*, pp. 532-3). The net balance of $0.4 billion added to the commodity total, $39.9 billion, yields a numerator of $40.3 billion. The ratio is, therefore, 3.7.

This ratio is for a commodity total that includes the elaborate items of producers' durable equipment and construction as well as highly fabricated consumers' durable products (automobiles, radios, household electrical equipment, etc.) that find little counterpart in pre-industrial economies. The ratio we need should have been calculated only for the sector of raw materials and finished commodity flow that comprises the simple types of product—foods, clothing, other nondurable goods, furniture, etc. A more elaborate calculation of this type, more directly relevant to our purposes, is beyond the scope of this paper. We therefore arbitrarily reduced the ratio from 3.7 to 3.25, to allow for the inclusion of these more complex commodities specific to an industrial country alone. This is a fairly generous scaling down, in view of the fact that consumers' durable commodities (not all of which should be omitted), construction, and producers' durable equipment (averaging per year $4.8 + 2.1 + 2.9) amount to only $9.8 billion, less than one-fourth of the comprehensive commodity total, $39.9 billion. The reduction of the ratio by about one-seventh associated with a presumptive exclusion from the total of somewhat less than one-quarter, means that the ratio for the excluded part is much larger than that for the non-excluded part (indeed, the implicit ratio for the durable part is 6.1).

Both to check on the commodity ratio just derived for 1931-36 and to demonstrate what a large proportion of the difference between crude materials and final cost of finished products is due to functions other than manufacturing proper, we calculated the components of the difference. As already indicated, total finished commodities average $40.3 billion per year 1931-36; the cost of crude materials, $10.9 billion. The absolute difference, $29.4 billion per year, may roughly be accounted for as follows:

	Annual value per year, 1931-36 ($ billions) (1)	Ratio (2)	Total ($ billions) (3)	Source DCS Table (4)
A Net income originating in				
1 Manufacturing	11.27	1.0	11.27	13
2 Contract construction	1.35	1.0	1.35	13
3a Trade	8.08	0.8	6.46	13
b Rr. transportation	2.25	0.8	1.80	13
c Highway, water, pipe line & related transportation services	0.80	0.8	0.64	13
d Business, banking, legal, engineering services	1.90	0.8	1.52	13
B Depreciation & capital consumption	7.58	0.8	6.06	4
C Business & sales tax	2.52	0.8	2.02	8
Total	35.75	..	31.12	..

The deduction of 20 percent for items A3, B, and C is intended as a rough allowance for the part relating to crude materials proper and entering their value, or to services not embodied in new commodities and hence not relevant to commodity ratio calculation.

The total for comparison is $31.12 billion (col. 3). No precise check with the $29.4 billion total is attempted here, nor is one feasible. But the rough congruence of the two totals shows that the huge difference between the value of crude materials and the cost to ultimate users of the finished commodities they enter can easily be accounted for by the sum of net income originating in the industries handling them and the additional items of depreciation and taxes.

Of more interest in the present connection is the fact that of the total spread, production activities proper account for little more than half. If of the depreciation total (in Item B) we allow about one-half as chargeable to manufacturing and construction (before being transported and distributed), the strictly fabricating functions account for $15.65 of the total, $31.12 billion. The rest is associated with transportation, trade, and other services. These figures make it easier to see that the very high commodity ratio characterizing a highly developed industrial economy is due in only small part to more elaborate fabrication; a great deal of it is accounted for by extensive transportation and intensive handling in distributive, credit, and other service channels.

4 THE ANALYSIS OF SERVICES

Of the annual volume for services, $28.1 billion for 1931-36, the major item is services flowing to ultimate consumers,— $22.6. The details in *DCS* Table 30 suggest the following rough functional classification.

The first group are services for which there is a clear counterpart in a pre-industrial economy, but of which a large proportion is carried on within the family and the community and perforce escapes measurement—domestic service, personal care, recreation, religion, funerals, etc., care of clothing and furniture, etc. For this category, labeled A, a rough calculation for 1931-6 suggests that they amount to 21 percent of all services flowing to ultimate consumers. Allowance must be made for the fact that many of them are performed within the family economy and are not reflected in orthodox estimates; and others (such as religion and recreation) are of a type, as suggested in the text, in which no clear case of greater per capita supply can be made between countries differing widely in social pattern. For purposes of comparison with a pre-industrial country the value of the services can at least be halved.

The second category, B, is the part of service flow to ultimate consumers that represents chiefly adjustments to the money economy. The foremost example is the large group of business services in the Department of Commerce classification (brokerage and bank fees, union dues, employment agency fees, insurance, foreign transactions, etc.). This category accounts for roughly 17 percent of total consumers' outlay on services; and the reduction for the extent to which it represents costs of an industrial economy rather than net returns must be large. We set the reduction at eight-tenths of the total.

The third category, C, comprises expenditures of urban populations on services whose value is grossly inflated by the extra problems and difficulties of urban life. The most conspicuous example is urban rents (cash or imputed). Others are commutation, communication costs, and the like. This category accounts for 50 percent of total services to consumers, and it should be cut at least in half if the real net product element in it is to be comparable with that in an essentially non-urban society—still disregarding price differentials for *identical* goods.

The fourth category in consumers' outlay on services, D, comprises services that contain no element of grossness, and that, on the whole, are likely to be as fully recorded in the ordinary estimates for pre-industrial countries as they are for industrial countries. The foremost examples are medical services or services of education. This category accounts for roughly 12 percent of total outlay by consumers on services, and no reduction should be made in it.

Finally, we come to services purchased by government rather than by ultimate consumers. As argued in the text, a major part of governmental activity is intermediate rather than final product, hence this category, E, contains elements of grossness not unlike those in category B. However, similar elements of grossness may also be included in the estimates for pre-industrial countries; and while in any comparison between the two some reduction may be in order, it should be fairly small—about one-fifth.

We thus have the following exhibit:

Service category	% of total flow to consumers, 1929, U. S. (1)	Reduction ratio suggested (2)	Col. 1 reduced (3)
A	21	0.5	10.5
B	17	0.8	3.4
C	50	0.5	25.0
D	12	0.0	12.0
E	24	0.2	19.2
Total	124	...	70.1

The following items were included in each category (the numbers for A-D refer to those shown for various service groups in *DCS*, Table 30).

A: II-5, 6, 7, 8, 9, 10, 11; III-2, 3, 4; V-10, 11, 12, 26, 27, 28; VI-7, 9, 12, 13, 14, 15, 16, 17; IX exclusive of all commodity components; XI.

B: VII-3, 4, 5, 6, 7, 8, 9, 10, 11, 12, 13, 14, 15, 16, 17, 18; XII—all excluding 1c.

C: IV-1, 2, 4, 5; V-20, 21, 22, 23, 24, 25; VIII-1d, 1f, 1g, 2, 3.

D: II-13; IV-3; V-13; VI-3, 4, 5, 6, 8, 10, 11; X.

E: *DCS*, Table 9, compensation of employees.

The ratio of the total flow of services to that considered truly net and comparable is as of 124 to 70.1, or 1.77. For purposes of comparison, any standard estimate of services for a pre-industrial country like China should be raised by some such ratio, even if price differentials for identical service items are disregarded.

5 RECALCULATION OF THE ESTIMATES FOR CHINA

We may now apply the results to the estimates for China, taking advantage of the data in Mr. Liu's book and the similarities in the concepts used by him to that of the Department of Commerce.

Crude materials flowing into domestic consumption can be

estimated first. The average per year, 1931-36, of the gross value of agricultural products (excluding urban-agricultural sales) and of mineral and metallurgical output, for the 22 provinces amounted to 16.89 billion yuans (for the former see Liu, Table 11, pp. 35-40; for the latter, Table 19, p. 51). With the allowance of 11 percent for the missing provinces, the total amounts to 18.75 billion yuans per year. Let us assume further that no raw materials were imported and that all commodity exports were raw materials—an assumption that tends to minimize the value of raw materials flowing into domestic consumption and hence the value of the national product. The average annual total of exports, including the adjustment for undervaluation, is 771 million yuans; deducting 10 percent for adjustment to the level of producers' values (a patently small deduction) the figure becomes 694 million yuans per year (see Liu, Table 28, p. 69). Subtracting it from the already derived annual average output of crude commodities, 18.75 billion yuans, leaves 18.06 billion per year.

According to Mr. Liu's calculation, the difference between prices of identical commodities in China and the United States, estimated from a comparison of crude commodities alone (rice, wheat, other grains, beans and peas, sweet potatoes), for 1931-36 results in undervaluing Chinese commodities 47 percent (see pp. 73 and 75). Before any conversion by means of the customary exchange rates, the value of Chinese crude material in yuans must, therefore, be raised 47 percent. The next step is to allow for the ratio calculated above of finished commodities to crude materials of 3.25. Hence, for an estimate in yuans, directly convertible by means of official exchange rates, the value of finished commodities in China's gross national product must be derived by multiplying the value of 18.06 billion yuans per year, first by 1.47, then by 3.25. The result is 86.28 billion yuan.

The service component of China's gross national product can also be derived from Mr. Liu's figures. The average annual value of professional service, 1931-36, is approximately 3,438 million yuan (see Table 27, p. 66); of value added by governmental and educational institutions, 882 million yuan (see Tables 23 and 24, pp. 55 and 58); of imputed house rent (farm alone), 1,620 million yuan (see Table 11, pp. 35-40). For 22 provinces the total of these services not embodied in new commodities is therefore 5,940 million yuan per year; and with the 11 percent increase for omitted areas, becomes 6.59 billion yuans.

This total must be raised to adjust for the differences in prices for identical services in the two countries; and further for the ratio, calculated above, of the gross to the net element in the services. Mr. Liu has no data for prices of services, and in fact employs the price differential derived from comparison of crude commodities. For lack of information we follow his practice. The adjustment then consists of multiplying 6.59 billion yuan first by 1.47, and then by 1.77. If the result, 17.15 billion yuans, is added to 86.28 billion, the total derived above for the commodity component, annual gross national product is 103.43 billion yuans.

These are yuans that are directly convertible to United States dollars by the official rate of exchange: 1 yuan = $0.2886. The total, i.e., $29.85 billion, can be compared with that derived by Mr. Liu as a result of his adjustment for differences in price levels, in the marketing structure of agricultural production, and in the extent of unpaid family services. With these adjustments Mr. Liu raises China's gross national product, 1931-36, to $16.68 billion per year (see p. 85). The present adjustment thus raises Mr. Liu's adjusted total by $13.2 billion, or another 79 percent.

In passing from gross national product to consumers' outlay, we may accept Mr. Liu's figure of 10 percent for gross savings (see pp. 86-7). Consumers' outlay per year amounted, in terms of equivalent purchasing power in United States dollars, to 26.87 billion. With a population taken at Mr. Liu's figure of 410 million, per capita consumption is $62½, rather than the $37 derived by Mr. Liu. For the same period, consumers' outlay per capita in the United States was estimated by the Department of Commerce to be $433.

6 CONCLUDING COMMENTS

The experimental calculation above is admittedly susceptible to criticism, and particularly revisions entailed by more specific and elaborate application of the basic assumptions. But if the latter are granted, one is justified in claiming that the magnitudes assigned to the adjustments are moderate. The grounds for increasing them, thereby reducing the difference between the national products of United States and China even further, are:

a) The coverage of crude materials in the estimates for China may well be less complete than in those for the United States, partly because of the assumption concerning imports and exports and partly because some agricultural and mining crude materials escape measurement in China to a greater extent than in the United States.

b) The ratio of finished products to crude materials, 3.25 may be on the low side. An increase would add proportionately to the commodity sector, and to national income.

c) The price differentials between China and the United States are probably underestimated, largely because the figure used by Mr. Liu is heavily dominated by basic foods freely entering international trade. The crude materials that do not move as freely, either because they are too perishable or bulky or because they supply local demand primarily, are likely to exhibit much greater price differentials. Even in Mr. Liu's five agricultural commodities, those moving in international trade—rice, wheat, other grains—show price differentials of from 27 to 50 percent of the price in China; whereas beans and peas and sweet potatoes which are of more local use, show differentials as large as 80 and 118 percent. A simple recalculation, in which the combined differential for beans and peas and sweet potatoes is given the full weight of all agricultural products except grains, would raise the five commodities price differential from the 47 percent calculated by Mr. Liu to 70 percent. This adjustment alone would raise the national product for China 15 to 16 percent beyond the $29.85 billion established in our calculation.

d) The price differential for services is likely to be greater even than the 70 percent just suggested. Mr. Liu estimates per capita income for professional services to average roughly 105 yuan per year (Table 26, p. 65). This, for a family of six, works out to 630 yuan per year, or at official exchange rates, to about $180. In the United States per capita compensation of employees in professional activities would average well over $1,000 and of entrepreneurs in a field like medical service well over $2,000. It is difficult to assume that the quality differential is such as to bridge the difference between some $300 ($180 x 1.7) and say $1,500 to $2,000.

These considerations suggest that further analysis might bring the per capita estimates for China and the United States even closer.

7

NATIONAL INCOME AND
ECONOMIC WELFARE *

I

By social welfare we mean some positive element in
the satisfaction of men's wants, men viewed as members of society; and for economic welfare we can adopt Pigou's definition as "that part of social welfare that can be brought directly
or indirectly into relation with the measuring-rod of money".[1]
Pigou indicates that the boundaries of the definition are elastic, as we interpret the word 'can' in a narrow or broad sense.
Indeed it is impossible to set precise boundaries in advance.
But one must be particularly aware of variations in coverage
of the measuring-rod of money, both over time and in space:
between the highly industrialized and market-bound economy
of the United States of today and the agricultural, self-sus-
tained economy of two hundred years ago, or between the
United States and China of today. If economic welfare is to
be a usefully measurable magnitude, even if only in terms of
more or less, we must interpret its connection with the measuring rod of money broadly—not limit the latter to specific
coverage in a narrowly defined area or period.

Some aspects of the definition will emerge more clearly in
discussing specific questions that arise in attempts to measure
economic welfare. Those questions may be treated most effectively if we accept, for the present purposes, some measure

* Reprinted by permission from *Boletin del Banco Central de Venezuela,*
Nos. 53-4, July-August 1949, pp. 11-21.
[1] A. C. Pigou, *The Economics of Welfare,* Third Edition, London 1929,
p. 11.

considered closest to a comprehensive estimate of economic welfare. Such a measure is national income, even though many official agencies responsible for the preparation of the estimates tend to deny it. Such denial of welfare basis is futile. The most widely accepted definition of national income equates it to the total *net product* yielded by a country's economy during a given period. But product is something that has a positive value in terms of human wants; and the attempt to measure it on a *net* basis implies a recognition of end-goals, of ultimate wants with reference to which final products can be distinguished from intermediate. That national income accounting distinguishes such groups as households, business firms etc., in itself implies a distinction between ultimate and intermediate consumers; and satisfaction of wants of the former by the use of scarce material resources organized with the help of the measuring-rod of money constitutes economic welfare. It is, therefore, not only permissible but necessary to view national income measures as approximations to economic welfare, since they are, by definition, appraisals of the yield of the country's economy from the standpoint of the wants of its ultimate consumers. Were we unconcerned with such welfare aspects, there would be no particular need to worry about duplication or to limit the total to positive product (excluding e.g. definitely harmful or illegal goods): we could take any well-defined total (e.g. the sum of gross products of all industries, the industrial classification being specifically defined; or the sum total of all transactions including or excluding those dealing with transfers of assets) and operate with it as a measure of economic activity, indeed as a measure of production as a process. For many analytical and technical purposes such totals would be more useful than national income. But the moment we attempt to measure net product, where *product* means something positive and *net* must have direct relevance to some final set of uses, we are, in fact, dealing with an approximation to economic welfare.[2]

[2] Unless we wish to assume some different set of end-goals. For a lengthier discussion of this problem see Simon Kuznets, *National Income, A Sum-*

The composition of national income or national product (we use the two terms interchangeably) of most interest for the present purposes is that of: (a) flow of goods to ultimate consumers, i.e. the individuals and households comprising the nation, (b) government product, (c) additions to capital stock. This threefold division is followed by the Department of Commerce estimates for this country, and by those of many agencies for other countries. We refrain from complicating the terms by various qualifying clauses, since our interest does not lie in technical details. The broad questions to be discussed can best be raised in connection with each of these three major components of a nation's net product—the estimates of which are our most widely used approximation to economic welfare.

II

Flow of goods to individuals and households means simply that the economic system yields, during the year or decade, so many pounds of bread, suits of clothing, millions of cars, and thousands of whatever units of professional, medical etc. services we can envisage. In the present connection it is not important whether we think of such flow as purchases by individuals or households or as use in actual consumption. But it is important that we look carefully at this flow, by far the largest part of any national product total, whether today or yesterday, in the United States or in the USSR, and observe the major questions that arise in defining the total—regardless of the technical questions which may arise in measurement.

Two major problems can be seen immediately. One, to be designated for convenience as that of non-market sectors, is most clearly illustrated by the perennial example of housewives' services. Should such services, which are presumably received by individuals and households, be included under economic net product? And what about the commodities that are

---

mary of Findings, National Bureau of Economic Research, N. Y. 1946, Part IV, and the references given therein.

produced by our amateur gardeners, whether flower or truck, or devotee photographers, cabinet makers and other people who practice such hobbies, however unskillfully? There is a general inclination on the part of economists, and particularly statistical technicians, to dismiss these questions as rather petty details and to confine measurement to goods produced for the market. But, in the long view, should not economic activity involving the use of limited means for wide ends, include at least all major flows of scarce goods, no matter how produced? That the item is not necessarily in the nature of a minor detail, can be seen from the fact that the value of housewives' services, whenever estimated, was, in the years prior to the present inflation, in the neighborhood of one quarter of the national income even in such an industrialized country as the United States.[3]

The second question is the opposite of the first. Do all goods flowing to individuals and households really represent final products in the sense of being sources of satisfaction to consumers as consumers? If a person must use trolleys and buses to go to work, buy banking services because he is a member of the money economy, pay union dues, live in a city—not for any personal satisfaction but as a condition of earning his living—should these services be counted as a positive return to him from the economic system? This is the problem of what may be called 'occupational expenses', although the term is unnecessarily narrow since it may cover even such items as the executive's big automobile or expensive membership in various clubs which may be considered indispensable prerequisites of his occupational status rather than freely made personal choices. That such occupational expenses are hardly in the nature of minutiae may be illustrated by a tentative calculation made in attempting a comparison of per capita income

[3] See Simon Kuznets, *National Income and Its Composition, 1919-1938*, National Bureau of Economic Research 1941, Vol. II, p. 431. For more recent estimates see Margaret G. Reid, The Economic Contribution of Homemakers, *The Annals of the American Academy of Political and Social Science*, Philadelphia, May 1947, p. 65.

in the United States and China and purifying the former for what may be called inflated costs of urban civilization: the inflation in question amounted to from 20 to 30 percent of all consumers' outlay in 1929 as estimated by the Department of Commerce.[4]

In dealing with this twin problem of non-market sectors and inflation by occupational costs, the following basic criterion may be suggested: the touchstone is the individual and his wants, as a member of society at large, and not the individual viewed as a market enterprise. In other words, we want to include under economic activities all those yielding scarce products, whether produced for the market or for consumption within the household; whether produced for profit motives, for the sheer pleasure of producing, or out of regard for the recipient. It also means that in evaluating those goods purchased by ultimate consumers which represent occupational costs rather than final products, we need to know the individuals' choices under conditions freed from the pure calculation of job needs. In either case, the criterion is not easily applied, nor is it meant to suggest that it can be applied automatically; but it calls for much more careful scrutiny and analysis than heretofore of the measures of flow of goods into ultimate consumption—a badly neglected area in economic research.

In actual practice, the national income measures in this country and in most others, whether by governmental or other agencies, for obvious practical reasons, tend to omit most of the non-market activities and to include items that represent occupational expenses or more broadly speaking, many costs associated with earning of incomes. For any given year and country, the omission of non-market activities and the inclusion of cost items, may offset each other at least partly. But in studies of economic progress over time, the two limitations augment rather than offset each other: in other words,

[4] See the appendix to the paper on National Income and Industrial Structure, presented to the International Statistical Sessions in Washington, D.C., in September 1947 (reprinted in this volume, pp. 145-91).

the movement of national income over time will be given an upward bias on both counts, because non-market activities shrink over time and this shrinkage is not measured, and because occupational costs increase with urbanization and swell the duplication in the flow of goods to ultimate consumers. Thus, the increased flow of goods to consumers as ordinarily measured reflects not a net increase in the positive contribution to consumers' welfare but partly identifies a change in form with increase, and partly identifies increase in costs with increase in returns. How large such exaggeration can be is a matter for further research.

The same two biases materially affect many comparisons of national income between urbanized, industrialized countries on the one hand, and agricultural underdeveloped countries on the other. Even with adjustments for differences in price levels, the current measures often yield the absurd result of a per capita income in underdeveloped countries, such as India or China, which *in terms of U.S. equivalents* amounts to $20 to $40 per year. With such *average* income persisting over a number of years, a population obviously could not survive. The answer to the riddle lies in the fact that the estimates for the non-industrialized countries are almost inevitably short on the non-market items, while those for the industrialized countries are long on occupational expenses and costs of urban civilization at large.[5]

III

The individual member of society as a touchstone of what constitutes a net positive yield of economic activity, as a touchstone of economic welfare, is even more important when we deal with government product. Here we see the government busily engaged in the production of all sorts of commodities and services: guns, planes, ships, roads, public buildings, judicial, legislative and administrative services as well as books,

[5] See the discussion mentioned in footnote (4).

forms and countless others. How much of all this is the mere cost of maintaining the social fabric, a *precondition* for net product rather than the net product itself?

The dispute in recent years as to the extent to which government activity may be considered to yield net final product, i.e. something positive to the individual members of society as consumers, or may represent only intermediate product, i.e. the actual cost of maintaining and keeping organized society as a pre-condition to economic product, is one in which I have become increasingly involved.[6] In this controversy, I have, on the whole, been on the minority side—the general trend in current national income estimation being to classify all government activities that involve commodities and services (rather than transfers) as yielding *final products*. This easy way out seems to me to do violence to the basic aim of national income measures—that of gauging the *net* positive contribution of the economy to some end-goals of social life. Certainly, in measuring economic welfare, it seems far-fetched to count as a positive contribution the outlay of governments on such activities as welfare, police work and the like—as if X billions expenditure on armaments means a positive contribution to the end-goal of society in the same way as X billions worth of food, clothing and other means of providing for individuals' welfare. Nor can we conceive of wars, increasing complexity of society with respect to internal management, and other basic factors in the recent major increase in government activities, as a natural calamity *unconnected* with the character of our social institutions. Quite the opposite, they may well be viewed as being, in large part, effects of the same forces that facilitated and induced the rapid growth of our material production. An overwhelming proportion of government outlay of real resources is thus in the nature of costs of those same social institutions that yielded the net product properly defined, and they must be viewed as costs, rather than

[6] See particularly the review of the recent work by the U.S. Department of Commerce under the title "National Income: A New Version," *The Review of Economics and Statistics,* August 1948, pp. 151-197.

added in as a net return. Only those parts of government activities of direct welfare to individuals as individuals (education, health services and the like), can be considered as yielding net product.

If this viewpoint be accepted, the customary estimates of national income extending over a long period would be subject to an upward bias if they were taken as gauges of economic progress—this time because they include an increasing proportion of government activity that may not be adding to, but at best may be just preserving the welfare of individual members of society. Likewise, in so far as the proportionate extent of such government activity, needed or feasible, is likely to be very much greater in the urban, industrialized societies than in the non-urban, non-industrialized countries, the full inclusion of government activities as yielding final products may contribute to an exaggeration of the totals for the industrialized countries or to the relative under-estimation of those for non-industrialized countries.

IV

We now pass to the problems involved in determining changes in the stock of capital—problems that bring us into an entirely different range. So far we have tried to find out what constitutes a positive contribution to some end-goals of economic and social activity—using the individual member of society as a touchstone. At this point we are confronted with problems of estimating the future.

This cryptic statement should be explained. Having measured how much flows to consumers either *via* their purchases, production within the households, or government activity, we want to know whether, in the process of supplying these goods, the economy kept its capital stock intact, added to it, or reduced it. In the former case, total net product, the total positive contribution of the economy is equal to the amount furnished to consumers; if capital is increased, the total net product is obviously larger than the amount furnished to con-

sumers; and if the capital is reduced, the net product is obviously smaller than the amount furnished to consumers.

But how do we know whether capital increased or diminished? In general, the magnitude of capital is indicated by
the future services such capital can render (with a proper dis-
count). If, in the process of current production, the total volume of such future services (discounted at an accepted rate),
has increased, there is an addition to capital stock. Clearly,
this involves an estimate of the future. At first it might seem
possible to avoid it by arguing that the total net product delivered by the economy, less the amount flowing to consumers,
will yield a residue equalling changes in capital stock. But in
estimating total *net* product, the amount of capital consumed
must be subtracted, and how can we estimate how much capital
was consumed (little of it is consumed physically), unless we
project *past* experience into the future?

In practical estimation of capital consumption, as an offset
to the total production of new capital goods, the income esti-
mator accepts, with or without a few adjustments, the depreciation estimates of business firms and extends the practice
to cover some durable capital in the hands of consumers (such
as houses) or in the hands of government.[7] But such depreciation practices yield, at best, a careful estimate based on past
experience, projected into the future. And such projections may
easily prove wrong.

As one thinks about this sector in our measure of economic
welfare, at least two major problems emerge. The first is suggested by the current hue and cry about exhaustion or threat-
ening exhaustion of irreproducible natural resources—be they
soil, forests, or minerals. It should be noted that a great deal
of this using up of natural resources is not recorded in the
national income estimates because they are not recorded by
business firms (e.g. the deterioration of the soil). But there is
the important question as to whether we should make allow-

[7] For a good discussion and analysis see Solomon Fabricant, *Capital Consumption and Adjustments,* National Bureau of Economic Research, New
York 1938.

ances for such using up of natural resources, other than amortizing any resources spent on their discovery. For to take this exhaustion at face value is to assume a certain fixity in our technology in the future—a continued dependence on these resources, the failure of human ingenuity to find reproducible substitutes. One may therefore argue either way on this question: pessimistically, in the Malthusian manner, that the pace of human improvement is too slow and that the exhaustion of natural resources will be felt; or optimistically, that natural resources will, in good time, be replaced by the products of human ingenuity. But regardless of the answer, the measures of economic welfare and progress assume a continuity of our technology, and cannot be so constructed as to reflect properly either exhaustion of natural resources or accretion to stock of knowledge (as distinct from stock of material capital). Consequently, one should either include both or exclude both. In practice, both are excluded, and as far as net balance is concerned, I am inclined to the judgment that the purely technological aspects suggest that our customary measures of national product *under-estimate*, rather than over-estimate economic progress and welfare.

The second problem is the possible unreality that attaches to all the customary estimates of capital accumulation, because of the projection of the past into the future. In measuring national product as a gauge of progress, to what extent can we accept the mechanical assumption that the future is going to be like the past? Granted that business firms and individuals must make this assumption if they are to have some defensible basis for their future estimates (many of these are needed for such purposes as income tax reporting), need we accept them in the broad and long term view of economic welfare and progress? And if we don't accept them, what can we substitute for them?

I have no answer to this question; but the very raising of it is important because it sheds light on some puzzling aspects of interpretation of national income as a measure of welfare and progress. One aspect is revealed in the judgment of the value of an increase in national income accompanied by a rise in population numbers and a constant per capita income, as compared with that accompanied by a lesser rise in population numbers and an increase in per capita income.[8] Assuming that the increases in the total national product in both cases are equal, real, and free from any biases discussed above, there would still be a general inclination to conceive of a situation accompanied by a rise in income per capita as somehow representing greater increase than that accompanied by constant income per capita. Why should we instinctively prefer the situation with increased per capita? One important reason, sometimes only unconsciously felt, is that an increased income per capita provides a better basis, if not for continued progress, at least for maintaining progress already attained—both because the pressure upon natural resources is less, and particularly because, with higher income per capita, a larger surplus is available for the type of exploratory and pioneer activity that served in the past as the main source of mankind's increasing command over material goods.

Another interesting aspect illuminated by the question is the paradox illustrated by the present in the United States. With all the duplication and biases affecting our current measures of net national product, it is fair to say that they reveal an unexampled record of economic progress—a remarkable achievement in the way of economic welfare. Nevertheless, there is little confidence in or satisfaction with the result: on the contrary, there is concern and worry, of a type seemingly absent, say half a century ago, when our total economic product was not much more than one half of the present, even on a per capita basis. The reason obviously lies in the fact that the implicit estimate of the future is quite different from that actually used in our current national income measures; that this widespread projection into the future, rightly or wrongly,

[8] It might be added that the concept of optimum population and the literature employing it, while directly bearing upon the question, have failed to evolve any acceptable criteria for providing a satisfactory answer.

does not assume an easy continuance of our 'normal' past. To put it differently, common opinion assumes a possible change, largely in international conditions, which represents a tremendous depreciation of our economic capital, and in that sense employs a figure of capital consumption that would reduce our national income as a measure of economic welfare to a level far below those presently appearing in official and unofficial estimates.

The burden of these comments is that our judgment of economic welfare concerns itself not only with the past but also with the future. Thus an apparently purely technical problem of estimating capital accumulation is like the peak of an iceberg that conceals a vast area below it, and the sooner we become aware of it, the better shall we understand the meaning of our measures and the more attention shall we direct, as we must, not only to evaluation of the past but also of the future. That this must be the case is implicit in the very inclusion of capital changes under *current* measures of welfare: the latter measure not only the recent past but the foreseeable future.

V

Let us assume now that we have managed to apply the criterion of welfare of individuals as members of society and to distinguish the net product contributed by an economy, and that we have found an adequate basis for gauging the future for the purpose of estimating net changes in capital stock. In order to quantify the total thus defined, study its movement over time and observe differences in economic welfare, relate component parts to the total, it is necessary somehow to find a basis for measuring the diverse parts—a common denominator by which to reduce individual commodities and services to comparable units.

We all know that this is usually done by reducing them to market prices or their equivalents, with adjustments for changes in prices over time and differences in prices in space.

Regardless of any defects in such a yardstick, it is the only one at all feasible, and it is the only one that comes at all close to an economic valuation. Any substitutes that have been offered so far, whether based upon experimental, natural science techniques or upon philosophical assumptions of the proponent, fall far short of the price system as an expression of wants and values by individuals as members of society. The concern here, therefore, is not so much with criticism of the price yardstick by some outside criterion, a patently easy task, but rather with bringing out some basic assumptions that underlie it.

The first assumption is apparent when we ask how we deal with goods that are the product of *changing* technology and society over time (or across space). By what legerdemain do we compare totals over long periods, totals that include such modern gadgets as automobiles, airplanes, refrigerators, radios etc., with those that are bare of all such items but include horse carts, antimacassars, and petroleum used for medicinal purposes? Or more strikingly, how do we compare, across space, totals comprised of our industrial products with those comprised of voodoo drums, ebony idols, and necklaces made of human teeth?

The answer is in the underlying assumption of the constancy of human wants. By such constancy we mean that the wants of men are sufficiently identical over time and similar in space to assume that they all want food, shelter, clothing, transportation, amusement, intellectual fare and the like; that the specific forms which these wants take differ from time to time and place to place with the technology and complexity of production and social organization, but that nevertheless there is essential parallelism residing in the identity of man as a member of the species *homo sapiens*.

This assumption is basic to any concept of economic welfare or progress, or for that matter of *any* welfare or progress. Unless we are willing to grant this essential identity of man, no comparisons are possible, no results that would relate to comparable entities. And considering the variety and elasticity of human experience in different places and at different times, considering that for one and the same human society it is possible to find the whole gamut from the most 'primitive' to the most advanced, the assumption finds wide support in observation. It is in the light of this that we can speak of people being better off at one time as compared with another, or in one place as compared with another. We may or may not agree with the assumption fully; we may wish to limit it to some periods or to some countries. But whenever we measure economic change over time or economic differences in space, we must use this assumption if our measures are to have any meaning—short of being satisfied with quantities of single, identifiable physical units.

But while this assumption permits the comparison of totals of diverse physical identities, another assumption is needed as a basis for measuring the *specific magnitudes* of the physical units included. We are accustomed to market prices as such weights; and markets are widespread in human society, provided we do not limit the concept to the highly developed money type that characterizes the industrial countries of the last century or two. They provide a valuable mechanism by which a social judgment is made of the magnitude of this or that item included in our total of net contributions.

This judgment may seem, at first, paradoxically wrong; and yet further reflection would reveal a high degree of validity in it. To illustrate this by a rather common, if often overlooked, aspect of our national income measures: in general, the really important things, those we call basic necessities, are relatively cheap, as far as market prices go, while the things we call luxuries are expensive. This seems like a topsy-turvy system of valuation, and as a result of it, the larger the national income per capita, the greater is the proportion in it of so-called trivialities. But when you come to think of it, economic progress, or an increase in welfare, does imply an increase in the proportion of trivialities; it does consist of the ability to satisfy basic wants with a small proportion of resources, and of the ability to spend a vast amount of resources on trinkets—whether they be cars, television sets, or horse racing. And as already indicated, the greater the surplus for such non-essential products, the greater is the hope that the welfare thus attained will be kept and increased.

It therefore makes sense for the price system to measure the various goods by the amount of resources which individuals and society are willing to put into them, rather than by the scale of physiological importance of wants which they satisfy. Provided that all the goods included are wanted, their relative weight is the amount of resources sunk into them, i.e. the over-all magnitude of foregone opportunities sacrificed for them, rather than some natural scale of indispensability. This need not prevent us from using a different scale if so desired, by the simple device of using a price system based on an earlier and a more 'primitive' set of prices, i.e. one closer to the natural priority scale of wants. Nor should the statements above be interpreted to mean that the price system, as currently operating, is free from those distortions which society —in the light of more efficient operation designed toward specified ends—might remedy. This discussion is meant to indicate only that the basic assumptions of the valuation involved in such measures of economic welfare and progress as national income—the constancy of human wants and the use of prices reflecting largely input of resources rather than primacy of wants—are both essential and contribute to, rather than detract from, the meaningfulness of the resulting totals.

It follows that from the standpoint of basic wants or needs, the system of valuation implicit in national income measures may lead to an under-estimate of the extent of economic progress or of the extent of economic superiority across space in satisfying primary wants. Because goods are measured, not by their importance in the scale of wants but by their costs in terms of resources, the magnitudes assigned to the satisfaction of primary wants are much smaller than if they had been set at the *ill-fare* associated with their non-satisfaction. In that sense, comparisons among periods or countries in which one term involves aggregates that may be below the margin of subsistence and others that may be well above it, would yield quantitative differences far short of those suggested by the notions of *welfare* and *ill-fare*. Just as the customary measures of capital accumulation under-estimate real progress over time or differences in space in the real stock of capital associated with technological knowledge and human capacity, so the use of prices as weights is likely to underestimate real progress over time or differences in space in the magnitudes associated with satisfaction or lack of satisfaction of *primary* wants. A national income of X units which means starvation of a goodly part of the population, is not one-half, but a much smaller proportion, of an income of $2X$ which permits fair living. In that sense, the price system is adequate only for income levels *above* a certain minimum.

Even with this limitation, the use of the price system as the best approximation to individuals' judgments in society raises some problems only hinted at so far. The first is that the system of weights involved in prices changes over time and differs in space; and that the results of valuation would differ as we use one or another system of weights. Comparisons, therefore, assume some choice of a single system, even though it be a synthetic composite. And if we wish to avoid such choice with its commitment to a single schedule of weights, the consequence is a variety of answers in the comparison, a range of results rather than a single, unique answer. The second problem is that any given system of prices is likely to reflect some distortions as compared with a hypothetically ideal system in which the individual members of society have free choice and are less encumbered by inequalities or monopolistic restrictions of opportunities that are often the unwanted heritage of historical development. One must be cognizant, therefore, of both the element of judgment involved in the use of any single system of weights provided by prices, and of the need for close scrutiny of the particular system used with respect to the extent to which it conforms to our basic touchstone—the judgments of the individual members of society when given free choice in a desirable social environment.

VI

One major problem remains. Assuming that we have adjusted our measure of economic welfare and progress for all the biases suggested, it is still that of contribution of the economy to the welfare of individuals, without any hint of the sacrifice and labor involved. Should not some account be taken of the possible changes over time, or differences in space, in the input of labor by individuals who are the active members of the economy viewed as a system of production?

The pertinence of this question is based upon two considerations. The first is the rather common attitude that participation in economic activity is a sacrifice, a disutility, the magnitude of which should be considered in appraising the net returns. The second is the common observation that in the past century or two, economic progress has been associated with substantial reduction in the amount of time spent by individuals in production proper and in the physical labor involved. Considering that human life is short and that time spent on unpleasant tasks is a negative element, should we not insist that economic welfare and progress be measured not only in terms of supply of wanted goods but also in terms of freedom from unwanted labor?

The argument seems plausible, and the resulting attempts to estimate man-hours of labor or other measures of input of human resources justified. Yet there is in the argument an equivocal element. Should we conceive participation in activity as a necessarily negative quantity? Granted that back-breaking labor carried to physiologically damaging lengths is to be so classified, to what extent should we disregard the instinct of workmanship and the value of participation in production as a pleasurable activity? Thus we are deterred from a hard and fast conclusion on the matter. True, the immemorial dream of mankind as expressed poetically in the myth of the Garden of Eden, is to be completely free from economic labor. But may not this dream be a reflection of the old times when labor had to be too long and too arduous? Can we carry over this judgment directly to modern times, and argue that the reduction of the working week from say 36 to 30 hours represents some positive accretion to economic welfare similar to an increase of one sixth in the supply of goods?

In raising this question, there is no wish to deny that the amount of labor involved in the net product is a corollary, inverted gauge of economic welfare and progress. But one may question the rough and ready assumption that economic labor *per se* is a sacrifice and can be measured in terms suggested by the arithmetical example above. Furthermore, the very fact that economic progress takes the form of an increasing supply of goods other than physiological essentials, as it ordinarily does in industrial economies of the recent past, implies an obvious reduction in time assigned to economic activity and an increase in time assigned to the process of ultimate consumption. For it takes time to utilize these "non-essentials," be they education, amusement, travel and the like. One might, therefore argue that in so far as economic welfare is measured by the growing volume of non-essentials, it must, *ipso facto*, reflect the release of men from long time devotion to the tasks of *production*. This does not necessarily free us from the need of scrutinizing every possible measure of hours and conditions of labor, as a check upon the character of economic welfare measured by the net product. But it does suggest that under certain conditions, the latter measure is adequate even without direct consideration of labor input.

VII

The discussion so far may have left the reader with the impression that he has been led into a labyrinth of value judgments and intangibles away from the observable hard core of economic reality. The natural reaction would be to dismiss all these questions of relevance of economic production to welfare, and to urge that we merely observe and measure what the economy does regardless of the relation of such activities to wants of individuals or to assumptions concerning the future.

I must confess to a strong sympathy for this viewpoint and to reluctance in raising such questions. If the total performance of a country's economy could be measured over the longer run or for comparisons with other societies without raising questions of relevance to end-goals, and with results that would be understood and accepted, it would be a most happy circumstance. But one can avoid these questions only on one of two assumptions. The first is that some specified congeries of tangible economic goods, measurable in comparable units, (say tons of steel plus bushels of wheat plus heads of cattle, reduced to some common denominator) is, in and of itself, a measure of the performance of the economy as a productive system. Such an assumption is obviously invalid. The second is that we are not really interested in the total performance of the economy but only in its distinguishable parts; and that in measuring the latter we are seeking for some invariancies that will permit us to get nearer to generalization. But to accept this assumption and, by disregarding the social valuation or judgment placed upon the economy—one of the most powerful factors in determining its course—to expect that we can still understand and predict is to be oversanguine as to our ability to understand economic life by a few mechanical outward manifestations.

To indicate that the questions raised here are directly relevant to many major policy and intellectual problems, a few illustrations might be helpful. They might also help us to understand the exact import of the points only briefly indicated above.

Consider the twin question of non-market activities and urban civilization costs in their bearing upon a proper understanding of the problem of industrialization of underdeveloped countries—a fashionable problem these days. Clearly, the fact that economic progress means a drastic reduction in non-market activity is a strong reminder that industrialization is not merely a painless process of piling up steel mills and electric power stations. It is simultaneously a destroyer of no mean magnitude, a painful process of breaking established patterns of life and of shrinking the portion that can be supported from within the household. And this emphasis leads to another. If one asks how industrialization ever comes about, the answer is likely to be that there are some groups or forces in society in a position to break the crust, to impose the painful dislocations that are involved in economic growth in a new pattern. And just as the whole emphasis on non-market activities focuses attention upon this element in any quantitative measure of economic welfare and progress, so the emphasis on urbanization costs urges attention to the process of building up a population capable and desirous of engaging in this modern type of economic activity—with its high returns and high costs. The all too-common practice of using national income measures of the customary type in comparisons of industrial and pre-industrial societies may distort the problem of industrialization; and it may easily leave us with a completely misleading impression of the essence of the problem—unless we are alert to questions of the type suggested above.

To illustrate further, consider the practical importance of whether and to what extent government activity results in final products, in providing for wants of individual consumers comprising the inhabitants of a country. Is it not fair to claim that the current practice, in official estimates, of automatically classifying *all* government activity as final product, is misleading, and discourages badly needed functional analysis of government outlays, careful scrutiny of the latter with respect to their service to some approved, ultimate end-goal of society? Is it not of vital importance that currently used measures of net product of our economy serve to reveal, rather than to conceal, the difference between net product and any gross totals that may have value for technical analysis but are misleading if interpreted as net product? It does not follow, of course, that such a distinction, consequent upon a functional analysis of government activity, would in and of itself produce a wiser public policy or prevent an increase in the proportion toward ends other than consumers' welfare. But there is some hope that a better understanding of these problems might help.

Consider again the bearing of the questions relating to the measure of capital accumulation upon our policy problems with regard to the future. The clear realization that these measures extrapolate our past experience into the future is necessarily a spur towards a more careful examination of this past as a basis for our judgment of the future. What in fact has been our historical experience in the way of capital accumulation? How important has been the sheer piling up of construction and equipment, and how important has been the whole framework of social institutions and the social milieu, including the international framework? Can we accept simply the conservative and mechanical judgments of business firms with reference to capital consumption? It is clear that the questions thus put force us to consider more thoroughly the technological and social framework of the economic system, even if, (for want of a better basis) we must accept for the time being the capital consumption estimates of business firms.

It should be repeated that there is no assurance of better understanding or of more valuable results by merely raising these questions. One can also argue that the problems illustrated could have been perceived, and actually were perceived, without specific application to national income measures viewed as gauges of economic progress or welfare. Nevertheless, if we are going to use such measures, and we must and will do so to an increasing degree, it is a necessary precaution to raise these questions as unmistakable signals of the deficiencies, compromises and arbitrary assumptions which these measures embody.

VIII

By way of qualification and conclusion, three comments are in order. The first stresses the fact that we have been discussing the *measurement* of *economic* welfare, not of social welfare at large; and that we have dwelt upon measurement rather than explanation of the factors that served to increase or augment economic welfare. That economic welfare as such is important enough to merit consideration, is itself a reflection of a certain scale of social valuation which puts a high premium upon the material performance of the economy, which does not view famines and material deprivations as an acceptable punishment of Divine Providence or an opportunity for purification of the human soul, and which is willing to consider economic satisfaction apart from the moral, esthetic, intellectual or religious attainments of mankind. It is important to see the limitations of a viewpoint implicit in dealing with economic welfare alone, and to realize that, because of these limitations, attainments with respect to economic welfare may well be accompanied by failures in other aspects of social and individual life. Furthermore, in viewing only one aspect of social life, we may well overlook certain conditions which are important in *explaining* (rather than observing and measuring) changes in economic welfare proper.

The second comment notes the fact that our entire discussion was in terms of over-all totals of national income, ignoring the *distribution* of the product among various groups in society. This omission is not due to a denial of the importance of such distribution as part of a proper gauge of economic welfare: clearly one and the same national income or product total, measured with due respect to the questions of inclusion, exclusion, and valuation raised above, may represent different magnitudes of economic welfare under different systems of distribution by size, by conditions of securing of income, or by stability or variability of such income over time. Limitation of space alone keeps us from discussing these questions here. But it is important to note that the obvious need for such distributions points in the same direction that is clearly indicated by the questions raised above: the need for refinement and articulation of the national income totals so that they can serve as better approximations to the basic purpose which they are intended to serve—gauges of economic welfare.

This brings me to the third and concluding comment. In

stressing the limitations of the current measures of national income as gauges of economic welfare, it is *not* intended to suggest that because of these limitations the measures should be discarded. On the contrary, they should be used more and developed further than heretofore. The answer to the questions raised here, and to the many others that become apparent when we consider problems of distribution, does not lie in fanciful speculations, nor in personal reflections no matter how emotionally and esthetically satisfying they may be. It lies rather in starting with the measures that we now have, and seeing how we can push them further, particularly in the direction where we can (1) gauge more distinctly the activities of individuals and households, (2) see more precisely the functional categories of government activities, (3) observe the conditions under which past decisions regarding capital accumulation have been made and how they provided the basis for an expanded volume of production, (4) note how international relations, under differing world conditions, linked or failed to link the economies of different nations, (5) distinguish the various groups of income recipients according to their shares in the current product of the economy and according to their control over the accumulated capital of the country.

Indeed, in the light of the questions raised above, all the work done in the past on national income measures is grist to the mill of better understanding; and regardless of any controversies concerning proper classification and semantics, the broad view of economic welfare and progress can only benefit from any addition to the knowledge of basic economic magnitudes contributed by the traditional work in the field of national income. Compared with the value of this contribution, constantly added to by the official and unofficial estimates of today, any difficulties created by the defects of the estimates from the broader viewpoint advanced here, pale into insignificance. And any country just entering upon the initial phases of such work should be stimulated rather than depressed by the questions and thoughts advanced above.

The main purpose of raising such questions is not to discourage work along traditional and official lines, but rather to call attention to the serious problems to which approaches along these lines pay insufficient heed. It is also important to note that cognizance of these questions directs work in the national income field into otherwise neglected channels. The emphasis on industrial distribution and final product classification; the careful scrutiny and compilation of price data; the accumulation of information on patterns of size distribution, consumption, and savings; the data on government revenues and expenditures; and many other streams of economic information are all required if our national income measures are to answer the simplest questions, let alone the more difficult questions raised above. This discussion should, therefore, not only re-enforce our need for national income measures, but stress the fact that their adequate use depends upon the intensity of penetration of these measures into the fabric of economic and social life. There is little use in playing with national income figures as single quantities unreduced to their component parts and unaccompanied by price data; there is much more use in the kind of national figures that are compiled by official agencies in the industrial countries of today. But their full use for the fundamental understanding of economic welfare and economic progress awaits a more explicit consideration of questions of the kind raised above; and depends upon experimental and analytical use of the data designed to provide at least approximate answers.

8

INTERNATIONAL DIFFERENCES IN INCOME LEVELS *
(Reflections on Their Causes)

I. INTRODUCTION

Recent changes in the world scene have produced a feeling of greater involvement of all countries with each other, a keener interest in their diverse economic and social structures and functions. When events in a remote corner of the globe affect the lives and destinies of people thousands of miles away, we cannot easily retain the feelings of separateness and independence that may have characterized our thinking half a century ago. Concurrently, the closer linking of the world, in peace and in war, in international organization and in military conflict, has resulted in more information and in a greater effort to reduce the apparent qualitative differences in life around the globe to some comparable, measurable basis. The marked recent increase in quantitative data on population, health, food supply, industrial production, and income is in response to a natural urge to measure the similarities and differences in the social and economic structures of various nations; and to provide for national and international policy a more reliable basis than can be supplied by impressions of travelers, qualitative accounts of historians, or appraisals of geographers.

The increasing number of countries for which national income is estimated and the attention in recent years to international comparisons of income levels, are thus only one strand

* Reprinted by permission from *Bolétin del Banco Central de Venezuela*, Nos. 65-66, July-August 1950, pp. 20-36.

in the whole fabric of the study of the world framework of human society. This particular way of learning about mankind is still in its early stages. True, several international compilations and comparisons were made in the 19th century; and even, though on a much cruder basis, in the late 17th. But by current standards, the earlier compilations and comparisons have at most only suggestive value and are often misleading as indications of orders of magnitude. Even today, a critical examination reveals unreliability and inadequacy in a goodly portion of the current measures, which are so misleading in the impression of quantitative precision that any figure suggests. Unless civilization suffers a serious relapse, the comparisons we draw today may look as crude to scholars fifty or a hundred years from now as the 19th century comparisons look to us. We should bear this qualification in mind and not attribute too much significance to minor quantitative differences or draw unwarranted conclusions from the estimates. Even if we accept the qualifications, our interpretations may well prove superficial in the long run, chiefly because our accumulation of information concerning the various parts of world society is still in an almost embryonic stage.

Nevertheless, the data on income levels in various countries are already sufficient for at least a rough picture of the differences and of the associated social and economic characteristics. And there has been enough speculation and assertion about the causes of these differences to merit a review. The notes that follow are, as indicated by the subtitle, reflections on the theme—not results of a thorough analysis. But they may serve the useful purpose of stimulating further thinking on this important subject; and, possibly, of suggesting directions of further data collection and analysis that may prove fruitful.

II. A BRIEF STATISTICAL PICTURE

We begin our discussion with a brief statistical picture of international differences in income levels. More as a matter of convenience than because of the greater accuracy of the figures, I use here the compilation made by United States Department of State in laying the foundation for its Point Four Program. These figures have several advantages: they refer to a pre-war year (1939) relatively free of the disturbances and havoc of World War II; cover 53 countries which together account for about 85 percent of the world's population; and provide data not only on income but also on various other characteristics. I have used the figures in the State Department report as given, supplementing them only by approximations to the shares of non-agricultural sectors.

The income figures are in US dollars, without correction for differences in purchasing power and minor conceptual dissimilarities. Since for many of the 53 countries the statistical basis for estimates is exceedingly thin, minor differences can be attributed little significance and the specific ranking of the countries is also to be disregarded. Only the major contrasts among the groups of countries are important for the present purposes. They can be summarized as follows:

(a) There are marked differences in per capita income levels among broad groups of countries. Even if the differences are exaggerated by peculiarities of income measurement,[1] and we should reduce the income ratio from over 10 to 1 (groups I to III) to perhaps 6 to 1, the range of differences is still substantial. These differences are not just a matter of a single year or two, but characterize the long term income levels of the various countries.

(b) The figures for the 53 countries in the table relate to only 85 percent of the world's population. The remainder (except the population of such countries as Spain, Portugal and Turkey which might fall in group II) would probably fall in group III, since it is for the economically less developed countries of the world that statistics are lacking. The exceptional position of group I, with about one-sixth of the world's population and over six-tenths of the world's income, would be even

[1] See the author's National Income and Industrial Structure, presented at the International Statistical Conferences in Washington, U.S.A., in September 1947 (reprinted in this volume, pp. 145-91).

more conspicuous were it possible to include the rest of the world. The position of group III, with almost seven-tenths of the world's population but only about one-fifth to one-quarter of the world's income would be similarly accentuated.[2]

INTERNATIONAL DIFFERENCES IN PER CAPITA INCOME AND
RELATED MEASURES, 53 COUNTRIES, 1939

	Groups of Countries by Per Capita Income				
	I	II	IIIa	IIIb	III
1. Per Capita Income (U.S.A. $)	461	154	86	31.5	41
2. Percent of Total Population	20	16	11	53	64
3. Percent of Total Income	64	18	6	12	18
4. Per Capita Income, Index	100	33	19	7	9
5. Average Population Type	1.1	1.5	2.8	3.0	2.9
6. Expectation of Life at Birth (Index)	100	82	..	..	63
7. Physicians per 1,000 Population (Index)	100	73	..	..	16
8. Percent Literate (Index)	100	77	..	..	20
9. Percent of Total Income from Non-Agricultural Industries	84	71	68	46	59
10. Average Income of Population Dependent on Agriculture (Index)	100	39	..	..	8
11. Investment in Industry per Worker (Index)	100	39	..	..	11
12. Energy Consumed per Day (Horsepower Hours per Capita, Index)	100	24	..	..	5
13. Miles of Railroads (Per 1,000 Square Miles of Area, Index)	100	72	..	..	32
14. Annual Freight Carried (Ton Miles per Capita, Index)	100	60	..	..	4

[2] Colin Clark's data for 1924-35 in his *Conditions of Economic Progress* (London 1940) yield similar results.

INTERNATIONAL DIFFERENCES IN PER CAPITA INCOME AND
RELATED MEASURES, 53 COUNTRIES, 1939

	Groups of Countries by Per Capita Income				
	I	II	IIIa	IIIb	III
15. Daily Per Capita Food Supply (Indexes)					
All Foods (Calories)	100	92	..	..	72
Animal Proteins (oz.)	100	56	..	..	18
Fats (oz.)	100	57	..	..	32
16. Net Annual Consumption of Textiles (lbs. per capita, Index)	100	40	..	..	26

Notes to Table

All entries, except for line 9, from *Point Four* (U. S. Department of State, publication 3719, released January 1950, Appendix C, pp. 103-124).

Groups of countries distinguished in the columns of the table are by size of per capita income. The following countries, arranged in declining order of per capita income, are included in each group:

   I (per capita income over $200): United States, Germany, United Kingdom, Switzerland, Sweden, Australia, New Zealand, Canada, Netherlands, Denmark, France, Norway, Belgium, Eire, Argentina.

   II (per capita income from $101 through $200): Union of South Africa, Finland, Chile, Austria, U.S.S.R., Italy, Greece, Czechoslovakia, Hungary, Bulgaria.

IIIa (per capita income from $51 through $100): Cuba, Yugoslavia, Poland, Japan, Venezuela, Egypt, Palestine, Costa Rica, Colombia, Peru, Panama, Ceylon, Mexico, Uruguay, Dominican Republic.

IIIb (per capita income from $22 through $50): Haiti, Nicaragua, Guatemala, Bolivia, Honduras, El Salvador, Brazil, Ecuador, Paraguay, India, Philippines, China, Indonesia.

All averages used in the table are, unless otherwise indicated, weighted arithmetic means. For entries other than income and population type data may be for fewer countries, especially in group III, than listed above.

Population types are identified as follows:

Type 1. Low growth potential. Birth rates below 25 per thousand. Low death rates. Small natural increase with prospect of relatively stationary population in the future.

Type 2. Transitional growth. Birth rates 25-35 per thousand. Both birth and death rates generally falling. Rapid population growth.

Type 3. High growth potential. Birth rates over 35 per thousand. Death rates (but not birth rates) generally declining. Rapid growth in absence of civil disturbance, famine, and epidemic.

The entries in line 5 are unweighted arithmetic means of entries for each country, given separately in the source.

Line 9 is based on data in *National Income Statistics, 1938-47* and *National Income Statistics, 1938-48*, both published by the Statistical Office of the United Nations (in 1948 and 1950 respectively), supplemented for one or two countries by Colin Clark, *Conditions of Economic Progress* (London 1940). In general, the ratios are for 1939 or the year closest to it, within a decade either way. The entries are unweighted arithmetic means for 13 countries in group I, 8 in group II, 6 in group IIIa, and 5 in group IIIb. Weighting by total income for each country would have produced even more striking differences.

(c) These differences measured by such a comprehensive *monetary* index as income per capita are corroborated by measures reflecting quantities of goods. The food supply per capita, especially if we deal with the more qualitatively select types, is, in group III, from one-third to one-fifth of that in group I; and the consumption of textiles per capita shows similar contrasts. Were data available on other consumer goods, more reflective of quality differences, the contrast would be even greater. In short, after allowances for roughness in measurement, real income levels per capita in group I (with one-sixth of the world's population) and in group III (with almost two thirds of the world's population) must still be in the ratio of about 6 to 1.

(d) These differences in real income level are associated with different patterns of population growth. The high income level countries have, on the whole, a low growth potential (low birth and death rates); whereas countries in group III have high growth potentials. An increase in per capita income levels in any country is contingent upon a rate of growth in total output exceeding that of population, unless the latter can be reduced by emigration. It will be thus seen that the problem

of raising the low per capita income levels in group III countries is aggravated by its high growth pattern of population.
Another correlate is the degree of literacy of population—high
in group I and low in group III, with group II in the middle.

(e) Differences in income level are also associated with
differences in industrial structure, as revealed by the shares
of non-agricultural industries in total income (line 9) and investment in industry per worker (line 11). Clearly the low
income levels in countries in group III are connected with
preponderance of agriculture in the economic structure, low
levels of productivity in agriculture, low rates of industrial
investment, low consumption of energy, and an undeveloped
transportation system reflected in railroad mileage and freight
carried. The opposites of these characteristics typify countries
in group I. The list of characteristics of the national economies
each viewed as a productive framework could be expanded,
but the few given in the table are sufficient to indicate the
major differences.

III. Association and Causation

In considering the factors that determine international differences in income levels of the magnitude just revealed, it is
a natural tendency to treat the associated characteristics as at
least in part causative. If this tendency is carried to its fullest
extent, it can be said that income levels in countries in group
III are low *because* the population follows the pattern of high
birth rates and high death rates; or because the population is
illiterate; or because agriculture, which tends to be a low income industry, is preponderant, and secondary and tertiary
industries (to use Colin Clark's terminology) are unimportant;
or because industrial investment per worker is low; etc. It also
follows from these statements that the way to get a higher
level of income per capita is to change the population pattern;
or shift working population from agriculture into non-agricultural sectors; or increase industrial investment per capita. Indeed, much of the discussion of industrialization of under-

developed countries smacks of such identification of associated characteristics with causal factors.[3]

There is undoubtedly some truth in this interpretation. A population with high birth and death rates is handicapped as a body of economic producers, if only because high mortality, particularly concentrated in the infant ages, means an exceedingly wasteful pattern of life—with energies of parents devoted to raising children of whom only a few reach productive ages. It is equally obvious that an illiterate population is more handicapped than a literate one in developing productive skills. Likewise a larger stock of productive capital is a prerequisite of high productivity. Somewhat less obvious is the relevance of industrial structure, i.e. the preponderance of non-agricultural industries. That agricultural industries *per se* are no less productive than non-agricultural ones is, of course, evident from a comparison of agricultural productivity in the United States or in New Zealand with say, the productivity of labor in manufacturing in India or China. But one can argue that greater industrial *diversification*, which implies a smaller share in the national economy of any single group of industries such as agriculture, is a factor making for higher over-all productivity since it permits a more balanced use of technical advances in a variety of industrial sectors.

But even if the above arguments are granted, the significance of these factors as *causes* of international income differentials is still to be considered. Taken in and of themselves, out of the full context of all aspects of social and economic life, differences in birth- and death-rates would scarcely have much effect on per capita productivity; and this may also be true of literacy, especially when one considers how superficial its level is even in the economically advanced countries of the world. And one certainly can ask whether the approach to industrial struc-

[3] This is certainly the impression given by Colin Clark in *The Economics of 1960* (London 1944) and by Louis Bean in International Industrialization and Per Capita Income, *Income and Wealth Studies, Vol. Eight* (National Bureau of Economic Research, New York 1946) —to mention but two authors.

ture suggested above and implicit in many writings on industrialization of underdeveloped countries does not put the cart before the horse; income is not high *because* a smaller share of the nation's economy is accounted for by agriculture and is not low because of the preponderance of agriculture, but in certain countries agriculture accounts for a smaller share *because* income is high and in other countries agriculture predominates because over-all productivity is low. The reduction in the share of agriculture accompanying a rise in over-all productivity is due partly to the permissive factor of a higher level of productivity in agriculture itself; and partly to the inducive factor that when the standard of living rises, human tastes are such that the proportion of agricultural products wanted declines and that of products of other industries rises. Quantitative proof of the former statement is supplied by the table where the contrast in productivity of population dependent on agriculture between countries in groups I and III is even greater than the contrast in per capita total income (compare lines 10 and 4). The second proposition, decline in the proportion of agricultural products wanted with rise in per capita income above a certain level, is demonstrated in any cross-section analysis of consumer budgets at a given point of time, where the proportion of income spent on food and clothing (the former particularly being an agricultural product) declines sharply as we pass from the low to the upper income groups.

What was just said of the industrial structure of the economy as a *consequence* of reaching certain over-all productivity levels, is also applicable to other characteristics. Literacy is perhaps as much, if not more, a consequence as it is a cause of high income levels; and the same is true of capital accumulation, industrial and otherwise. Population patterns with low birth rates and low death rates, too, are just as much consequences of a higher standard of living and higher income levels as their cause. Certainly in the historical development of countries during the last 150-200 years the rise in over-all productivity came first, followed by reduced death rates and then with a substantial delay, birth rates, increased literacy, capital accumulation, etc.

Because of this interaction of income level and other characteristics, the *statistical association* between them is no basis for assuming that these characteristics are causative factors. The increasing emphasis on quantitative measurement in international comparisons naturally makes it easy to translate close statistical association into significant causal relationships. In view of the continuous interplay of income levels and these associated characteristics, in which the former rather than the latter is often the determining variable, this simple translation is a logical trap that should be avoided lest it lead to intellectual sterility and to a dangerously mechanistic approach to policy implications.

Two conclusions can, I believe, be safely drawn from the discussion so far. (i) Factors such as population growth pattern, literacy, industrial structure, and capital investment are of *some* importance in determining international differences in levels of income. But their importance, *per se,* is much more limited than their close statistical association with per capita income suggests. Their *net* effect, if it could be measured, might account for but a small part of existing differences, and therefore leave much room for further search and explanation. (ii) These characteristics are associated with income levels, both as causes and consequences, and together, with many others not specifically indicated in the table, form an interrelated complex. All policy measures to raise per capita income levels are implicitly steps in producing the whole complex into being, and should be so viewed. They must, therefore, be conceived as measures designed to raise income levels, *and* to change population patterns, *and* to increase levels of literacy, *and* to permit a different industrial structure of the economy, etc. The realization of the extent to which per capita income level is only a symbol of a whole socio-economic complex of conditions is important for any intelligent policy approach, as well as for analysis of causes.

IV. 'Natural' Factors

Since mankind is part and parcel of a physical world, a biological species living in conditions provided by nature, it seems reasonable to ask whether economic differences among human societies are not reducible to differences in either natural environment or biological characteristics. The temptation to look for such 'natural' factors is great: if it were found that such factors beyond human control determine international differences in say income levels, the difficulty of disentangling the interrelated complex of economic and other social phenomena could be avoided. The finding of such 'natural' factors would also provide solace to minds and hearts of men who are perturbed by many aspects of human society but are reluctant to face or despair of the painful task of amelioration: if these troubles could be charged to inexorable nature (as they used to be charged to inscrutable ways of Divine Providence), man could only bow to fate in the spirit of sadness and resignation.

Whatever the reasons, and some of them are warranted in the light of empirical observations, natural factors such as climate, topography, presumptive biological characteristics of particular groups of mankind (races, etc.) have appeared recurrently in attempts to explain international differences in political, social, and economic structures. On the surface, they also seem relevant to international differences in income levels. Without presuming to treat them adequately, we discuss them under two heads: (a) location-race factors; (b) irreproducible economic resources.

(a) By location-race we mean factors represented by climatic-land aspects of the location of human societies, or by the presumptive biological characteristics of one human group as distinct from another. While differences in climatic and land conditions of various human societies are obvious and the so-called racial characteristics are subject to dispute and doubt, for purposes of discussion here, we take both for granted, and inquire whether they can be of significance in determining international differences in income levels.

The answer would seem to me largely in the negative, for two obvious but often neglected reasons. The first is the striking disparity in time between the location-race factors and their presumed consequences—international differences in economic performance. Climatic and land conditions at a given spot of the globe change exceedingly slowly on the scale of history of human society. Few significant changes in climate or state of the land have occurred within the five thousand years covered by the known historical stretch of human society (except those caused by man himself, in which case they are hardly 'natural' factors). Yet economic performance in many parts of the globe has changed rapidly. Indeed, only a few portions of the globe have not been, at some time, at least quite high on the relative scale of economic performance, if not in the vanguard. Certainly, China and India, now classified among the lower of the countries in group III, were in this category; and the same is true of some of the predecessors of the present Latin American republics. As historical knowledge increases, we find more examples of outstanding economic and social performance in the past in places far outside the present orbit of economic leadership. Of course, there may be areas on the globe where climatic and land conditions are forbiddingly difficult, e.g. in the Arctic Circle. But the contribution of these factors to the explanation of current, or even of past, international differences in income levels is obviously small.

Exactly the same argument applies to presumptive racial characteristics and differences. Even if we accept for purposes of discussion the dubious proposition that innate, biological differences exist among various sectors of mankind, the time span of these differences—because they are assumed to be innate and biological—is exceedingly long on the scale of human history. Yet no matter what racial, etc. groups have been identified during the known historical stretch of human society, each has at some time or other been among the economically advanced societies: the Mongol race during China's leadership; the American Indians during the Mayan and Incan civilizations; the Negro races in some of the Ethiopian, Egyptian, and Berber kingdoms; the Semitic races through much of human history. I do not feel competent to pursue this subject in detail, nor is such detail needed here. The time spans between the location-race factors and inter-spatial or inter-group differences in economic and social performance are obviously too great for the former to play a significant part as a determinant of the latter.

But, granted this disparity, one may still contend that the location-race factors may be significant in that they effect genuine differences in natural conditions, thus limiting the adoption of methods by which high incomes are *currently* attained. To illustrate, assume that high levels are achieved only with the kind of exertion that is possible in temperate climates alone; or only by scientific endeavor, the capacity for which is claimed by some to be limited to the white races.

The speciousness of this argument is revealed by the second broad consideration that should lead us to deny much significance to location-race factors. Any historical distinctiveness in recent methods of attaining high income levels lies in the enormously increased power of man, developed by a diversified system of empirical science. Climatic and land conditions, as obstacles to human effort, are much less forbidding today than in the past; and the very growth of human technology means that location factors are less important today than they may have been in periods of more primitive technology. Likewise, the varieties of mental effort and capacity that go into the technology of today are much greater than they may have been in the past, so that it is even more doubtful today than it ever was, that some presumptive differences in innate, biological characteristics of different groups of mankind significantly affect the acceptance and use of the diversified corpus of modern economic practices.

Dismissing the race factor as an empirically unestablished element and confining our attention to the obvious location differences in climatic and other conditions, we reach two conclusions. (i) Location factors, in the current and recent past state of technology and human knowledge, could not, in and of themselves, have contributed materially to international differences in income levels. Whatever difficulties natural conditions presented could, for the most part, presumably have been overcome by concentration upon the problem of human ingenuity and science. (ii) The natural conditions of many countries in group III are no more unfavorable to high income levels than those of many countries in group I. It would be difficult, for example, to demonstrate that nature *per se* is much less favorable in China than in Sweden or Australia; or that it is so much more favorable in England than in Mexico. At any rate, the burden of proof is upon the proponents of such theories; and no proof has been provided that takes full cognizance of the potentialities of human technology in dealing with even the most unfavorable aspects of land or climate.

(b) The discussion above touched only implicitly upon a natural factor that is important in many analyses of international differences in economic performance—the supply of such irreproducible productive factors as cultivable land and minerals. Economic technology always, and modern economic technology is no exception, leans heavily upon extraction of certain irreproducible resources from the earth; and it has been claimed that a poor supply of such resources, *relative* to existing population, is a major factor in explaining low per capita income levels, and a rich supply relative to existing population, high income levels.

This claimed dependence of international differences in economic performance upon the relative supply of irreproducible resources cannot be examined in great detail here. The reflections that follow lead to a somewhat more critical view of this dependence than usually prevails, and suggest the limitations of the hypothesis adopted.

i) 'Economic resource' is a concept relative to a given state of technology. Until man learned to use coal for heating a steam engine or smelting iron ore, it was a domestic consumer good but hardly an important industrial fuel. When man learns to grow his food in trays of synthetic chemicals, the importance of land as a resource for the production of food will dwindle. Examples abound of many hitherto important economic resources that have lost almost all importance, and of many formerly unimportant or valueless parts of the earth that have recently become exceedingly valuable. Even more telling are cases of relative scarcity in the past of some irreproducible resource, strategic within the framework of an older technology, that have been overcome not by finding more of the scarce resource but by a change in technology and substitution of a new resource, more plentiful and usually more effective. The conspicuous case, which in a sense laid the basis for modern economic technology, was the way the Industrial Revolution overcame the shortage of wood, as both fuel and industrial material, and of animal and wind power. More recent cases are the substitution of fixed nitrogen for natural guano and of synthetic for natural rubber. Hence, any emphasis on relative scarcity of irreproducible resources, as a factor in determining low levels of economic performance extending over a *long* period, must be countered with the question why no successful effort has been made by the victim of such scarcity to overcome it by changes in technology. To be retained, the hypothesis must, therefore, be rephrased: the have-not societies are poor because they have not succeeded in overcoming scarcity of natural resources by appropriate changes in technology, not because the scarcity of resources is an inexorable factor for which there is no remedy. And obviously human societies with low levels of economic performance are least able to overcome any scarcities of irreproducible resources by changes in technology; but this is a matter of social organization and not of bountifulness or niggardliness of nature.

ii) Our knowledge of the supply of irreproducible economic resources is inadequate. This is true even of resources that, because of their strategic importance, have been investigated and explored most intensively—as the continuous upward revisions of world supply of petroleum clearly indicate. It is even more true of minerals that have not been as intensively explored; and may also be true of the oldest resource available, viz. cultivable land, the knowledge of whose chemical and other properties is a recent addition to the stock of scientific information. This limitation of data on irreproducible resources, data that can be amassed only by considerable effort and by application of technical skill and knowledge—all scarce in the underdeveloped countries—is, unfortunately, greater for these countries, so that shortage biases are likely to be greatest for just the countries with low income levels. It follows that all our current estimates of the supply of irreproducible economic resources are slanted to minimize the supply in countries in groups II and III compared with the estimates for the developed countries in group I.

iii) The irreproducible economic resources that do exist in the countries with low income levels are not used as effectively as those in countries with higher income levels. Statistical support for this statement is readily available, ranging from measures of yield per acre of land for agricultural crops to comparisons of the rate of extraction of mineral resources with their estimated deposits. We cite one illustration, of interest because of its broad coverage. Recently, Professor A. P. Usher prepared estimates of world resources of mechanical energy (represented by reserves of oil, coal, and water power) as well as world output of such energy (extraction for minerals and production for water power).[4] From these estimates, largely for 1939, the proportionate shares of countries in groups I, II, and III were calculated, after allocating roughly to group III the countries not included in our table but covered by Professor Usher (except for Turkey, Spain, Portugal, and Rhodesia which were placed in group II). Countries in group I accounted for 44 percent of total world stock of mechanical energy resources; in group II for 19 percent; and in group III for 37 percent. The index of per capita stock of energy resources was,

[4] See his summary in "The Resource Requirements of an Industrial Economy," *The Tasks of Economic History,* 1947 Supplement to the *Journal of Economic History,* N. Y. 1948, pp. 35-46.

therefore, measured by about 2.5 in group I; 1.25 in group II; and 0.5 in group III. The contrast in relative supply between groups I and III is thus measured by a ratio of 5 to 1.

But the range in energy *consumed* per day per capita between groups I and III is much wider than that—about 20 to 1 (see table above, line 12). Moreover, Professor Usher's data indicate that in terms of production of mechanical energy resources (extraction, not use) group I accounts for 73 percent of the world total, group II for 12, and group III for only 15 percent. That production by countries in group I of 73 percent of the current supply, with a resources share of only 44 percent, indicates that their rate of extraction relative to stock is much greater than in the world at large. It would, of course, be theoretically just as possible for countries in group III to extract their irreproducible resources at a greater rate than the world at large, i.e., they could compensate for a smaller supply by drawing upon it at a faster rate. Yet their extraction rate is much lower—an indication that under existing circumstances and for some time to come an absolute shortage of irreproducible resources is *not* a limiting factor.[5]

iv) Finally, many industries and economic activities do not need irreproducible natural resources; and if they are needed, a country with a scarce supply can presumably secure them in trade, given a minimum network of international economic relations. England developed a flourishing cotton textile industry, without possessing the basic natural conditions for producing the raw material; and the same is true of the rubber product industries of the economically advanced countries of the world. To claim strategic significance for the relative supply of irreproducible resources is unwarranted, so long as many

[5] It is somewhat misleading to deal with all countries in group III (or groups II and I) as a unit, since within each group, energy resources are unevenly distributed among the individual countries. But the general tenor of the argument would remain the same were we to deal with individual countries (e.g., China and India); and so long as the statements made in the text are not literally translated as applying to *every single* country in group III (or in the other groups), no harm is done.

industries do not need them; and so long as international trading relations permit one country to compensate for shortage in irreproducible resources by specialization in other sectors of economic production.

All these arguments should not be interpreted as denying that under given conditions of technology, the possession of a large stock of natural resources by a country is an economic advantage; and the complete absence of such resources a disadvantage. They are intended to suggest only that, in explaining *long term* international differences in levels of income, the relative supply of irreproducible resources is not a dominating factor; that our data on the presumptive relative scarcity of such resources in the underdeveloped countries are faulty to the point of being misleading; that in fact countries in group III fail, by a wide margin, to utilize the stock of resources which they do possess; and that, after full allowance for this factor is made, there is still a wide range of international differences in income levels to be explained.[6]

V. The Factor of Size

International comparisons are almost always in terms of the existing nation-states that differ widely in size, whether size is in terms of area, population, or some economic magnitude. Thus the list of 53 states distinguished in the data underlying the table, includes huge units like India and China, each with

[6] Specific figures in Professor Usher's tables suggest that the supply of irreproducible resources in many smaller countries in group III accounts for an income level *higher* than it would otherwise have been. In many, the fortunate existence of deposits of strategic raw materials (particularly petroleum) results in an active interest of firms from industrially advanced countries and in a higher level of national income than would otherwise be the case. Most common references to shortages of natural resources are to those of coal and iron. But a fairly high level of income can be attained without them, if only peaceful economic life is considered; and as a general rule, most of the large countries in group III have such resources but fail to utilize them at sufficiently high rates.

over 350 million of population; and relatively small units like New Zealand and El Salvador, with less than 2 million each. Is the mere factor of size important in determining levels of economic performance per capita?

The question implies that even with international trade and other flows across boundaries, the existence of a separate state organization means at least partial isolation of the economic complex, barriers to an easy flow of goods and resources. Even if we assumed a world of free trade and free movement of capital and people, the several states, with their different languages and historical and cultural traditions are societies that think of themselves as different and separate from each other; and economic flows among them, even in the absence of legal restrictions, would not be easy because of these barriers of language and different historical antecedents. If we add the realistic consideration of barriers to migration either of men or of capital and the various impediments in the way of a free flow of goods that are in fact created by a separatist state organization, we must conclude that the state structure does result in separate units, whose existence, because of the obstacles to free economic flow that they impose, may be an important factor in determining differences in over-all economic productivity.

This inference as to the possible importance of size of state in producing inter-state differences in levels of economic performance is reenforced by somewhat more specific arguments. First, some industries associated with modern technology require a minimum size of market to warrant the application of efficient methods of mass production. In such industries, e.g. iron and steel, aluminum, automobiles, shipbuilding, etc., the scale of units is quite large. For a country with a small population and a correspondingly small domestic market, such industries are feasible only if they can count, in the long run, on relatively free access to markets outside their country's boundaries. Under existing and even past conditions of the world, such access is precarious. It follows that countries below a certain minimum size cannot develop such industries (except sometimes at extra cost), and take advantage of some of the more advanced methods of economic production.

Second, some industries *must* locate within a country's boundaries, since no substitution for their products by imports is feasible. This is obviously true of the industry represented by the state itself, and of industries rooted in the country's area and population (e.g., educational and other services, the construction industry, and the like). If we add the need for other domestically located industries induced by a desire to be independent of unreliable sources outside (particularly in case of disruption of normal channels of international intercourse), it is clear that a *minimum* complex of industries must be maintained within the state, and will be maintained regardless of size (excluding splinter units like Monaco or Luxemburg). But if the state has a small population, the need for a diverse industrial structure may well lead to an uneconomic scale of operation in many industries—even when the latter, unlike the giants of the type discussed in the preceding paragraph, have an absolutely low optimum scale of operation.

On the other hand, a small state may enjoy some advantages. It is easier for a small than for a large state to find a favorable position in the interstices of international economy. It is easier for a Norway, a Denmark, or a Switzerland, by taking advantage of some of its resources, to attain a high level of income per capita than it would be for a bigger state unit, say of the population dimensions of Italy, let alone a huge one like China. Also, it may be easier for a small state to achieve the degree of internal unity and cohesion of the population which so facilitates economic progress and prevents sharp internal conflicts from developing. On general grounds, one cannot assert that, given a relatively peaceful state of international relations, the balance of advantages is definitely against the small and in favor of the larger state unit. Such a negative conclusion would certainly be safe if we excluded the extreme ranges in size—the tiny units in which the basis for economic independence is almost completely absent, and the huge units in which the problem of economic and social organization is of grave magnitude indeed.

In the light of this discussion, we can look at the figures and see what they suggest. For the 53 countries covered in the table the level of per capita income can be correlated with the size of the country as measured by its population. The coefficient of rank correlation (used to avoid the assumption of normality in the distribution of units by size or by per capita income),[7] calculated for all 53 countries is + 0.18, indicating some positive association between level of per capita income and population size; but not large enough to be significant. However, if we exclude India and China, where huge population masses are associated with very low per capita incomes, the coefficient rises to + 0.30, a value which for the 51 countries is statistically significant. If we could include more state units, the positive correlation might be even closer, because most of the additional units would be both small and characterized by low levels of per capita income.

There is thus some statistical evidence, for states below the line of huge population units, of a positive association between per capita income levels and size. In general, the larger the state, the higher its per capita income. But the association is far from close. Even as a purely statistical result, it may be shaky: there are altogether too many notable exceptions. While the factor of size in and of itself may contribute to international differences in income levels, at the present stage of our knowledge and analysis, no great weight can be attributed to it.

However, the importance of size as a factor may well be increasing. For the growing cleavage among states in the world today may mean that the disadvantages of small size may be sharply and catastrophically increasing. Indeed, within the orbit of the USSR these disadvantages are so great that small states as separate entities are fast disappearing. Where they remain, the restrictions on normal international economic in-

[7] The formula used is $1—6$ (Sum of d^2)/n ($n^2—1$), where d is the difference in ranks, and n the number of pairs of items in the comparison.

tercourse may mean a serious deterioration in the relative position of small states, which may be only partially counteracted by already observable efforts to merge them—for some purposes—into larger units.

VI. A HISTORICAL VIEW

The limitations of the analysis developed so far, and the meagerness of its contribution to the explanation of international differences in income levels, may well be due to the author's ignorance or prejudice. But it may also result from the restriction of the analysis to *cross-section association* of income levels with other variables; and hence to its neglect of the historical antecedents of these levels. All the units whose economic performance we are comparing for a given year or decade are results of a long process of historical development; and our comparison is thus a cross-section in the stream of historical change, with divergent trends and different levels at whatever point we start tracing these trends. The question to which we seek the answer might be illuminated if we view the broad trends in historical development of which the current income levels are the outcome. Such a view, while necessarily superficial, may lead to certain broad conclusions that would provide at least a framework for a potentially more fruitful inquiry into the problem.

The suggestions yielded by such a broad historical view are stated *seriatim* without any effort at detailed documentation.

a) First, the range of international differences in income levels must be much wider today than it was say 150 to 200 years ago. This impression cannot be corroborated statistically, since our measures do not reach that far back; but its plausibility follows from the current figures. In countries in group III per capita income levels are close to minimum subsistence and it is clear that it would have been *physically* impossible for past income levels to be a fraction of the current levels in any country in group III. By contrast, per capita levels in countries in group I are far above any minimum subsistence and the more developed countries in the past (not necessarily those that are now in group I) could well have had income levels that are fractions of those now prevailing in group I. We know, in fact, that in the countries in group I the past century to a century and a half were marked by rapid growth in income per capita. And it is plausible to assume that the low per capita incomes in countries in group III are not due to an *absolute* decline of income levels during the last century or two; or that whatever secular decline in real per capita income occurred was relatively small. We can thus infer that the range in per capita income levels was much narrower about two centuries ago than it is today. To illustrate: if in countries in group III (allowing for the shift in identity) per capita levels two centuries ago were at the lowest say 50 percent of the present, about $20, and if in countries in group I (again allowing for shift in identity) per capita levels were say one-seventh of the present, $65, the range narrows from over 10 to 1 to about 3 to 1. The narrowing of range in fact may well have been greater than in this illustration.

To put it differently, much of the current international spread in income levels is due to diversities among countries in the rate of growth of per capita income during the last 150-200 years: in some countries per capita income grew quite rapidly, in others very slowly if at all. Therefore, from a starting point of more equal levels, marked inequalities in per capita income have developed. Hence, current international differences in per capita income may be due in large part to diversities in the rate of growth of per capita income during the past two centuries. What factors induced and permitted some countries to attain a high rate of growth in per capita income, and why were the same or similar factors not operative in other countries?

b) The use of a span of one and a half to two centuries in the preceding section is not an accident: history suggests that the factors that operated in some countries and not in others are those associated with the 'industrial system'—a concept used to designate a wide application of knowledge, based on empirical science, to the problem of economic and social technology. It is the adoption of the industrial system, combined with certain social and political concomitants, that is at the basis of the rapid growth of per capita income in some countries. And the industrial system dates from one and a half to two centuries ago.

It is important to emphasize here that, given an organization of the world into separate and competing states, there is *bound* to be inequality in the rate of spread of any new type of economic and social mode of life; and, consequently, inequality in levels of economic performance among countries. If a new economic system is ushered in, it certainly will not be 'invented' and adopted simultaneously in all the countries of the world: such simultaneity could be attained only by some planned imposition of the change by a single world authority. The new type of economy, the secular innovation, will necessarily arise first in one or two countries in which historical antecedents and pressures combine to break through the crust of the existing economic and social habits toward a new and more productive mode of operation. Given this limitation of the origin of a secular innovation to one or a few countries, and its slow spread to others; given the significance of the secular innovation as a basis for a higher per capita income, it follows that its gradual spread across the face of the globe means *at any given time* differences in income levels among various countries—associated with the degree to which these countries have adopted the new and more productive mode of operation.

Economic history of the longer lived human societies provides several examples of this process of initial limited impact and then gradual, uneven spread of secular innovations. The successive effects of the discovery of the new world, as they filtered through first the pioneer explorer countries of Western Europe and then the others, is one conspicuous example. The spread of the system associated with the medieval town economy is another. In this sense, the originally limited impact of the industrial system (marked by 'Industrial Revolution' in

England) and its gradual and uneven spread to other countries, is only another example of the introduction of a secular innovation in a world organized in competing states.

c) To repeat, the industrial system is the application of empirical science to basic and ever increasing areas of economic and social technology. That it is the basis of high levels of economic performance in countries in group I can be seen easily by comparing their industrial structure and mode of operation with those in countries in group III. In countries in group I many industries have developed whose basis is some recent scientific discovery (ranging from steam and steel to electricity, internal combustion engines, electronic communications, and atomic power as the most recent example), whereas in countries in group III they are, on the whole, either completely absent or present in minuscule amounts. Furthermore, the technical procedures used in the oldest industries, e.g. agriculture and construction, in the more advanced industrial countries utilize, to a much greater extent than in the countries in group III, the contributions of the empirical and rational approach that is the hallmark of modern science.

The feasibility of using the results of modern science and empirical knowledge in economic production is not merely a matter of availability of a stock of discoveries contributed by original workers or practical minded adapters. Let us disregard for the moment the importance of social and economic organization as a precondition for adoption on a wide scale of the contributions of science to economic technology. A minimum of cultural adaptation is still required, regardless of the economic and political organization of society. Widespread use of scientific technology is impossible without a literate population, and in a society whose general outlook has not been sufficiently secularized to place a high value on rational calculation and material welfare. The very development of science, and the effective application of its results, requires a cultural milieu in which existing values do not impede an open-minded view on nature, a dispassionate consideration of empirical findings, and a strong desire to enhance the material welfare of man. It is hardly accidental that the growth and spread of science in the modern world was accompanied by and closely tied to broad secularization of those societies that led in the development; and that widespread application of science required and was accompanied by a shift in the general outlook of ever growing proportions of the population toward an acceptance of rational calculation, toward greater habituation to a life governed by the conventions of scientific measurement. Clearly, the development of science and widespread application of its results would have been impossible in the early Middle Ages in Western Europe, with an illiterate population, dominated by religious tenets and emphasis on the hereafter, completely unaccustomed to living by the clock and by rule, and reconciled to a status view of life where traditional patterns of economic procedure and behavior seemed hallowed by inviolable precepts of religious origin.

Whether under a system of private enterprise or communistic organization of the economy, of political democracy or authoritarian state, the adoption of an industrial system is thus not merely a matter of having a stock of scientific knowledge embodied in books or pamphlets; or even of the physical embodiment of such knowledge in machines and plants. Its effective use involves as a minimum an adaptation of the culture and mores of the population. Part of this adaptation we have already observed in discussing the relation between high income levels, literacy, and population type 1 (the latter reflecting a more rational approach to family life). But it has many more ramifications, most of which cannot be put into quantitative terms. Obviously, a change in cultural milieu, when needed for an effective adoption of the industrial system, may well be a slower and more painful process than the accumulation of savings and capital, or other material prerequisites of a higher level of economic performance.

d) The successful adoption of the industrial system, resulting in high levels of per capita income, has been limited, in fact, to countries that combined with it private enterprise as the main unit of economic organization and the democratic state as the dominating form of political organization. In all 15 countries in group I (except possibly Argentina, which is the lowest on the list, and even there the greatest development was under the aegis of private enterprise and political democracy), private enterprise was the main engine in introducing changes associated with the industrial system; and during the periods of rapid growth that brought them to high income levels, the state was a democratic organization. In fact, all of them are deep in the long standing tradition of Western European development, part and parcel of the historical milieu out of which science and rational thinking, freedom of economic enterprise, and political democracy, grew. It is dangerous to assume that this association of rapid growth in income levels with free enterprise and political democracy was an historical accident.

Of course, the association is not hard and fast. Some countries in the same tradition and with the same antecedents, like Italy, Austria, and Czechoslovakia, failed to reach the levels of group I. And, more important, because such an association existed in the past, it does not necessarily follow that an effective adoption of the industrial system as a base of economic organization requires free enterprise and political democracy. At any rate, the communist states of today proceed on a different premise: they assume that a more effective adoption of the industrial system is possible in combination with enterprise controlled by the state and an authoritarian structure of that state (I am disregarding the misuse of the term 'democracy' in its application to states that have no free press, no free political parties, and none of the other basic characteristics of democracy). But history, while naturally subject to bias, leaves one with the distinct impression that a heavy burden of proof lies on those who think that an effective adoption of the industrial system is possible without free private enterprise and political democracy, granted the possible initial role of the state as aider and abettor. Certainly, the experience of those countries in the past that did introduce the industrial system with but an inadequate provision for freedom of enterprise and political democracy (Japan, and somewhat less so, Germany) is not encouraging. Their record, when viewed in the large, *necessarily* including the results of wars that could not be avoided precisely because of the failure to eradicate authoritarian and feudal elements from the past, is hardly indicative of a successful attainment of high income levels *in the long run*. However, we are on highly problematical grounds, and should perhaps only stress the connection in the past between effective adoption of the industrial system and freedom of private enterprise and political democracy; and ask whether this connection is indispensable, i.e. whether without it the use of the industrial system to raise the long term levels of per capita income would be much less effective.[8]

VII. Obstacles to the Spread of the Industrial System

In so far as high income levels result from a rapid rate of growth in income per capita associated with the adoption of the industrial system, the range in current international differences is partly a function of the *slowness* with which the industrial system spread over the face of the globe. A rapid spread, say, in a decade or two, would bring a generally high level of income per capita and a much narrower range of differences in income level among countries. Because over some

[8] Many aspects of the interrelation between an effective adoption of the industrial system and private enterprise-political democracy, argue for its indissolubility. The drive for profit and personal gain that animates economy under private enterprise; the supremacy of the consumer in a political democracy; the fostering of the spirit of inquiry and critical examination of evidence—are all powerful means of breaking resistance to change, encouraging extensive application of knowledge, and building industrial society on the lasting and solid base of a high standard of living of ultimate consumers. In contrast, the recent experiments in grafting the industrial system to a society deprived of personal freedom and with the ultimate consumers' needs forcefully subordinated to state imposed goals, seem much less effective—particularly as bases for peaceful economic growth for the long run.

two centuries, the spread of the industrial system was limited to a small portion of mankind and because so many countries have as yet failed to take full advantage of it, the low income levels for most of the world and the high levels in countries in group I are in marked contrast. What are the obstacles to the adoption of the industrial system that may account for its slow spread, and thus partly account for the existing differences in per capita income levels among various countries?

a) One is tempted to think of the stock of technical knowledge as a free resource, fully available to all countries; of the contribution of science and empirical study as a universal possession of mankind. In a sense it is: most of it is overt and open to study and adoption by anyone. But this impression of universal availability of technical knowledge is partly an illusion. Scientific discoveries, and particularly their practical counterparts in inventions and technical improvements, are often the solution to a specific problem in a specific country adapted to the resources it possesses. The major technical changes at the core of the Industrial Revolution in England were partly colored by conditions in that country. The agricultural revolution of the 18th century, with its introduction of continuous crop rotation, scientific livestock breeding, and another wave of enclosures represented adaptations of already known advanced practices to conditions of British agriculture. It is not clear that these technical changes would have been as valuable, or as relevant, to the type of intensive agriculture followed in China in the 18th and 19th centuries. The adaptation of coal in the Industrial Revolution in England to serve as the major fuel in iron smelting was a technical change eminently suited to British needs, with the country's abundant supply of coal. But it could not be directly useful to a country in which the main supply of energy is water power. And passing to less basic types of technical change, the series of inventions and improvements that went into organizing the United States methods of mass production (standardization, analysis of work tasks, continuous conveyor and assembly belts, plant organization, etc.) were obviously geared to large scale plants well adapted to the huge domestic market—and not as easily adapted to smaller countries, even of the size of Great Britain.

Since inventions and technical changes bear the specific stamp of the originating country, their use by other countries is not a matter of taking over by direct imitation but of modification and adaptation. The magnitude of this modification may vary widely, from one type of technical change to another and from one country to another. But where it is required, sufficient will and talent are needed in the follower country, whenever such capacity and talent cannot be imported—and it cannot always be imported—from the originating, leader country. The slow spread of the industrial system is thus, in part, due to difficulties involved in modifying the original technical change to fit different conditions.

The important implication of this observation is that the spread of modern industrial technology outward from its originating country most easily reaches such other countries as have either similar material conditions, or are closely associated by social and cultural antecedents. It is hardly an accident that so many of the countries in group I have close ties, blood or culture, with England, the leader of the industrial system. Australia, New Zealand, Eire and Canada are certainly in this category; the United States bears a strong imprint of its original association with England; and a fair number of the European countries in group I are within the orbit of British economic influence (Denmark, and less so, other Scandinavian, countries). In all these cases, connection with the originators of the industrial system was sufficient to provide, often on the spot, the talent necessary for the technical modification of the English industrial system.

b) Another reason for the slow spread of the industrial system may be the fact that in this competitive world, the pioneer countries use their economic superiority to impede growth elsewhere. The dynamics of economic and social growth in a world organized in competing states are such that success within a country often results in attempts to extend influence and dominate elsewhere. The aggressiveness of Western Europe through the centuries of its growth is an old story, and need not be retold. It is clear that the advance of the industrial pioneering countries was accompanied by impacts upon the rest of the world that partly corroded and distorted the then current economic and social organization; and frequently resulted in political subjugation, hardly a favorable condition in the politically inferior countries for a rapid adoption of the industrial system. The story of imperialistic domination over countries in Asia, Africa, and Latin America is all in point. While such domination had some economic advantages, it certainly served to block the way to a concerted effort on the part of the dominated countries toward adoption of the industrial system. This is not to say that, free of foreign control, they would have seriously attempted to or succeeded in adopting the industrial system and laying the foundation for higher levels of economic performance. All that is meant here is that even if there were forces in these countries bent upon such attempts, necessary political independence had first to be acquired. And, in some cases, the very effort to secure political independence in turn strengthened forces in the country that in the long run were inimical to the effective adoption of the industrial system (*vide* the case of Japan).

c) But the most serious obstacle to the rapid spread of the industrial system is one that it shares with many major innovations: it means a marked break in established patterns of social and economic life; it destroys established interests; it requires a system of social values and a cultural milieu quite different from those that are the heritage of a long historical past in many countries. In short, it is a thoroughgoing revolution, in the full sense of the word. And revolutions are neither easily made, nor successful without long preparation.

Industrialization and economic change in the major countries that went through it successfully engendered painful dislocations, and the long preparation of the cultural and social milieu (as well as some happy historical accidents) accounted in large part for a relatively successful solution of the difficulties. Especially in countries with a rich historical heritage, this impression of industrialization as a process of destruction, as well as of creation, is particularly strong. In England, in Germany, in other European countries adoption of the industrial system meant dislocation of the peasant off the land; the destruction of the artisan; the reduction in importance of the landed nobility; and a change in social values that was painful to many groups who lived by the old traditions. Only in the new, relatively 'empty' areas to which European immigrants brought their training and skills, but not the full force of historical tradition and the rigidities of class structure, was the process less painful. But even here it meant the destruction of the aborigines; and in the United States, a civil war had to be fought before agreement was reached on the adoption of the industrial system with all its social and other concomitants.

The slowness of the spread of the industrial system is then the slowness with which, in old human societies with established traditions and social values and entrenched class interests, a new class is formed which views the industrial system as its ideal; which is willing to exercise pressure for the social changes requisite for the introduction of the system; and which becomes powerful enough to impose its interests, considered by it identical with the interests of society at large, upon the country. That this is far from an easy task, and that conditions favorable for the formation of such a class are not common, is evident after only a brief glance at the social structure and history of many of the countries now in groups III and II.

If, in addition, free enterprise and political democracy are considered prerequisites for and necessary accompaniments to the successful adoption of the industrial system, the obstacles imposed by historical heritage over the major parts of the globe become only the more obvious. Nor is it surprising that the countries with the oldest historical background, with the highest attainments in the past of economic and social performance within the *old* framework of technology and cultural values, are the ones in which the difficulties of a revolutionary transition to the new mode of life are the greatest. China and India are conspicuous illustrations, although other factors contribute to the extreme difficulty of adopting an industrial system evolved by and geared for countries of a size and material conditions so vastly different from these Asiatic agricultural empires.

d) The statements above do not mean that in countries in group III (or group II) avenues toward an increase in per capita income levels are few or completely barred. On the contrary, any country at any time, even the group I countries, can find various feasible ways to raise their income levels. For example, in China the rebuilding and extension of the inadequate railroad network; the reorganization of the property framework of agriculture; the establishment of an honest government administration; the application of relatively small amounts of technical skill and knowledge; and a vigorous campaign for limitation of family size—would go quite a way towards increasing per capita income. Similar observations, perhaps with different specific contents, could be made concerning most countries in group III. All that the arguments suggest is that the attainment by countries in group III of a per capita income level at all approaching those in group I is a process that requires a thoroughgoing revolutionary change in economic and social structure, in the cultural complex, and possibly a series of technological innovations so large as to be neither easily nor promptly securable.

One implication of these obstacles should be stressed. The spread of the industrial system is often assumed to be a process that will take its inexorable course in due time,—like a slowly moving glacier whose course cannot be stopped or avoided. In the light of history such a picture is largely an illusion. True, *some* of the elements in the industrial system are likely to spread to all parts of the globe: e.g. the more important technological artifacts, like railroads, automobiles, electric power stations etc. will find their way eventually, even if in moderate quantities, wherever there is room for them. But it is quite possible that for centuries to come these and other products of industrial civilization will be available in many countries in amounts far smaller relatively than they are now available in group I countries, and that the elements of the industrial system will constitute but small islands in the sea of a pre-industrial economy in many countries of the world. If by an industrial system we mean the full and effective utilization of the potentialities of empirical knowledge and science in economic production, even of the imperfect type now realized in countries in group I, its spread to all or even most countries of the globe is far from inevitable. For it is quite possible that many countries will not have the spearheading group, with sufficient power to break the crust of historical heritage and to evolve the forms of adaptation of the industrial system necessary for the relatively effective utilization of its potentials.

History provides several examples of secular innovations which have run their course *without* penetrating into or significantly affecting all countries, even those close to the origin of the innovation. The feudal system was a well nigh general institution in medieval Europe, and yet the Italian peninsula was not fully dominated by it. The idea of political democracy is over two centuries old at least, and its application in Western Europe over a century and a half old; but Spain and Portugal never had it to any significant extent, and never shifted to a system of social values free from the domination of religion. Yet these countries were geographically near the locus of the secular innovations in question. True, with the growth in power of transportation and communication, the world has become a smaller unit. But by the same token, the world as a whole is a more greatly diversified complex than just Western Europe, a complex whose parts bear the deep impress of different series of historical experiences and antecedents. That a universal spread of the industrial system, in a relatively efficient form, to all these historically different parts of the globe is an inevitable process, is highly problematical. The assumption that it is, just as the assumption of the inevitability of human progress, may well be a misconception that originated in the rationalistic theory of the 18th century and was reenforced in the 19th by the impressions made upon Western thinkers by the remarkable economic and social progress in countries directly within the field of their vision.

VIII. Some Implications

The task of inference from the variety of historical experience is difficult at best; and it is particularly difficult and treacherous when attempted without detailed documentation and thorough data. The suggestions advanced here concerning the historical bases of international differences in income levels are but general impressions, which may well be, and probably are, colored by the author's personal judgments. They are, to repeat the warning made at the outset, merely reflections on the problem. But it is hoped that these reflections have some foundation in recorded data and facts; and that they will, therefore, at least provoke serious thought in directions that have heretofore been little emphasized in the statistical literature.

If these reflections are of some validity, they have a variety of implications, for both policy and further research. The implications for policy neither need nor can be discussed here in detail. We mention only the most obvious—that attempts at raising economic levels in countries that have so far failed to take advantage of the potentials of an industrial system are not merely a matter of adding a few plants (which without the necessary background are merely junkpiles of brick and steel), and not merely of importing a few technical experts who are more than likely to be ignorant of the history and institutional background of the country. It is more a matter of finding within the country whatever groups among its population are aware of the need for and the ways in which elements of the industrial system can be adopted; and of mobilizing support behind these groups in the difficult effort which they will necessarily face. Above all, policy action must be made in full cognizance of the social and cultural corollaries of higher levels of economic performance, and of the implicit destruction of long standing and entrenched interests and attitudes which the adoption of these corollaries threatens.

But I am not competent nor in a position to examine the policy implications adequately. My interest lies more in the suggestions for further study—which are, in a sense, the *raison d'être* of this whole discussion. The main lesson can be put briefly: instead of confining ourselves to mechanistic, cross-section comparisons of quantitative indexes, let us pay adequate attention to the historical trends which cumulate in the kind of international differences in income levels that we currently observe. All that has been said concerning these trends in explaining existing differences was a tentative summary of what little one can learn. It is more important as an indication of directions and questions around which further and more thorough inquiry into the processes of economic growth of nations can be built.

This inquiry into economic growth in various countries would utilize quantitative data on secular changes in population, national income and its structure, many of the components ordinarily distinguished in studies of national income and wealth, foreign trade and investment, and a host of other aspects of economic and social structure. But the inquiry cannot, and should not, be limited to quantitative data alone, even apart from the difficulties to be encountered in the scanty supply of such data for most countries. The historical heritage of the several countries as embodied in patterns and values dominating social behavior, their political structure, their attempts, successful and otherwise, to adapt the elements of the industrial system to conditions within their boundaries, would have to be examined. Much of the raw material for a systematic inquiry of this type lies in historical monographs and studies; much is still buried in the primary historical materials; and much may be lost beyond recovery. More significant, a proper analysis of data of this kind, in conjunction with quantitative data, would impose upon the scholar problems for which the tools of his particular discipline—whether it be economics, political science, sociology, anthropology, statistics—may not be adequate. And much of the effort spent in this direction may yield primitive and limited results, at least at first.

We cannot be too optimistic that this, or other similar, inquiries will establish some invariant pattern of economic growth of nations, or succeed in clearly distinguishing between the necessary and accidental conditions of the effective adoption of the industrial system. Indeed, one must beware of premature generalizations because of the temptation they create to disregard much of the variety and mutability of historical experience. But what alternatives are there, except an examination of the only raw material of experience that we have for studying human societies, their structure and activities as revealed in the past? One can hope that a better understanding of the latter, scanty as the resulting tested generalizations may be, would at least prevent us from placing too much confidence in a succession of theories that so often magnify partial and transient conditions into universal and immutable factors.

9

RETARDATION OF
INDUSTRIAL GROWTH *[1]

I

A glance at the world from the end of the eighteenth century suggests a process of seemingly unslackened growth. There is ceaseless expansion of production and trade, continuous growth in the volume of power used, the amount of raw materials extracted from nature, and the quantity of finished products. But if we single out various nations or industries, the picture becomes less uniform. Within a single country or industry (on a world scale) growth has not been uniform and unretarded. Great Britain yielded her supremacy in economic matters to Germany and to the United States towards the end of the century. The textile industries ceded their place to pig iron, to steel, and then to the electrical industries. And within one industry we find further variations. The rapid development of English cotton textiles came much earlier than in the United States. While Belgian coal output had reached nearly stable levels in the beginning of the twentieth century, American and German coal production was still showing substantial growth.

* Reprinted by permission from the *Journal of Economic and Business History*, Cambridge, August 1929, pp. 534-560. The first few paragraphs have been omitted. This article presents a preliminary summary of findings published later in greater detail in *Secular Movements in Production and Prices*, Houghton Mifflin Co., Boston 1930.

[1] This article is part of the study undertaken by the author while a Research Fellow for the Social Science Research Council (1925-27). Throughout the study, and in the writing of this article, the author has profited by the kindly, critical advice of Professor Wesley C. Mitchell to whom he expresses his sincere gratitude.

Since historical records and our statistical data show events and changes mostly within a national branch of an industry, it seems advisable to resolve the general problem of economic growth into the narrower question as to the general course of long term changes that can be observed in various national branches of production. The general impression of this course may be summarized as follows. As we observe various industries within a given national economy, we see that the lead in development shifts from one branch to another. A rapidly developing industry does not retain its vigorous growth forever but slackens and is overtaken by others whose period of rapid development is beginning. Within one country we can observe a succession of different branches of activity in the vanguard of the country's economic development, and within each industry we can notice a conspicuous slackening in the rate of increase.

To test this observation statistically we take the volume of output or of consumption for an industry, average it for nine years (or seven where the data are short at the ends of the series) centered around the year ending with o or 5, and divide one average by the preceding. We thus obtain the percentage rate of increase or decrease by five-year periods. These percentage rates of change do not move uniformly. To see whether the general tendency is to decline, rise, or to remain stable, we divide the entire period covered by each series into halves, and obtain an average percentage rate of increase for each half. The table that follows summarizes the results. Of 35 series only one showed an increase in the average percentage rate of increase. It is obvious that we are dealing with an important characteristic.[2]

[2] Another test of this characteristic was carried through in the more refined statistical analysis of the series cited, as well as of about 10 more. We fitted to all of them the simple Logistic or Gompertz curves, of which the most conspicuous feature is that they assume a decline in the percentage rate of increase. The fits obtained were all satisfactory first approximations, most of them good, thus demonstrating again that the decline in the rate of increase is a generally observed trait of industrial

The observation that an industry cannot grow indefinitely at the same rate and must eventually show retardation is so obvious that it is not likely to be disputed. But when placed next to our general belief in continuous and unlimited possibilities of economic progress, it raises a frequently overlooked question. Why are the forces of growth and development concentrated in one or two branches of production, often creating them, and why do they forsake the older industries after a certain period of their history is passed? Why is there no uniform progress in all branches of production?

These questions can best be answered by inspection of the historical records of industrial growth, a survey that would reveal the processes that underlie economic development. The above generalization concerning the slackening of expansion to be observed within separate industries of a national economy will serve as our guide through the maze of concrete data available.

II

Of the numerous factors discussed by economic historians in tracing the history of an industry, three groups stand out as dynamic: (1) growth of population, (2) changes in demand, and (3) technical changes, including both technical progress and improvement in business organization. They are of course not independent but are each conditioned by the others in a chain of relationship.

The growth of population seems to be a self-generating process, independent in itself, although influencing nearly all social phenomena. But in the industrial system of a country, population is another productive factor, and its size from year to year is of significance for analysis similar to that, for instance, of the annual output of pig iron. To treat the growth of pop-

growth, when we take the latter for single industries and separate countries. We did not apply the test to wider series, i.e., either for world-wide industries, or for national economies, because reliable statistical indices were lacking.

AVERAGE RATE OF PERCENTAGE INCREASE DURING FIVE-YEAR PERIODS, SHOWN
BY INDICES OF THE VOLUME OF PRODUCTIVE ACTIVITY IN VARIOUS INDUSTRIES,
IN THE UNITED STATES, GREAT BRITAIN, BELGIUM, GERMANY, AND FRANCE

Country and Nature of Series	Period Covered	Average Rate of % Increase		
		During 1st Half	During 2nd Half	Relative Decrease (% of (3))
1	2	3	4	5
United States				
1. Wheat Crops	1866-1924	20.4	7.3	64.2
2. Corn Crops	1866-1924	17.7	6.7	62.1
3. Potato Crops	1866-1924	17.6	11.5	34.7
4. Cotton Crops	1866-1924	24.2	5.6	76.9
5. Anthracite Coal Shipments	1825-1924	70.8	16.3	77.0
6. Bituminous Coal Output	1840-1924	62.9	33.9	46.1
7. Crude Petroleum Output	1860-1924	70.5	51.4	27.1
8. Pig Iron Production	1856-1924	46.7	29.4	37.0
9. Crude Steel Production	1866-1924	157.7	46.2	70.7
10. Portland Cement Output	1880-1924	337.4	90.0	26.7
11. Cotton Consumption, Domestic Mills	1871-1924	30.4	19.0	37.5
12. Raw Silk Imports	1866-1924	66.0	41.8	63.3
13. N. Y. City Bank Clearings, Deflated	1876-1923	15.2	8.0	47.4
14. Locomotives Produced, Baldwin Locomotive Works	1836-1923	47.9	22.3	53.4
Great Britain				
15. Coal Output	1856-1913	16.2	10.4	35.8
16. Pig Iron Production	1856-1913	15.4	4.0	74.0
17. Raw Steel Output	1876-1913	39.3	20.4	48.1
18. Tonnage of Ships Cleared, All Ports	1816-1913	24.8	18.9	23.8
19. Raw Cotton Imports	1781-1913	35.4	11.1	68.6
20. Tea Consumption [a]	1810-1919	14.8	12.6	14.9
Belgium				
21. Coal Output	1831-1913	25.6	6.9	73.0
22. Pig Iron Output	1851-1913	18.8	21.6	+14.9
23. Steel (Crude) Output	1881-1913	58.9	46.8	20.5
24. Zinc Production	1846-1913	29.0	14.5	50.0
Germany				
25. Wheat Crops	1881-1913	14.7	6.7	54.4
26. Coal Output	1861-1913	28.6	25.7	10.1
27. Pig Iron Consumption	1861-1913	36.7	25.5	30.5
28. Steel Output	1881-1913	73.8	67.8	8.1
29. Zinc (Crude) Production	1846-1913	24.7	10.5	57.5
30. Raw Cotton Consumption [b]	1836-1910	43.5	22.8	47.6
France				
31. Wheat Crops	1825-1913	7.8	2.0	74.4
32. Coal Output	1811-1913	29.6	15.9	46.3
33. Petroleum Consumption	1866-1913	57.9	26.6	54.1
34. Pig Iron Output	1825-1913	24.3	16.8	30.9
35. Steel Output	1871-1913	47.3	35.4	25.2

[a] 10-year averages until 1854. [b] 10-year averages through the whole period.

ulation as an independent dynamic factor is a delusion as to the specific function of man in his productive and procreative capacities. As labor, men are just as much conditioned by the product of the industrial system as the latter is conditioned by labor. Human procreation, being a kind of production, is influenced and determined by material surroundings as much as the production of steel or portland cement.

This thesis seems less shocking when we look at the factors that have controlled population growth during the last century and a half: birth rate, death rate, and immigration. With growth of wealth the European birth rate has declined, and the great increase in population has been due to a fall in the death rate, for which modern science has been mostly responsible.[3] Immigration is also conditioned by the same forces that make for economic growth.

While the increase of population is not independent of industrial and technical development, it may in turn influence the latter. A large population in the industrial economy, made possible only by the preceding expansion of the industries, may in its turn account for the further growth in the volume of productive activity. Here it is interesting to note that, according to latest investigations, in most European countries there was, in the course of the nineteenth century, a definite decline in the rate of increase of population.[4]

Were changes in population the only factor in industrial development, this tendency towards a smaller rate of increase would both confirm and explain our hypothesis concerning a similar tendency in the growth of industries. Population showing a decreasing rate of growth, the volume of industrial output should show the same. But other factors enter in and we see per capita output rising in most countries, and in various branches of production within the national economies we find a variety of rates of increase and retardation. To account for this we must turn to the two other groups of factors, changes in demand and changes in technique.

[3] See M. C. Buer, *Health, Wealth and Population in the Early Days of the Industrial Revolution* (1926).

[4] See the studies by Raymond Pearl and others.

In the discussion of demand it is well to distinguish between ultimate consumers' demand and producers' demand. The needs of manufacturers often provide a direct stimulus to technical progress, while the reverse is true when changes in the demand of ultimate consumers are brought about because technical innovations have brought a new or improved commodity within reach. Demand for tea, electric light, and automobiles appeared only after the progress of technique had made these commodities available at a price that stimulated large demand. Consumers' demand is a passive force and when saturated may slow down the growth of an industry.

But in general, demand is elastic and depends on the cost of the product compared with available purchasing power. Both are a reflection of the state of the productive arts. Lowering of costs by technical progress may expand demand considerably, and the same result may be brought about by an increase of purchasing power through expansion of production due to improvement of technology. Therefore technical changes loom as the most important factor in an industry's development. While all three factors are interdependent, the changes in technique condition most clearly the movements in both population and demand, while the dependence of the former upon the latter is not as clear and immediate. In the interconnection of the three, this link seems to be the most important because it seems to offer a most promising way toward significant findings.

III

In every industry there comes a time when the basic technical conditions have been introduced, a fundamental change has taken place, and a new era may be said to have begun. In manufacturing it is frequently the period when the machine process has supplanted labor to a substantial extent. In the extractive industries it is either the moment when the sources and use of a commodity have been discovered, as in the case of petroleum, or when a new, wide use has been opened up for a hitherto little used commodity. The cotton textile industry in Great Britain in the decade 1780-90, steel in the decade 1860-70, the anthracite coal industry of the United States in the 'thirties, petroleum in the 'sixties, and, in our own time, the automobile and radio industries, are concrete examples. In all these cases a revolutionary invention or discovery changed the industrial process fundamentally.

With this condition established, the industry grows rapidly. The improvements in the quality of the product and the other possibilities offered by the new techniques permit a larger output. The innovation is rarely perfect from the start, and further improvements take place continually after the main invention or discovery has been made. The use of the continually improving and cheapening commodity spreads to larger areas, overcoming obstacles that may have limited demand in the past. Population grows and helps to swell the total volume of output. Nevertheless vigorous expansion slackens, and after a time growth is not so rapid. What are the processes that underlie this change?

In an attempt to answer this question we have grouped together trends observed in the histories of a number of industries:

A. Technical progress slackens, changes in methods of production being more numerous in the early period.

B. Slower growing industries exercise a retarding influence upon the faster growing complementary branches.

C. One nation's industry may be retarded by the competitive influence of a branch of the same industry emerging later in another country.

The slowing down of technico-economic progress was noted twenty years ago by the German economist Julius Wolf. One of his four "Laws of retardation of progress" reads: "Every technical improvement by lowering costs and by perfecting the utilization of raw materials and of power bars the way to further progress. There is less left to improve, and this narrowing of possibilities results in a slackening or complete cessa-

tion of technical development in a number of fields." [5] Wolf
illustrates the thesis by a number of examples, but undertakes
no study to show that retardation of technical progress had
actually taken place. An attempt to do so must begin with a
distinction between the manufacturing and the extractive industries. In the former, the spectacular technical development
that has taken place during the last century and a half has to
be observed rather closely before its tendency toward retardation is apparent. In the extractive industries, technical progress
has been less conspicuous. Moreover, its failure to overcome
the limiting influence of exhaustion can be demonstrated in a
direct manner.

IV

A thoroughgoing study of technical changes in manufacturing industries cannot be presented within the limits of an
article. We can only cite a few observations concerning several industries by way of illustration; and even then the absence of reliable up-to-date material prevents our presenting
these observations as final.

The textile industries offer the best illustration of an apparent decline in the rate of technical progress. The cotton, wool,
and worsted manufactures are among the branches of production in which the Industrial Revolution took place long
enough ago to allow sufficient time for the tendency toward
retardation to manifest itself.

Most of the revolutionary inventions in the cotton manufacturing industry were bunched together in the last thirty
years of the eighteenth century. The spinning jenny was invented by Hargreaves in 1767, patented in 1770, and introduced immediately after that. Arkwright's first patent for the
water-frame was taken out in 1769, and his mill built at
Cromford in 1771. In 1779 Crompton invented the mule. In
1785 Arkwright's patents were thrown open to the public, but

[5] See *Die Volkswirtschaft der Gegenwart u. Zukunft* (Leipzig, 1912),
pp. 236-237.

they had been used widely before that time. Meanwhile a pressing need for raw cotton developed, in response to which Whitney's cotton gin was invented in 1793. In 1792 Crompton's mule had been greatly improved by Kelly. In 1785 Cartwright had invented the first power loom, which was not efficient and did not spread until essential improvements were introduced much later. A number of subsidiary machines were invented during the last quarter of the eighteenth century. The carding machine (cylinder), was introduced in Lancashire in 1760, and was greatly improved in 1772 by John Less. The scutching machine was invented in 1797.

There were, however, serious defects in some of the important machines, and a number of gaps in the mechanical equipment of the industry. Most of these were remedied during the first half of the nineteenth century. The mule was made self-acting by Roberts in 1825, and the throstle was introduced into the water-frame. The final improvement that made the power loom practicable was carried through by Kenworthy and Bullough in 1841. Major improvements in the carding machine were made in 1823, 1834, and 1850.

Few important inventions were made after 1860. Of course, there was marked improvement in the machines already in use by 1860, but the bulk of the mechanical equipment was available by that time. In spinning, no important new mechanisms were introduced. In spooling, however, two new devices appeared: Wade's wire bobbin holder (invented in the 'seventies) and the Barber Knotter (1900). In warping and sizing, the same machines were used after 1860 as immediately before it. The single revolutionary invention after the 1860's was the Northrop automatic loom (on the market in 1894). It combined a number of important features and cut the labor cost of weaving in half, "a fact which is particularly significant since the labor cost of weaving previously constituted one half of the entire labor cost of manufacturing cotton cloth." [6] The automatic loom was improved later and adapted to the weav-

[6] M. T. Copeland, *Cotton Manufacturing Industry of the United States* (1912, 1917), p. 86.

ing of cloth from different colored threads (Crompton and Knowles). In converting and finishing, most of the processes have remained essentially unchanged. The only recent development of importance has been in the mercerization process. In the drying and finishing processes, machinery has been considerably improved, but there have been no new inventions.

The general impression conveyed by such a survey is that the bulk of the machine equipment was introduced into the industry before 1860, and after that date there were few important inventions.

The economic effects of technical improvements are reflected in the cost of capital and labor required to produce a pound of cotton yarn as the following table indicates:[7]

Yarn 40 hanks to the lb.			Yarn 100 hanks to the lb.		
	Shillings	Pence		Shillings	Pence
1779	14	0	1786	34	0
1784	8	11	1796	15	6
1799	4	2	1806	4	2
1812	1	0	1812	2	10
1830	0	6.75	1830	2	2.75
1860	0	6.25	1860	1	5
1882	0	3.375	1882	1	0.375

As measured in absolute savings the effect of technical progress seems to grow progressively smaller. But even the rate of decline in the cost of capital and labor has been diminishing, although not continuously. Thus for the first fifty-one years this cost (for yarn, 40 hanks to the lb.) declined from 14s. to 6.75 d., or 96%; for the next fifty-two years to 3.375 d., or only 50%. The same is still more obvious in the case of yarn, 100 hanks to the lb. The cost of raw cotton did not exhibit the same decline. For yarn, 40 hanks per lb., it was 2 s. in 1779, 7.75 d. in 1830, and 7.125 d. in 1882. Thus, the cost of cotton constituted 12.7% of the selling price in 1779, 54% in 1834, and 68% in 1882.

[7] Thomas Ellison, *The Cotton Trade of Great Britain* (1886), p. 61.

The woolen and worsted industries received most of their machinery from the cotton industry. The two important exceptions were Kay's flying-shuttle and the wool combing machine. The mechanization of operations in the industry was thus completed quite early, and after 1860 no great inventions were introduced.

We may cite a few details. The Burr picker was introduced in 1833-34; the Burr cylinder was attached to the carding machine about 1846. The carbonization process of cleaning was introduced in Germany in the 'fifties. In washing and scouring, the modern processes were also established some time ago. The slashing machine (invented in 1835) was improved to its modern form by 1860. The carding machines were essentially in their modern form in the 'thirties, as was the machinery for spinning. The automatic loom did affect the process of weaving after 1860, but it was not nearly so important as it had been in the cotton industry. In finishing machinery there was progress in the size and efficiency of the apparatus. Gig mills and mechanical shearing were pretty much established by the beginning of the nineteenth century. The latest important inventions were in the worsted operation of combing. The first machine technically suitable for wool was achieved by the introduction of the "nip" process by Heilman (about 1840), and brought to its final efficient shape by Donisthorpe and Lister (1851). Other important changes were made by Isaac Holden and Noble.

The decline in the rate of technical progress in the woolen industry has recently been noted by A. H. Cole. After sketching the vigorous technical advance in the American industry, he says in a general summary, "but this early advance has not persisted. . . . Advances have been progressively less significant as the years have gone by, until recently improvement has chiefly taken the form of refinements upon existing mechanisms, coming either from within the domestic industry or from abroad. . . . Moreover, with regard to both woolen and worsted machinery, one should note the recent advent of the automatic loom,—a significant exception to the statements just made. Though this mechanism does in fact promise less for the wool manufacturing industry than a similar machine has already accomplished for the allied cotton cloth manufacture, . . . still it must be viewed as a notable improvement. On the whole, however, marked changes and conspicuous advances have been rare during recent decades in the mechanical equipment of either the woolen or the worsted manufacture. In short there appears to be a tendency toward stability in technological form,—observable, I believe, in other industries as well. Progress undoubtedly will come in the future, but seemingly at a generally slower rate. The Industrial Revolution has here about spent its force." [8]

Steel presents another good example of the course of inventions. In 1856 it became possible to produce cheaply good steel from iron by the Bessemer process; and immediately upon this came the improvements and inventions of other efficient methods of production that account today for the imposing output. If we divide into two periods the sixty years that have elapsed since the decade in which the modern steel industry really began, we see that most of these improvements and inventions fall into the first half. The Siemens furnace was patented in 1856, and the Gilchrist-Thomas de-phosphorizing process was patented in 1877. This concentration of inventions in the period 1855-1890 does not mean that no improvements were made afterwards. But the essential processes of manufacture, those establishing the possibility of its modern large-scale production, were all introduced in the early period of the history of the industry.

We have no space to discuss the development of the other industries even as briefly as the three presented above. We can only mention that a similar analysis of the technical history of the shoe manufacturing and paper industries produces the same impression. A similar tendency may be observed in the development of the steam engine. It was modified, improved, applied to different uses, mostly in the period before 1850.

[8] *The American Wool Manufacture* (1926), vol. i, pp. ix-x.

An important exception to our tentative generalization can be observed in the case of copper smelting. Since the 1880's when it entered the modern era, we can observe no slackening in its technical progress. This may have been due to the rapid exhaustion of ore resources and the consequent deterioration of the raw material. In such conditions there was ever present pressure upon the manufacturing processes for adaptation to the deterioration of the raw ore. We might thus have in such cases unabated progress in the technique of the industry, but since it is called forth by the exhaustion of the raw materials, the checking effect upon the output stems from the latter.

This brief presentation, in the nature of illustration rather than of proof, shows that the number of important inventions within an industry with an unretarded supply of raw material tends to diminish in the later periods of its history. The reasons for such a trend are fairly obvious. The introduction of the initial invention exercises a stimulus to bring about, as soon as possible, corresponding changes and improvements in the other processes within the industry. As the industry advances technically, the economic stimulus to further innovations becomes progressively weaker.

Technically a branch of production is a series of separate operations that lead in an invariable sequence from the raw material to the finished product. Once an important process in this chain is revolutionized by an invention, pressure is exercised upon the other links of the chain to become more efficient. Any disparity in performance at the different stages precludes full exploitation of the innovation made. Many important inventions have come in response to such pressure. It may take a long while before the necessary improvements are made, but the initial invention itself paves the way by standardizing the product at the stage at which it is delivered for further processing, and indicates the mechanical mold into which the raw material is to be cast. And this standardization facilitates further technical progress.

While the stimulus for further inventions appears early, the number of operations to be improved is limited and is gradually exhausted. When all the important operations are performed by machines that have reached comparative perfection, not much room is left for further inventions. And if, in addition, the chemical processes are brought to a relatively efficient state, no great new improvements can be expected.

This gradual exhaustion of the protracted "industrial revolution" is accompanied and furthered by the weakening of the economic stimulus. When the reduced price of a commodity has taken it out of the luxury class, a low unit price renders the demand for it largely inelastic, and further possible reductions are too slight to have any marked effect.

So much for the tentative generalization concerning the decline in the number of important inventions. But we must consider other technical changes in an industry, such as the gradual improvements in the inventions themselves and the changes in labor.

The usual historical description of inventions presents them at the period when their first practical form has been reached. After that, numerous improvements in detail take place, whose cumulative effect is quite often much larger than that of the first application itself. But the essential content of the invention usually remains unchanged. The modern steam engine uses exactly the same principle of steam expansion that Watt used. The modern combined mule and frame embody the same mechanical ideas and forms that were introduced by Crompton and Arkwright.

The improvements that come with extending practical use are thus each minor in character. The possible stock of these improvements is limited, for finally there comes a time when the machine or the process is practically perfect. Improvements, which appear rapidly at first, occur less and less often, until finally there is practically nothing left to improve. This statement can be partly substantiated by the statistics of patents which indicate that for specific inventions or even for whole fields of inventions, the emphasis upon improvement declines rapidly. The cumulative effect of improvement can thus be presumed to increase at a diminishing rate and to approach gradually a stable level.

Of the third element in technical progress, the changes in labor, we know least. The first thing a new industry requires is to develop a more efficient labor group, which means teaching the formerly unskilled workers greater promptness, care of expensive machinery, and concentration on their work. Not until the younger generation had grown old enough to enter the factories, did the pioneer builders of steam engines, of spinning machines, and others have at their disposal a reliable working force. But this problem is usually solved early in the industrial development.

With the growth of the industry comes a lessening dependence upon the labor supply, for the introduction of automatic machines enables the performance of operations by relatively unskilled workers, though calling for an increased number of skilled machinists to keep the "automatics" in order. This suggests the possibility that, even after the technical equipment and processes of the industry have reached stable levels, there may be continued improvement *via* closer analysis and more scientific planning of the manual operations still to be performed.

These two streams of change in the labor element, coming, one immediately after the technical innovations, the other after the industry has reached comparative stabilization, seem to defer the decline in the rate of technical progress that might otherwise result. But consideration of the labor factor provides no basis for denying the tentative conclusions as to the existence of such a decline inferred from specific evidence and general reasoning concerning changes in industrial technique.

V

In discussing technical development in manufacturing industries we have considered the succession of important inventions within specific branches, the tendencies toward the improvement of these inventions, and the change in labor, in order to indicate the basis for the tentative generalization concerning the decline in the tempo of technical progress. In the extractive industries, however, the weakening effects of technical development in the face of exhaustion are reflected clearly in pertinent statistical indices. The few available statistical series suggest, with rare exceptions, a diminution in rate of growth, a definite approach to stability or even decline.

The best index available for analyzing the effects of the development of agricultural technique is the yield of crops per acre. Specific data on this point, in the form of decennial and quinquennial averages, present the following picture:

YIELD PER ACRE, FOUR CROPS, U. S. A.[a]

(Ten-year Averages, 1866-1875 = 100 base)

Years	Wheat	Corn	Potatoes	Cotton
1866-1875	100.0	100.0	100.0	100.0
1876-1885	103.3	97.3	87.3	96.9
1886-1895	105.8	91.2	79.4	100.4
1896-1905	111.7	98.9	91.7	107.3
1906-1915	125.8	102.7	105.1	105.7
1916-1925	115.0	105.0	109.2	97.2

[a] *United States Department of Agriculture Yearbook 1922* (1923) pp. 583, 571, 668, 711; *ibid., 1925,* pp. 743, 788, 913, 952.

The yield per acre of wheat rose continuously until the final decade. In the other cases, however, the increase in the yield per acre was neither continuous nor certain. It declined during the first decades (cotton during the first only) and rose thereafter, but absolute increment diminished. The presence of long, 30-year swings obscures the character of the underlying trend. On the whole, except for the yield of wheat, the American data indicate a growth in yield approaching a limit.

The data for other countries support this generalization much more clearly, for instance the German series for three crops:

YIELD PER HECTARE, THREE CROPS, GERMANY [a]
(Five-year Averages, 1878-1882 = 100 base)

Years	Wheat	Rye	Potatoes
1878-1882	100.0	100.0	100.0
1883-1887	101.8	101.4	114.3
1888-1892	104.3	100.0	106.0
1893-1897	129.1	140.4	153.0
1898-1902	141.7	149.1	169.7
1903-1907	151.7	162.6	171.7
1908-1912	158.7	180.2	174.4

[a] The data for 1878-92 are from *Statistisches Handbuch für das deutsche Reich,* pp. 448-449, the rest from *Statistisches Jahrbuch für das deutsche Reich* (1908), pp. 30, 32, and *ibid.* (1914), pp. 43-44.

Here we find a retarded movement in the yield per acre with the possible exception of rye; although even in this case, if the first two stable averages be disregarded, the rise is larger (absolutely) from 1888 to 1898 than in the following decade.

The French series, covering a much longer period of time, indicates the same tendency.

YIELD PER HECTARE, FRANCE [a]
(in Hectolitres)

Years	Wheat	Years	Wheat
1815-1818	10.0	1860-1869	14.4
1820-1829	11.8	1871-1880	14.2
1830-1839	12.4	1881-1890	15.6
1840-1849	13.7	1891-1900	16.2
1850-1859	14.0	1901-1910	17.6

[a] *Annuaire statistique, Ministére du Travail et de la Prévoyance Sociale,* vol. xxxv for 1916, 1917, 1918 (1919), pp. 50-51.

In undeveloped countries there is a rapid increase in the number of acres under cultivation, the extensive margin being pushed further and further out, and the yield per acre does not usually exhibit any conspicuous rise until territorial expansion stops. Australia presents a good example of this point.

ACREAGE AND YIELD PER ACRE, WHEAT, AUSTRALIA

(in Absolute Figures)

Years	Acreage (ooo's acr. omitted)	Yield (bushels)
1860-1861	644	15.91
1865-1866	818	11.80
1870-1871	1,124	10.75
1875-1876	1,423	13.15
1880-1881	3,054	7.65
1885-1886	3,277	8.37
1890-1891	3,229	8.40
1895-1896	3,774	4.84
1900-1901	5,667	8.53
1905-1906	6,123	11.19
1910-1911	7,372	12.90
1915-1916	12,485	14.34
1920-1921	9,072	16.08

While the area cultivated was increasing along a concave line, the average yield declined considerably through the first thirty-five years, and began to recover only in the second half of the period. Thus, for the whole sixty years, only the growth of acreage contributed to the increase in total volume of the crop.

In the second group of extractive industries, mining, output per worker is a good indication of the long-term trend in technical changes, or rather in the effect of these changes reduced by the adverse influence of gradual exhaustion of resources. If the rate of technical progress shows a constant tendency to increase, enough to overcome the deterioration of the natural conditions of production, the output per worker will show a continuous increase. If it shows a retarded growth that turns soon towards a decline, one may be justified in inferring that the course of technical improvement is not strong enough to overcome the exhaustion of resources. While the statistical data cannot provide a complete proof, since other factors may be responsible for the decline observed, they are nevertheless strong evidence in favor of the hypothesis.

The data for Germany on the annual output per worker in four of its most important branches of mining illustrate our point.

ANNUAL OUTPUT PER WORKER [a] FOR FOUR MINERAL ORES, GERMANY

(Five-year Averages, 1860-1864 = 100)

Years	Bituminous Coal	Iron Ore	Copper Ore	Zinc Ore
1860-1864	100.0	100.0	100.0	100.0
1865-1869	116.4	134.6	136.4	99.9
1870-1874	115.9	161.3	169.2	116.4
1875-1879	128.5	201.6	200.5	138.7
1880-1884	152.2	232.2	194.2	142.5
1885-1889	158.6	300.0	167.5	151.8
1890-1894	147.5	345.3	183.4	145.7
1895-1899	153.8	438.9	221.9	139.7
1900-1904	142.3	500.1	217.7	128.4
1905-1909	145.7	595.4	202.0	123.7

[a] Total output for the year divided by total working force (*mittlere Belegschaft*).

Three of these series (coal, zinc, copper) show a rise along a convex curve up to a point and a distinct decline thereafter. Thus, for these three minerals technical development made for increased output up to a certain point only, and, from then on, the approach to the limit became apparent. Even while per capita output was increasing, the size of the absolute increment was already declining. The net effect of technical progress, as expressed by these indices, was gradually diminishing; and thus, naturally, progress was greater in the earlier periods of the industry's history than in the later. This was not true of iron ore, for which the abundance of resources put no limiting pressure on the increase of output.

The data for other countries pertain only to coal output. In Belgium the movement was similar to that in Germany, output

per worker increasing until about 1890 when it began to decline. A similar long-term trend can be observed in the output
per worker in the coal industries of Great Britain and France.[9]
Unfortunately we do not have series for the United States satisfactory for the present purpose.

The evidence seems to indicate a generally prevailing decline
in the rate of increase of per-worker output of coal, and of
copper and zinc in Germany. But, in the case of mining, the
statistical proof may be superfluous. For here we have the
ideal example of an industry where limited deposits are being
gradually exhausted, and where the difficulty of production
increases as we approach the limit.

The discussion above of the dynamics of technical change
in industry can now be summarized. In manufacturing industries, which have profited more than any others by the development of technology during the last century and a half, the
"industrial revolution" has been a protracted process of a
gradually retarding character. The same tendency to slackening improvement and retarded spread has been observed in
the history of such an important single invention as the steam
engine. Technical progress of some industries was continually
stimulated by the impoverishment of the raw materials, and
consequently the same slowing down of rate of technical change
was not perceptible. In the extractive industries the slackening
effects of technical progress were shown by the curves of yield
per acre and of output per man.

VI

The slower growth of extractive, as compared with manufacturing, industries suggests another retarding force operative
within specific branches of production. In the economic development of a nation the industries are interconnected, and the

[9] Rowe, J. W. F., *Wages in the Coal Industry* (1923), p. 13; Saitzew, M.,
*Steinkohlenpreise und Dampfkraftkosten, Schriften des Vereins für So-
cialpolitik*, vol. 143, pt. 2 (1914), p. 141.

slow development of one eventually exercises a check upon the growth of the others.

Let us take the not-altogether-probable case of an industry whose processes are being technically improved, while the state of the industrial arts in the other branches of production is at a standstill. Let us also suppose that we deal with an isolated industrial economy. The increase in the total volume of product A will obviously find a check in the stability of technical conditions in the other industries. For, in the production of A, the developing industry consumes as raw materials commodities B, C, D, etc. With the growth in the volume of production of A, there is a larger demand for B, C, D which can be satisfied only by diverting a larger supply of labor and capital to the industries producing B, C, D, and thus making available less capital and labor for A. The savings which are realized by the technical progress in the latter do not all come back to be reinvested in the industry, but are drawn upon to subsidize the increase in the industries that supply A. The larger A grows, the larger is the diversion of labor and capital to the technically stable industries; for we are assuming an isolated economy with limited resources. There evidently comes a point when the technical improvement in A cannot liberate any more funds to make for its own further growth.

This last statement will be clearer when we look at the changes in the cost composition of A. The economic effect of continuous technical improvement will be that the "value added by manufacture" will grow smaller, while the "cost of raw materials" will either remain stable or grow larger. In the final price of the product, the component of value added will thus form a smaller and smaller percentage. And while technical progress may go on at an unabated rate (which we have seen above to be improbable), the *economic* effects of such technical development will become progressively smaller. There will come a time when the "value added" forms such an insignificant percentage of the total price of the product that no further change in the productive process, be it ever so important technically, will be of any economic effect in expanding demand and permitting a larger output. Without technical changes in the related branches of industry, a given branch A cannot go on expanding indefinitely, no matter how great its own technical progress. At a certain point saving from any further technical improvement would just balance the extra effort that would be needed to supply the additional quantities of raw material.

We have taken the extreme case of an industry developing within an otherwise stable economy. But the same reasoning applies to a case where, in respect to technique, we have rapidly changing branches of production and slowly changing ones. The difference between the rates of change within the two groups will serve to provide the same kind of check in both of its aspects, the technical and the economic. This applies directly to the contrast between the extractive and the manufacturing groups. Undoubtedly the latter group has enjoyed greater technical progress than the former; but in the long run the slow development of the one group tends to become a check on the development of the other. Therefore, the ratio of "value added" to value of raw materials ought to decline in the industries that have developed faster technically than the others. The table on the next page illustrates this point.

Of the five branches of metal production cited only one, blast furnaces, stands in immediate connection with the underlying extractive branch. Until recently steel mills used pig iron as their principal raw material, the other three branches mostly steel. It is interesting to observe the difference in the movement of the ratio in these five cases. The most definite and precipitous decline is in the ratio for blast furnaces. The decrease in value added in the steel mills just kept pace with the cheapening of pig iron, the ratio on the whole being stable. The three other groups were also technically improving, but the pace of technical changes was much slower in these than in steel and iron, their ratios consequently showing a definite upward trend. This example thus supports the statement made above: that the value added by manufacturing industries as over against the cost of the materials supplied by the extractive

RATIO OF VALUE ADDED TO COST OF MATERIALS, METALS, U. S. A.[a]

(Cost of Materials taken as 100)

Year	Blast Furnaces	Steel Mills Rolling Works	Cutlery and Edge Tools	Safes and Vaults	Hardware
1849	79.0	....	165.0	....	130.7
1859	69.8	....	170.5	152.0	147.6
1869	53.1	52.8	175.0	181.8	142.0
1879	52.4	56.2	149.1	134.2	124.3
1889	32.3	53.4	220.7	152.1	162.4
1899	57.2	52.8	190.5	132.6	145.4
1904	29.6	52.8	208.8	144.8	175.2
1909	22.1	49.9	216.5	146.6	154.4
1914	20.1	55.5	212.0	174.3	152.2
1919	27.9	68.3	242.1	131.4	164.0
1921	16.3	47.4	229.5	165.1	193.6
1923	21.8	54.3	322.4	169.6	168.0

[a] Abstract of the *Census* for 1921, checked by that for 1923.

groups declined. True, as we go up the industrial ladder, we may find that the rate of improvement in the production of the semi-raw product has been higher than in the processes of its further manufacture. But this evidently only acts as a check upon the continued technical progress within the most rapidly developing stage of production.

In studying more complicated mechanisms we find that the value added by manufacture has steadily decreased. With 100 representing cost of materials, we find that value added in production of sewing machines in 1859 was 556.89 but in 1923 only 158.85; value added in production of washing machines was 252.0 in 1859 and only 95.72 in 1923. A similar decline is observed in the case of typewriters, automobiles, and furniture. Of the other industries investigated, slaughter and meat packing, dairy products, linen goods, and knit goods showed a decline in the ratio of value added to cost of raw materials while in bread and baking products, woolen goods and silk goods the ratio was either stable or rising.

On the whole the data show that in the manufacturing industries technical progress resulted in a diminution of the proportions contributed by those industries to the price of the product. This is the statistical expression of the fact that the slower developing industries supplying the raw material check the growth of the industries more favored by benefits of technical development.

If in complementary industries, such as discussed above, the slower growth of one retards the growth of another dependent upon it for the supply of raw materials, in competitive industries, it is the *rapid* growth of one that serves as a brake upon the development of the other. And the field of competitive industries is wide and constantly extending with the increasing margin of spending power and the resulting range of choice among commodities.

VII

In looking at industrial development from a national point of view we must consider another factor, the effect of growing international competition. The best illustration is provided by the industrial history of Great Britain. The main inventions of the second half of the eighteenth century were made in England. Less affected by the French Revolution and the Napoleonic wars than the continent of Europe, it was the first country to develop industrial capitalism, and in the early periods of the nineteenth century supplied goods to nearly all of Europe. The insufficiency of its natural resources was overcome by extensive imports from other countries. Although this became more of a burden, when iron ore had to be imported in large quantities and when the copper and tin mines became relatively exhausted during the first half of the nineteenth century England enjoyed an undisputed leadership in industry and trade. But in the second half of the century it began to feel the competition of the United States and Germany whose superior natural opportunities and ability to take advantage of already developed techniques caused a rapid development which was a large factor in the retardation of British industry.

Let us now summarize the factors that tend to make for a decreasing rate of growth of an industry within a nation. As an industry starts from small beginnings and develops rapidly to substantial output, it is enabled to do so mainly by progress in technical conditions of production. But the effects of technical progress show an unmistakable tendency to slacken due either to retardation in technical progress itself or the pressure of exhaustion of resources, or both. Added to that is the check exercised by groups of productive activity whose industrial arts do not improve as rapidly and as significantly as in the industry in question. And finally, if the country is the first to benefit from the introduction of some new inventions, the development of other countries may form a serious obstacle to the growth of industry in the older country with an unabated rate of increase.[10]

[10] The hypothesis developed above must be taken with some caution. We have paid attention mostly to technical conditions, and to economic conditions in their technical aspects. We have not studied many other forces which influence the stream of events that constitutes the history of an industry.

Nor can the proof of the hypothesis advanced be considered complete. In one most important generalization, we adopted the crude method of listing and dating important inventions. The possibilities of omission and misplacement in such a procedure are numerous. In other cases the data cited are far from exhaustive. The most that can be claimed for the suggestions developed is that they supply a bare sketch of the general course of development within an industry, and offer plausible grounds for expecting a retardation in the growth of every national branch of production from the time its modern technical conditions are first established.

10

ECONOMIC TENDENCIES,
PAST AND PRESENT *

I

In times when the pace of history accelerates, it becomes important to know which of the many changes that confront us are transient and which have come to stay. In such times there is a strong urge to interpret the present in terms of the past and thus segregate the persistent from the passing, the long term trend from the shorter term cycle, the vagaries of accidental circumstances from the breaks indicative of major shifts in underlying forces. This urge becomes stronger when the impact of current events is unpleasant and disturbing. For then we are driven to analysis of current happenings by anxiety and by a desire for a more reassuring long term outlook.

It may seem that this concern with the past, present, and future, shared by every thinking citizen, is a far cry from those specific and technical problems that confront the statistician in his professional activities. Yet the solution of many of these technical problems is closely conditioned by the statistician's view of the continuity of historical events and the likelihood of the persistence of tendencies observed in the past. To take a specific example: if a statistician measures secular movements in industry X, he can interpret the results and carry through the measurement itself only by accepting implicit assumptions concerning the homogeneity and continuity of the process of historical development. For in fitting a single curve

* Presented before the Philadelphia Chapter of the American Statistical Association, October 24, 1941.

278

to the years from 1860 to 1940 he assumes that this period is homogeneous in that, within it, the process of growth has been produced by roughly one and the same set of factors. And if he extrapolates the curve, even for a short period beyond the given series, he assumes the continuity of historical development, that the processes that have shaped the past will shape this immediate future.

The same assumption underlies statistical analysis not only of secular movements but also of other patterns of temporal change which we distinguish in time series analysis (cycles, seasonal variations and the like). Nor is the analysis of frequency distributions and sampling theory free from such assumptions, simply because these tools, when applied to social data, relate to temporally changing realities. The practical significance of any inference based on samples hinges upon the assumption that knowledge of the universe today will not become obsolete tomorrow. Hence in considering questions of broad import suggested by the topic under discussion, we are not indulging in broad generalities of little relevance to problems we face in our everyday professional work. On the contrary, these questions deal with the basic conditions of statistical research, conditions that govern the validity of our inferences in the field of social statistics.

Before passing to the topic proper, it might be well to specify the time limits of the past and the present to be discussed as those embracing the economic trends in the advanced industrial countries of the world since the end of the 18th century, with primary emphasis on the more recent decades. And diagnosis of the present will here be applied to the prospective development for the next generation, that is for the next twenty-five to thirty years. The general question that we face is, to what extent can we consider the secular movements observed in the past and stretching into the present, as continuous and persistent? The answer to this question must be largely guesswork; but naturally it must take into consideration the forces that produced these secular movements in the past, for upon our view as to the persistence of these forces must rest our judgment as to their continuity in the future. I shall then first, state briefly what seem to be the most important economic tendencies in the past; next, indicate what the effect of the present emergency on these tendencies is likely to be; and third, conclude with a judgment as to the likelihood of their persistence.

II

The major economic tendencies in the past, as here defined, and for the industrial countries here dealt with, may be listed as follows:

1. The rapid growth of population was accompanied by a rapid decline in the percentage rate of growth. For most countries this high rate of population growth was due largely to a significant cut in the death rate, the result of technical and medical progress that took place in the latter mostly between 1780 and 1820 and between 1880 and 1930. The decline in the percentage rate of population growth in the countries here dealt with, especially observable since the 1880's, was due to a substantial cut in the birth rates. Since these industrially advanced countries could have increased their population by allowing and promoting immigration, another factor in the decline of their population growth was their restrictive immigration policy.

2. The extensive expansion of the industrial system that we associate with industrial capitalism has reached certain limits, limits true within the present social framework. Given our organization in national states and international relations, the areas for extensive expansion have been preempted so that widening their limits can be effected only by revolutionary changes in national and international organization. It is quite possible that such changes are imminent; and that at least one factor contributory to the disturbances that we witness today is this limitation of extensive expansion by political and economic organization and the resulting attempts to break the fetters in order to open up areas for more intensive exploita-

tion. But as far as the past is concerned, the disappearance of the frontier in the United States, the partition of Africa at the end of the 19th and during the 20th centuries, and the apparent complete absorption of the free areas in the world into the network of national sovereignties, all these mean that expansion of the industrial system into backward areas is contingent upon radical changes in public policy in these areas.

3. In the industrialized countries of the world, the cumulative effect of technical progress in a number of important industries has brought about a situation where further progress of similar scope cannot be reasonably expected. The industries that have matured technologically account for a progressively increasing ratio of the total production of the economy. Their maturity does not imply a complete cessation of further technological improvements, but it does imply that economic effects of further improvements will necessarily be more limited than in the past. Vigorous economic growth and technical progress in the immediate future are, therefore, contingent upon the appearance of new industries. Statistical studies of these industries in the recent past showing the rapidity with which they become absorbed in the general stream of economic development indicate that the periods during which these industries serve as expansive impulses for the national economy are, as a whole, becoming progressively shorter. There are obvious reasons why this should be the case, for the increased supply of free funds and capital stock of a country means that any promising innovation can be fully exploited in a much shorter period than during the decades when the industrial system was young and the supply of free capital limited.

4. With the growth in national and in per capita income there have been definite shifts in the composition of the national product. There has been secular stability in the share of capital formation in national income; but in some of the older countries, such as England, there is little question that the relative share in the 20th century has been lower than in the 19th. This is especially true if we include domestic capital formation alone and exclude the flow of funds abroad for

capital investment. In this country the decline in the share of capital formation appears only in connection with the recent depression. Whether this betokens a lasting trend is a matter for serious conjecture.

5. A correlated shift occurred in the composition of the part of national income called consumers' outlay, in favor of goods termed semi-luxuries and in general dispensable, at least over short periods. This meant an increase in the share of durable consumers' goods as well as of certain types of services not embodied in commodities.

6. There has been a notable reduction in the fully competitive areas of the national economies. This reduction was produced by: (a) the appearance of monopolistic tendencies in industries that had been freely competitive earlier, a trend observable in this country since the 1880's; (b) the growth in relative importance of industries that, because of their cost and demand structure, are not competitive and so call for close regulation. These are primarily the public utilities, whose significant growth in the industrial system began with the steam railroads and which have become increasingly important with the growth of utilities connected with power production and various types of urban service. (c) There has been a definite increase in the economic activity of governments as a result partly of these same monopolistic tendencies in the private sector of the economy, partly of changes in international relations. This increasing degree of restrictive organization of the system of economic enterprise was accompanied also by increasing organization among the laboring classes, as well as among other groups in the economy.

7. Some interpreters of the economic scene have suggested that these various trends in the contents and organization of economic activity have resulted in increased relative overcapacity, i.e. the relative share of both capital and human resources that, in the long run, remains unused in the production of goods. But this is a matter for which no general and tested statement seems possible at present. Monopolistic organization, high overhead costs, greater cyclical and other

short term variability in demand, do tend to be accompanied by a lasting core of idle capital and labor. But, on the other hand, free and vigorous competition, stimulated or accompanied by rapid technical changes, also produced in the past considerable obsolescence of capital and human skills and contributed to structural unemployment of resources.

8. In the area of international relations one notes the most spectacular shift of all. The period of comparative peace and of free movement of commodities, capital, and people, which characterized the 19th century from the 1830's to the 1880's or 90's, proved to be short-lived. In historical retrospect this situation appears to have been due to a fortunate combination of circumstances in which the industrially advanced country, England, was ready to export its surplus on a peaceful exchange basis to industrially less advanced countries. With the emergence of other industrialized countries—the U.S. on the one hand and Germany on the other—this period came to an end, and the world returned to the state of chronic armed conflict that characterized the European scene for most of the centuries prior to the 19th. The impediments toward free flow of goods, capital, and people have become progressively more formidable in recent decades, and there is no need to document the story with references to high tariff walls, restricted immigration, imperialistic tendencies of the flag following trade, etc.

This, in sum, is a picture of the most prominent economic tendencies observed in the immediate past and in the present. Obviously, the list is incomplete, and does not dwell upon certain corollary trends. Some of these are quite apparent in the field of credit and banking relations, in the disturbance of the international organization of trade and the international monetary standards; in the shift in the role of the banking systems from that of suppliers of short term business credit to suppliers of government and consumer credit; in the changed role of the stock market, formerly so important as the engine for mobilizing savings, and later for facilitating the formation of economic giants. Other tendencies are apparent in the general psychology and motivation of both business enterprises and economic activity in general—a shift from an atmosphere of free progressive expansion to one of uneasiness that further opportunities were being exhausted, a greater desire for stability and for the safeguarding of gains already made. Nor does the picture stress interrelations among the various tendencies noted. Obviously, the emergence of monopolistic characteristics in some industries depended upon the relative slowing down of revolutionary technical changes, and in turn affected the latter. The growth of domestic monopolies had a significant effect upon changes in the character of international relations, which in turn served to intensify restrictions upon free competition within national economies. Changes in population growth conditioned other tendencies affecting the volume and composition of the national product and the characteristics of economic organization and were, in their turn, conditioned by them. But these interrelations are quite obvious, and with this picture of the economic tendencies of the past and the immediate present before us, it should be possible to discuss, next, the probable impact of the present emergency, and then the question of continuity of these tendencies, of their possible persistence in the future.

III

In considering emergencies such as the present (allowing for this country's participation in the armed conflict), we are led to fairly determinate results if we exclude rigidly any of the post-emergency consequences, (such as armed victory or defeat and their corollaries). While the emergency exists, while the conflict is being waged and its successful or unsuccessful solution is not yet determined, some changes reenforce and others offset the secular tendencies so far noted. Thus the armed conflict, while it lasts, reduces materially the rate of population increase by restricting the birth rate, by increasing the death rate, and by barring immigration. The strains that accompany conflict also reenforce the tendencies toward restriction of free competition. The larger enterprises are likely to gain in importance because they are more ready and able to expand rapidly in response to pressing needs, and because the public authorities can deal more easily with a few large plants than with a multitude of small ones. Thus the inevitable expansion of government activities during war emergency not only represents in itself a marked increase in the weight of monopolistic and authoritarian elements, but serves also to increase them in the private sector of the economy.

However other peacetime trends are retarded during the war emergency. The tendency of technical progress to be damped as the industrial system reaches maturity is offset by the pressure for vigorous technical changes to overcome the limited capacity of the industrial system. The share of consumers' outlay in national income is restricted and that of capital greatly increased, even though it is the type of capital that contributes only partially to the country's peace time productive capacity. The peace time shift in consumers' outlay towards the more dispensable goods is blocked and even reversed by the pressure of war needs and the necessity of tightening the belt.

It is thus possible to observe and foresee the *direction* of the effects of a war emergency. But it is difficult to evaluate the quantitative magnitude of these effects, to estimate them in terms of reduced birth rates and increased death rates, of reduced free economic initiative and increased authoritarian elements, of reduced ultimate consumption and peace time capital formation and of increased outlay of scarce resources on armaments, and on other items that cannot directly contribute to present or future ultimate consumption. Yet any view of the economic tendencies in the post-emergency future must be determined, in part, by the assumed magnitude of the dislocations produced by the emergency. For the first phase of the post-emergency period will obviously be dominated by the need to repair the damages and to satisfy the long starved peace time needs. And we must always bear in mind the possibility that the dislocations produced by the present emergency may be so grave as to result in a drastic and lasting change in the whole style of social organization.

It is thus necessary to posit some limits to the magnitude of possible dislocations produced by the present emergency before we can evaluate economic tendencies in the future. And we must also postulate an outcome of the present conflict in terms of some distribution of economic and political power and some general characteristics of international relations in the immediate future. For unless we do so, there is little point in trying to consider the economic trends in the future development of any one national economy.

Finally, it is necessary to make assumptions with regard to another important element in the economy viz., technological change, before we can see clearly any lines of economic development ahead. Can we assume that a revolutionary change in the technological basis of our economy is likely? And the economy here dealt with refers specifically to mature and industrially advanced countries, with fully developed technologies of the modern style, rather than to countries in which the Industrial Revolution is still to come, and in which a *new* technological revolution is not of such immediately vital import.

IV

The three questions raised just now are, as to the likelihood of: first, an internal revolution in the characteristics of economic organization; second, of a revolution in international relations; and third, of a revolution in technology. Without postulating an answer to these three questions, it is impossible to discuss economic tendencies in the immediate future. Now the answers given to these questions will determine whether or not the secular tendencies discussed above are likely to continue into the future. If we answer all three questions for this country by saying that neither an internal, international, nor technological revolution seems likely, it follows that the economic tendencies observed in the past are likely to continue into the future. And it is precisely this answer that I am inclined to give, for reasons stated below.

1. As to the magnitude of the effect of the present emergency, I shall assume that it will be substantially greater than of World War I. It took this country well over five years to readjust after 1918; it may well take us a decade to recover after the present emergency. But I also assume that the attendant strains and dislocations are not likely to be sufficiently grave to produce a revolutionary change in the social system. In short, the most likely assumption for this country is the survival of the capitalist system characterized by private property, domination of profit incentives, freedom of labor and a democratic system of government.

The basic reason for this assumption is briefly that the magnitude of the strain faced by this country is not so large, nor the dislocations involved so grave, as to threaten the social fabric. True, a defense outlay of over $100 billion is not to be neglected. But in a country free from armed invasion and with our productive potential it is not such an overall burden that it may lead to a breakdown of a social system of long standing and acceptance.

2. I shall assume that this country will survive the war emergency; that whether or not totalitarian systems will remain in the world after this war, organization into national or supranational (but not world wide) units will survive; and that international competition between young and old, growing and mature countries will continue in one form or another. The reasons for these *obiter dicta* differ. I have already mentioned why I expect this country to survive this emergency. And the lesson of the historical past, if there be any lesson, certainly points to continuation of international competition and strife. Nobody has yet succeeded in disproving the wide benefits of the fullest free trade, provided that human beings of different national or cultural groups are viewed as equal. Yet mankind has never accepted this assumption. We cannot analyze here the factors that make the horizon of group consciousness so limited on the part of human beings. The fact

is that through centuries mankind lived, hunted, and fought as distinct groups with members of one treating often the members of the other groups as beyond the ken of rational and reasonable behavior. To proceed on the more realistic assumption—even if mankind succeeds in abolishing sanguinary armed conflicts there will still be an element of effective international competition which will lead to struggle between national or supra-national groups for a better place in the sun.

3. The answer to the question bearing upon the likelihood of a technological revolution is most difficult. And yet if by a technological revolution we mean a radical change in the laws of production, such as a change to a new and widespread source of power or more widely used industrial raw materials, it seems most plausible to assume that there will be no such revolution in the immediate future. What with all the reports of bombarding the atom and of uranium 235, etc., one can never be sure. Yet, lacking a more plausible and interpretable assumption, I shall have to assume that there will be no such revolution.

Given survival of the present form of social organization, continuance of international competition, and absence of revolutionary changes in technological bases of civilization, most of the economic tendencies observed in the past and reenforced by the armed conflict will persist in the future and perhaps become more prominent. The damping of the rate of population growth produced by a declining birth rate is likely to continue if only because the war itself will have introduced an element of uncertainty, shaken up the customary expectations sufficiently to make the opportunity costs of raising children higher than before. It should also be noted that the lower birth rate is a process that began in the upper social circles and has gradually penetrated downwards, that this process of the small family habit affecting wider and wider groups of people has by no means exhausted itself, and that there are no apparent factors likely to terminate it soon. The German experiments with raising the birth rate, while temporarily successful, have been obviously attained at a considerable vital cost elsewhere.

In general, so long as the social system places much emphasis upon the achievement of the individual as an individual, the obstacles toward the individuals' proper functioning as members of the race will always be formidable.

It also seems plausible to assume that restriction of free competitive areas and increased spread of monopolistic and authoritarian tendencies are likely to continue. The immediate post-war emergency will require much greater public participation in economic activity and control than before the war. The combined residues of the depression and the war will leave public authorities with budgets and activities that for a long time to come will represent a larger share of the national income than before 1929. Industries reaching maturity and acquiring monopolistic attributes will continue to gain in proportional weight. And it is doubtful whether the only element that might offset the increasing weight of these rigid elements in our economic life—a rapid and vigorous growth of new industries or new areas in which conditions favorable to free competition exist—will be easily attained.

This brings us to one of the most moot questions concerning the economic tendencies in a forecastable future. What is the likelihood of a satisfactory emergence of new industries, of new areas of expansion that would carry forward the vigorous development of the national economy of industrial countries? This question is raised with reference specifically to mature countries such as Great Britain and the United States. For the younger countries that possess the population and resources for vigorous industrial development, the future economic task is quite clear. For such countries as Russia, India, China, the obvious economic task is to introduce elements of the industrial revolution and attempt to bring these potentially rich countries up to the level of other advanced countries of the world. The question applies to the developed countries. Can we expect in them a growth of investment opportunities sufficient to carry forward the national product at the rapid pace at which it has grown in the past?

The stagnationist theory, advocated most vigorously by Alvin Hansen, has become rather prominent of late. It claims that, because of the damping in population growth and the exhaustion of opportunities for extensive expansion, we are threatened with a dearth of private investment opportunities sufficient to absorb savings, and hence with a danger that the national product will chronically fall short of the levels warranted by our productive capacity. To offset this, a greater development of public works, i.e. of public investment opportunities to supplement the private, is recommended. Though we grant that population is not likely to grow as fast in the future as in the past, that the frontiers of extensive expansion have disappeared, that monopolistic tendencies in the private sector of the economy are likely to grow stronger rather than weaker, yet the likelihood of secular stagnation, if by this we mean a failure of *per capita* income to continue its rise, does not seem inevitable. Even if we do not allow for the possibility of a basic technological revolution, the intensive technical changes that have occurred or will occur during the war emergency may provide a sufficient backlog of change to warrant adequate private investment for one or two decades after the emergency is over (even disregarding the stimulus of demand starved during the war). There is no basis for assuming that the contributions of scientific progress will not be sufficient to sustain the increase in per capita income enjoyed by us in the past. It is true that with a marked damping in population growth and restriction of opportunities for extensive expansion, our *total* national product may not grow at as rapid a rate as in the past. But this does not mean that the secular rise in the per capita income will not continue.

In this connection the claims that may be made upon this country by virtue of its international position after the war should not be overlooked. It is quite possible that after the war, we shall be forced to devote a larger share of our national product to capital formation substantially different in character from that which characterized our economy heretofore. We may have to invest more in military expenditures; and while such investment will be necessarily public in character, it will be undertaken not to supplement private investment opportunities but because pressing considerations of safety will compel us to do so. We may also be forced to consider the whole question of investments abroad, partly because of our place in the concert of nations and partly as a contribution to the further economic development of such other areas in the world as need it badly. The question may well arise as to the extent to which the United States should follow in the footsteps of England and devote a large proportion of its capital surplus to the industrialization of the undeveloped countries, thus providing an outlet for its products and permitting work at full capacity. Both possibilities carry with them claims upon our savings, demands for capital investment that will be additional to the private investment opportunities within the country, even if we do not assume a public works policy designed to fill the gap between private savings and private domestic investments. Under such conditions, secular stagnation in the sense of a significant decline in our *per capita* production does not seem an imminent threat.

If then we continue with a total national product growing at perhaps a slower pace than in the past, but with per capita product increasing at a satisfactory rate, some tendencies in the distribution of the national product observed in the past may well continue. The share of the product going into capital formation may remain fairly stable, or may decline but slightly. The continued growth in per capita income may mean a continued shift in the distribution of consumers' outlay in favor of the more dispensable goods, thus unfortunately increasing the areas in which ultimate demand is sensitive to fluctuations in business conditions and contributing to greater short term instability.

V

If we consider this prospective development, and look beyond the task that will face us immediately after the war emergency is over, two large groups of problems loom ahead.

The first concerns the international situation and the role
played by this country in it. It seems fairly clear that the
U. S. will have to play a more active role in the concert of
nations than it did in the past. It is likely to emerge as the
industrial leader in a disturbed world, with complex responsibilities; and looking beyond, if the growth of the total national
product and our population is likely to slow down, and if we
cannot envisage a basic technological revolution in which this
country will be the pioneer, then it is likely that the rate of
our economic progress will become inferior to the rate of economic progress of some other countries, and that we shall suffer
a recession in our differential economic standing similar to that
experienced by England (particularly prominent after 1880).
Both eventualities mean the abandonment of a condition of
splendid isolation and the extension of the sphere of active
foreign policy as steps designed to prevent unpleasant consequences of irresponsible leadership or of a lessening advantageous differential economic position. The problems that will
arise will concern primarily the best ways and means of pur-
suing such a foreign policy. And we badly need some imaginative thinking in this field, to grope towards a system of
international policies in which the natural shifts among major
national units in their leadership in economic progress could
be accomplished without the drastic consequences that armed
conflict brings in its wake.

The second group of problems refers to the domestic situation and relates to ways and means by which a high per capita income economy, with its attendant high level of consumption per
unit and its dynamic area of private investment, can be kept from
suffering drastic cyclical depressions of the type we experienced
in the 1930's. This problem will have to be attacked with due
cognizance of all other longer term trends that will accompany
this growth of income and consumption per capita.

In wrestling with these two groups of problems, public agencies will have to be called upon to assume greater and more
varied tasks than in the past. Governmental activity may thus
have to be more extensive than heretofore. A more vigorous

foreign policy necessarily means a more active and potent central government; and to develop various offsets to the undesirable short term variability of domestic levels of economic activity requires a government that is much more than a mere night watchman of our security and property. Inevitable as such increased governmental functions are, the possible dangers are also great. The difficulties inherent in the two groups of problems mentioned above and the need for imaginative and constructive work in evolving the proper methods for their solution are due to the danger potential in further extension of government activity. The danger lies in the possibility of control of the governmental apparatus by interests and goals not in accord with those of society at large. In this country, as in many others, the development and crystallization of monopolistic groups reenforces elements that are not actually interested in preservation of economic freedom and individual initiative. We must recognize that foreign policy, even in democratic countries in the past, is an arm of governmental activity imperfectly controlled by the desires and interests of the wider groups of the population. The prospective increase in governmental activity, both in domestic and foreign areas, raises the problem of how to strengthen the mechanism of control to offset the dangers of authoritarianism. And it need not be stressed that domestic and foreign policy are interrelated, so that maldirection of one means maldirection in the other.

Thus, even if we assume, as we do, the absence of revolutionary changes in both domestic organization and international position of this country in the concert of powers, and whether or not we assume a revolutionary shift in the technological basis of our economy, the continuation of the present economic tendencies will raise a series of formidable problems. Familiar institutions and patterns of economic life may prove inadequate to deal with maladjustments created within the country by a high consumption, high savings economy, and in the international scene by our new role as industrial leader in a disturbed world.

In these circumstances, social scientists, statisticians among them, are charged with important responsibility. All of us, immersed in our technical specialties, are involuntarily tempted to accept what *is* for what *should be,* and too easily take for granted the continued existence of the framework within which we solve our special problems. Just as the classical economists tended to identify the system which they saw around them with the immutable and natural state, and tended to extrapolate boldly tendencies observed within the narrow confines of the English isles into the distant future; just as the marginal utility theorists, in ostrich-like fashion, refused to deal with the problems of long term changes in the economy and spun out their analysis on the assumption of constancy of the social system; so we statisticians are all too prone to deal with special problems on the easy assumption of the persistence of the wider framework, and turn away from scrutiny of these larger areas. There is no one as revolutionary as a scientist within the narrow field of his specialty, and no one potentially as conservative in the broader field that provides the basic postulates for his specialty. The result is that the broader problems have often been approached primarily by people with axes to grind, and important and established bodies of evidence fell neglected by the wayside.

In the social sciences we have need of a new group of workers who combine the mastery of detail and careful procedures essential to the specialized research scientist with the wider horizon of the historian and social philosopher; and we have need on the part of our specialist groups of greater awareness of the variety of historical experience and the mutability of the social framework within which lie the more narrowly defined phenomena that they study. With specific reference to the statistical tools and techniques for dealing with social data, one might suggest that the statistician needs to be receptive to the results of the analytical theorist, to the suggestions of the student of the historical scene, and even to the claims and clamor of the reformers. And he must beware especially of the danger of identifying mechanically derived lines with trends; calculated ratios with immutable and natural laws of constitution, and correlation coefficients with inviolable laws of causation and association.

11

FOREIGN ECONOMIC RELATIONS OF THE UNITED STATES AND THEIR IMPACT UPON THE DOMESTIC ECONOMY *

A Review of Long Term Trends

I. SETTING OF THE PROBLEM

A given country's view of the rest of the world reveals a picture of variety and complexity. In this rest of the world, nations differ widely with respect to size and composition, ways of managing the economy and attitudes to other national units. This diversity is, in turn, the result of differences in the supply of natural resources, in historical heritage, in the pattern of social institutions governing economic life. And the picture never stands still; nations wax and wane in economic power, and apply this power in changing ways to other members of the world community.

The impact of the rest of the world upon the domestic economy of a given country may be viewed as the sum total of three types of change. The first is change in the given country as compared with the rest of the world. If a country grows more or less rapidly than others, if the volume or composition of its production exhibits trends different from those of the

* Read April 22, 1948, before the American Philosophical Society in the Symposium on the Relation between International Affairs and the Traditional American Scene.

Reprinted by permission from Proceedings of the American Philosophical Society, Vol. 92, No. 4, October 1948, pp. 222-243.

world at large, this in itself would change the economic relations between it and other countries—even if these latter stand still. The second is change in other countries; even if we unrealistically assume perfect stability of economic life in the given country, change in the rest of the world would force changes in the relations between the given country and the sum of all others. Finally, there may be shifts in the technological and institutional means for economic contacts among different countries: other conditions being equal, changes in techniques of transportation or communication or in institutional devices by which economic contacts among nations are made will spell changes in a country's international economic relations.

Still by way of introduction, one must recognize the various forms that economic relations of a given country with the rest of the world assume. On the narrow definition of "economic," such relations are confined to movements of commodities and services across national boundaries, and to the complex network of claims and obligations built up in connection with this trans-boundary movement of goods. These are the flows recorded in what economists call the international balance of payments—on both short and long term accounts. But to confine the relations of a given economy with the rest of the world to just these flows of goods and correlative claims and obligations is to miss some important channels of interaction. We should, in the first instance, add the movement of men, immigrants and emigrants—not tourists (whose expenditures are covered in the international balance of payments). These movements of men, in addition to those of goods and capital, comprise the peaceful type of economic relations—peaceful not in the sense that they could not be employed for warlike purposes (as they have been by some countries in recent years), but because they *can* be used for peaceful intercourse; and in fact have so been used until the very recent two or three decades.

Wars have not been usually treated as economic acts. They were ordinarily viewed by economists as aberrations that might temporarily modify the working of a country's economy, but that are otherwise too transient and "irrational" to merit analysis as integral parts of economic processes. However one might sympathize with such a position, one cannot exclude wars from consideration of the recent impact of the rest of the world upon a country's domestic economy. War conflicts also involve movements of men, commodities, services, and capital —but not by the type of consent that is expressed in a free market. The warring nations export men, commodities, and capital not because their enemies (the importers) want them, but because the exporters hope to achieve thereby a forceful change in the international situation favorable to themselves. It may seem fanciful to talk of war as export, and involuntary import, of men, commodities, and obligations. But it is because wars involve tremendous expenditures of economic resources and result in a changed network of claims that they are so important in any consideration of *economic* relations of a given country with the rest of the world. If wars were fought by oratorical contests involving few economic resources, resulting in purely symbolic gains and defeats (such as occur in the Olympic games), there would be much less reason, if any, for economists to be concerned with them.

Our attention is confined to the *material* flows across boundaries, with little discussion of spiritual flows—in spite of their importance. But even with this limitation, the picture is complex. The separate and combined effects of changes within the country, changes in the rest of the world, and changes in the techniques of international contact must be traced both in the various peaceful types of flow across boundaries (migration, foreign trade, other current transactions, capital flows) and the warlike types. Clearly, the analysis below can be little more than a sketchy outline, raising many questions to which no definite answers can be given.

II. Pre-World-War I Trends of Migration, Trade, and Capital

A long look back carries with it the danger of oversimplifying the past and creating a nostalgia for its simplicity as contrasted with the vexing complexity of the present. Nevertheless, in dealing with the recent impact of international conditions upon the domestic economy of the United States, we must take a look at the long term development of this country, and at the pattern of economic relations with the rest of the world that accompanied such development. It is only against the background of such a past that one can see clearly the recent trends and raise questions as to their implications.

The development of the United States, like that of all countries that grew as economic units during the last one and a half to two centuries, can be described as industrialization, i.e., extension in application of technical and social arts based upon empirical science. Beginning with a stage in which the country was predominantly agricultural, the extension of more advanced techniques served both to raise productivity in agriculture and to develop new industries (industries here being understood broadly) which permitted a better utilization of agricultural products and the employment in other pursuits of the growing population and of the labor force released from agriculture. Because the nature of human wants is such that, with the growing supply of goods per capita, an increasingly smaller proportion of consumer needs is satisfied by agricultural products, the growing product per capita meant a decreasing proportion in the national economy of agriculture and extractive industries in general; and a correspondingly higher proportion of non-agricultural activities—manufacturing, construction, and transportation in the earlier phases; service industries (trade, professional and personal services of various description, and government) in the later phases. Industrialization can be defined formally as a sustained increase in the proportion of a country's economy devoted to pursuits other than agriculture, accompanied by a marked increase in total production and associated with the spread of techniques based upon empirical science. All three elements are important in the process; but the spread of modern technology, physical and social, was the base; growth in production its most important result; and the diversion away from agriculture a corollary consequence, even though superficially most conspicuous.

The economic growth of the United States can thus be defined on the quantitative side as a sustained increase in total output; and on the structural side, as the extension of scientific technology resulting in diversification away from agriculture, the emergence of a host of new industries of urban character, rapid growth of productivity in all industries including agriculture, and the urbanization of the country. Such a diversified and ramified process would obviously affect also economic relations with the rest of the world; and we may consider briefly what these effects were on the movements of men, commodities, and capital across boundaries; and on the more warlike type of contact, either in aggression or in defense.

(a) The effect of economic growth upon voluntary emigration and immigration would be different according as the impact of industrialization is upon an old and settled country or upon a young one, with a large supply of free land. In either case, industrialization would result, at least in the early phases, in cutting death rates without an immediate decline in birth rates thus producing what demographers call the "swarming" of population; and also in dislocating agriculture wherever it is already settled, by the introduction of new techniques in the settled areas or by the extension of agriculture to new areas where higher productivity would mean disastrous competition to the old areas. Hence in both old and new countries the early phases of industrialization are accompanied by considerable population pressure, with dislocation in the old agricultural areas—both factors producing a strong flow of population to the cities and the new industries, a movement that feeds the rapid process of urbanization. But while these internal trends were fairly common in character, if not equal in magnitude, in both old and new countries, their effects on external migration were different. In the old countries, these movements resulted in emigration. At least a portion of the dislocated population moved out of the country rather than undergo the trials and tribulations of proletarization in their native cities. In the new countries, the effect was immigration. Not only was the available free land sufficient for internal migration of population dislocated from the settled areas, but the demands of the growing economy called for more population than natural increase alone could provide.

The unusual record of free international migration during the century preceding World War I, and the major role played by the United States as the main recipient of these voluntary migration flows, are well known.[1] They were not completely free; immigration from Asia was restricted in the 1880's. But with this significant exception, the flow was limited only by economic and technical factors both of which tended to become obstacles of diminishing importance. There was a happy conjunction by which, as one older European country after another entered the orbit of industrialization, at least part of its displaced population found room in the New World; and the New World, United States in particular, found use for the labor force thus made available.

The role of free immigration in both the economic development of this country and in setting the pattern of economic relations of thé United States with the rest of the world has

---

[1] A statistical account of nineteenth and twentieth century migrations is presented in *International migrations,* edited by Walter F. Willcox, I and II, National Bureau of Economic Research, publications Nos. 14 and 18, N. Y., 1929 and 1931. For the United States proper, a brief summary and analysis are given in Thompson, W. S. and Whelpton, G. K., *Population trends in the United States,* Chap. IX, N. Y., McGraw-Hill, 1933. A useful estimate of net immigration into the United States is also provided in Rossiter, W. S., *Increase of population in the United States, 1910-1920,* Appendix C, Census Monograph I, Government Printing Office, Washington 1922. Data for recent years can easily be found in the annual issues of *Statistical Abstract of the United States.*

never been fully analyzed. The literature in the field, charac-
teristically classified under the heading "immigration problem," with emphasis on *problem,* would appeal to impartial
analysts as largely a tissue of prejudiced opinions and garbled
statistics. True, in the short view, immigration was a problem;
and the long view seldom finds adequate representation in the
vociferous discussion that day-to-day questions arouse. I am
not concerned here with controversial questions as to whether
immigration has inhibited reproduction of the native population, or as to presumptive differences in quality among various
immigrant stocks. But for the purposes of the present discussion it should be emphasized that immigration did provide an
important force in the rapid economic growth of this country;
that it constituted outlets in the solution of problems of economic growth in European countries, clearly reflected in the
shift of immigration sources from one area to another following the shifting course of industrialization in Europe; and that
it made for a climate of international relations, economic and
other, that goes far to explain both the relatively peaceful
character of the century and the advantageous position which
the United States occupied in the world. Free immigration
meant free enterprise and political democracy in their most
conspicuous manifestation; and its cessation is an important
element in the retrogression of these institutions in recent
decades. The very diversity of national origins in the immigration to this country, a diversity that was much less characteristic of the immigration to other new countries (such as
parts of the British empire or the Latin American republics)
meant an exemplification of one world in the United States
which gave this country much greater weight in the affairs of
the world than either its economic or political magnitude,
vis-a-vis other great powers, warranted.

(*b*) We turn now to the effects of economic growth and
industrialization upon the flow of commodities and services
across boundaries. One obvious effect was the marked increase
in total output and the rapid improvement in means of transportation and communication which led to much larger move-

ment of goods across boundaries than would have been feasible in earlier times. Another effect is also clear, although less obvious. As a country enters the phase of industrialization and advances industrially more rapidly than the rest of the world, the composition of the goods that move across its boundaries changes. Whereas in its pre-industrial phase it exports raw materials and imports industrial products, with its industrial advance its imports gradually shift to raw materials and its exports to manufactured articles. Similarly, in pre-industrial or early phases of industrialization, the balance of services (as distinct from commodities), mainly for international transportation, communication, insurance, and investment are against the country; as it becomes industrialized, the balance of services might begin to move more in its favor. Last but not least, a country that enters the phase of industrialization later than others ordinarily tries to protect its young and growing industries against the competition of older and more industrialized countries by a system of tariffs—which it may or may not retain upon reaching a high state of industrialization.

All these trends, with some modifications, characterized the development of the United States.[2] Its foreign trade and other items in its current transactions grew prodigiously in absolute volume as the country grew and as its production expanded; foreign trade shifted from exports chiefly of raw materials and raw foodstuffs to exports dominated by manufactures, accompanied by an opposite shift in the structure of imports. The role of the country as the champion of protection is well known. The distinctive element lay in the sphere of services. After the Civil War, this country did not regain its important position in oceanic transportation; nor has it attempted, until after World War I, to play much of a part in other interna-

[2] The basic summary data on the volume of foreign trade can be found in the annual issues of the *Statistical Abstract of the United States*. The pioneer and only basic study of the balance of payments of this country for the long term period prior to World War I is that by Bullock, C. J., Williams, J. H., and Tucker, R. S., The balance of trade of the United States, *Rev. Econ. Statistics*, July 1919.

tional service industries. The main reason seems to lie in the absorption of all resources in rapid extension over the continent and in the growth of the domestic economy—an effort that left little room for challenging England or some of England's later competitors as international carrier, factor, or investor.

Some consequences of the gearing of trans-boundary flow of commodities and services to the needs of rapid growth of the domestic economy in this country deserve emphasis. The United States played a major part in the international movement of men during the century preceding World War I. It played a much smaller part in the international movement of commodities and services. Data are easily available for commodity trade alone, for the period since 1876.[3] But for this limited canvass, some important conclusions emerge. The first is that the share of the United States in total world trade is much less than its share in the world's total production. Thus, for the period extending roughly from the middle of the 1920's to the middle of the 1930's, the share of the United States in total world production was close to 25 per cent; the share in world trade was only somewhat over 10 per cent. In the case of manufactured products, the discrepancy is even greater. Our share in world manufactures in the inter-war period was roughly 40 per cent; our share in world trade in manufactures, between 10 and 12 per cent. This means that the rest of the world contributed a proportionately greater share of its output to world trade as a whole than did the United States. This fact is easy to explain. Total production in the rest of the world, particularly of manufactures, was in the hands of countries smaller than the United States. The ratio of across-the-boundary trade to domestic production varies, in general, inversely with the size of the country; a high ratio in small countries

[3] The data are taken largely from *Industrialization and foreign trade*, League of Nations, 1945. The estimate of the share of the United States in total world production is approximate, and is based upon the estimates by Colin Clark (see his *Conditions of economic progress*, London, Macmillan, 1940).

(like Belgium, Netherlands, Switzerland, Sweden, etc.) and a low ratio in countries with large land masses and huge population and production machines. Once the United States expanded from the strip of land along the Atlantic coast to a vast continental country, its proportionate rate of participation, i.e., the proportion of its total output directly engaged in foreign trade was bound to be low.

The second statistical conclusion is somewhat unexpected. The share of the United States in world trade has been quite steady through the decades preceding World War I, hovering at slightly above 10 per cent. Even after World War I, the increase in that share to 14 per cent in 1926-1929, accounted for by the pressure upon the United States to contribute to world reconstruction, disappears during the depression; and the pre-World-War II years are marked by percentages again not much above 10. Such stability was maintained in spite of the fact that during the decades since 1870 the United States was growing more rapidly than the rest of the world. This suggests that the stable share was the resultant of two trends that offset each other: the growth of the share of the United States in total world production and a decline in the share of foreign trade to total production in the United States, a decline that was much more marked than the trend in the ratio of world trade to world production.

Both of the preceding conclusions seem important in understanding the foreign trade relations of the United States with the rest of the world. This country relied less than the rest of the world on foreign trade, strategic as the latter may have been to it; and its relative contribution to the world's foreign trade remained stable through the decades back to the 1870's. Whatever increasing independence from foreign countries this country was establishing, and whatever limitation upon international economic cooperation *via* trade this country's tariff policies were imposing, these were offset by its very rapid growth. One might claim that in a sense the world, as a partner in international trade, was not a loser because the United States chose to force the growth of its domestic economy by protective policy, as over against an alternative policy of less protection and of possibly less rapid growth of its domestic economy. This is a challengeable thesis. Yet there is some ground for arguing that a free trade policy would have kept the United States more predominantly agricultural, growing at a much slower rate; and that this slower growth, even if combined with our greater participation in international trade, might not have yielded larger foreign trade volumes than the combination, actually realized, of more rapid economic growth with a lower rate of participation in world trade.

(c) Like most countries that were in the nineteenth century in the early phase of industrialization, the United States enjoyed the assistance of foreign credits in assembling the resources needed for the development of its industries. The consistent net debtorship position of the United States on international accounts prior to World War I is well known.[4] Less widely recognized is the fact that neither the gross international indebtedness of this country nor the net (i.e., after deducting U. S. claims upon foreign countries) has been large, either in comparison with the total pool of international capital investments; or in comparison with the total capital in this country owned by its residents, even if we limit capital to reproducible wealth alone (i.e., exclude land and other nonreproducible natural resources). Prior to World War I our *gross* foreign obligations amounted, at their peak, to some $7 billion, and, in so far as crude estimates of wealth permit a comparison, were never more than one tenth of reproducible wealth (or one twentieth of total wealth); *net* foreign obligations never exceeded $4 billion, and accounted for a correspondingly lower proportion of domestic wealth. Moreover, while the statistics of total international capital investment are none too adequate, it appears that placements in this country never amounted to much more than one tenth of world placements by creditor countries.

[4] A full treatment of the position of the United States on international capital accounts back to the early nineteenth century is provided in Lewis, C., *America's stake in international investments*, Washington, Brookings Institution, 1938.

Since a rapidly developing country provides such splendid opportunities for capital investments, it may at first appear surprising that investment funds did not flow into the United States in much greater volume during the century preceding World War I. But it must be remembered that prior to the recent era of direct investments (i.e., when foreign investment takes the form of direct purchase and ownership of plants, land, and other real assets) credits in a foreign country could be accumulated only by importing commodities or services without a *quid pro quo* in commodities or services received. This meant that a borrower country could build up a foreign debt only by a consistently unfavorable balance in commodity trade, or in the flow of services, or in both. Prior to the 1870's the United States did have a fairly consistent unfavorable trade balance (i.e., an excess of imports over exports). But even this excess was relatively small, and the possession of a merchant marine capable of active participation in international trade served to keep down the unfavorable balance on the service account. During this period also, European countries imported a great deal of capital, and provided competition to the United States as an international borrower. After the Civil War the vigorous growth of production in the United States, combined with the protective system, resulted in a consistently favorable balance of commodity trade, and under these conditions accumulation of a debt balance on the international account could come only from either the service account or from direct investments. The former is naturally a limited source of international indebtedness because of the small ratio of international services to the total product of any country of fair size; and the latter was inhibited by the distance between the would-be direct investor (in the European creditor countries) and the United States, as well as by the fact that funds available for direct investment at that time were only a limited proportion of all funds available for placement in the international investment market.

Whatever the reasons, and the suggestions advanced above merely offer a tentative explanation, the fact was that the United States played a limited role in the network of international capital investments; and that, as in the case of foreign trade, its share of participation in it was fairly low relative to its size. In summarizing this and other aspects of peaceful flows across boundaries as they appear in the long view, one may state it, perhaps too simply, as follows: The United States told the rest of the world, "we shall take your men and women freely and let them participate in the rapid economic growth that we expect and look for; we shall export as freely as we can, and import subject to restrictions designed to force the pace of our industrial development; and while we shall borrow from those of you who can lend, we do not need too much credit—for it is in the process of rapid expansion that we shall find, within our country, the means needed for successful industrialization."

III. Pre-World-War I Trends in Expansion and Conflict

A rapidly growing country displays a tendency towards expansion of territory under its sovereignty, and of economic penetration into other areas, where, without acquiring sovereignty, it tries to assure favorable conditions for economic intercourse. Such expansionist tendencies are a natural consequence of economic growth so long as that process is sparked by aggressive individuals; and so long as economic production cannot occur in a vacuum but must depend upon the use of land and other natural resources. The extension of new methods of production, whether or not based upon empirical science, is a difficult and risky task—in either old or new countries. Such a task is likely to be assumed, with the tacit or explicit consent of society, by individuals or groups willing and capable of running the risks and tackling the difficulties involved. These individuals and groups are not likely to forbear from taking advantage of facilities provided by the wider territory and the greater natural resources that can be acquired by their own state; or from forcing openings in other states where the possible advantages of trading or investment are obvious.

In its rapid growth during the nineteenth century, the United States provided a clear example of such tendencies towards territorial expansion at home and economic penetration abroad. While the record is familiar, it can do no harm to recall that the nineteenth-century history of this country is punctuated at frequent intervals by sizable additions of territory under its sovereignty. The Louisiana Purchase of 1803, the Florida Purchase of 1819, confirmation of the claim to Oregon in 1846, the annexation of Texas and the cessions from Mexico (and the Gadsden purchase) in 1848, the purchase of Alaska in 1869, the annexations resulting from the Spanish war towards the end of the century, and, finally, the acquisition of the Panama Canal Zone at the beginning of our century constitute a record of rapid external expansion. And to this list, comprising only changes involving other sovereign states, should be added the continuous encroachments on the aboriginal rights of the Indian tribes.

While the record with reference to economic penetration, sometimes backed by force, into other countries is not as striking as the above, it still shows that this country was scarcely free from this tendency. Our initiative in opening Japan is a familiar fact, as is the economic penetration into Mexico, and particularly into the Central American republics. Like all countries that, in the process of their industrialization, come to rely upon raw materials from other states, the United States was anxious to assure the possibility of ordinary commercial intercourse, unhindered by pre-industrial patterns of political and social institutions in the underdeveloped countries.

That vigorous extension of territory under its sovereignty and its penetration into other areas in order to assure itself a minimum of the necessary economic traffic were vital elements in the long term growth of this country is a fact that need not be labored. This phase of growth parallels that for others, whether in England, the original habitat of industrial capitalism, in later followers such as Germany or Japan, or in the USSR, the most recent example of industrialization, this time under authoritarian auspices. But the distinctive characteristic of the American example of this aggressive aspect of economic growth was its accomplishment without major armed conflicts, and thus with little outlay of resources. Much of the extension of the area was with the consent, reluctant or eager, of the powers involved; and such as involved armed conflict never called for exertions that impeded significantly economic efforts toward peaceful internal growth. The same was true of economic penetration abroad. With respect to this relatively peaceful type of external expansion, the record of the United States is fairly similar to that of Russia in its movement eastwards.

The basic conjuncture of circumstances that permitted this relatively peaceful process of external expansion was the absence of powerful neighboring state units and the favorable or relatively indifferent attitude of those powers that could have impeded the process or made it a relatively costly one (particularly England). This also explains another characteristic peculiar to the long term development of this country. In spite of the gains of extensive expansion, the United States was marked by the freedom of its economy from either the tradition or burden of militarism—the usual concomitant of such expansion in other countries. Unlike England who had to maintain its fleet to insure its lines of communications; unlike Germany who inherited a strong military group from its pre-industrial phase and used it for aggressive expansion across its boundaries; unlike Russia who maintained a large military establishment partly for internal security, but largely with an eye to its European and Minor Asiatic boundaries; unlike Japan who retained the military cast of its pre-industrial society, and used it both to free itself from Western penetration and for its own conquests, the United States neither inherited the military cast from its feudal past (of which it had little), nor saw much need for it as a tool of growth or security. Except during the Civil War decade, military expenditures of this country were in minor fractions of one per cent of total national income—a record practically unparalleled among other major countries within the orbit of industrial capitalism in the nineteenth century.

One must also not overlook the fact that the infrequency of major conflicts (there were in fact only two during the span of more than a century, of which by far the more important was the Civil War) meant freedom not only from direct economic burdens but also from distortions in the structure of the economy. In countries organized along lines of free enterprise and political democracy, even successful wars, so long as they call for a major economic effort, involve changes that are serious impediments to continued peaceful growth. Freedom from such impediments was an important element in the unusual record of economic growth of this country.

The trends in external expansion and international security just noted serve to explain, at least as permissive factors, the trends already indicated in the across-the-boundaries flows of men, goods, and capital. A large volume of immigration was made possible by the prevailing and prospective security of this country on the one hand, and by at least a benevolent or neutral attitude of countries of origin, on the other. The whole structure of foreign trade, as well as its growth in volume, cannot be explained without relating it to the rapid growth of the country's domestic production in turn related to its expansion of territory and the turbulent growth of its population. The relative lack of dependence upon foreign capital was due to internal economic strength on the one hand, and the lack of any purely *political* inducements for would-be creditor countries on the other. This interrelation between the peaceful currents across the boundaries, and the developments in the realm of international relations with respect to balance of power and the possibility of conflict, must be clearly kept in mind. Cognizance of it is indispensable in analyzing the economic relations of the United States with the rest of the world, for the longer period briefly sketched above; and even more for understanding the major changes in these relations that occurred since World War I.

IV. Post-World-War I Trends in Migration, Trade, and Capital Investment

In considering trends in the economic relations of the United States with the rest of the world since World War I, we must shift our emphasis in a significant way. The foregoing skeleton outline of trends during the century preceding 1914 emphasized primarily the growth of this country, as the major factor that made for changes in international relations, so that we could, justifiably, pay little attention to shifts in the rest of the world except as a permissive factor. In treating the recent three to four decades, the emphasis must be on changes in the international scene. It is the latter that catch our eye; and it is they that largely determine changes in the economic relations of the United States with the rest of the world. From a permissive factor, trends in the rest of the world become a compelling factor. This does not mean that trends originating within the United States proper can safely be neglected. But it does mean that they recede in importance in comparison with changes in the international scene.

These changes are a sadly familiar story needing little elaboration. Out of some thirty odd years that extend from 1914 through 1948, major wars of unparalleled intensity account for fully a decade, little less than one third. The period is also marked by accelerated industrialization of Japan, with disturbing consequences in the Far East, and of Russia, with disturbing effects in Europe. Perhaps most important is the fact that, contrasted with the expansion of the system of free enterprise and political democracy in the nineteenth century—exemplified by almost all countries reached by the industrial revolution in that century—there is a definite advance of authoritarian types of social and economic organization—sweeping out of Russia, Italy, and Germany, affecting Japan, and, in recent years, penetrating into other countries, mostly those underdeveloped economically. Contrasted with this, there is the apparent failure of the nineteenth-century type of industrialization in many major areas of the world—among which China is most notable. Finally there is progressive and striking disorganization of the whole network of economic relations among nations, originally based upon a relatively peaceful movement of men, commodities, and capital. And this list omits the distortions of economic and social institutions *within* the countries still marked by free enterprise and political democracy.

It is against these marked changes in the international scene that recent trends in the economic relations of the United States with the rest of the world must be viewed. These trends are clearly apparent and can be summarized under four headings: (*a*) the reduction and virtual cessation of immigration; (*b*) the reduction in relative size and the drastic change in the character of foreign trade; (*c*) the shift from debtor to creditor position on international account, and the distortion of the whole system of international capital relations by political types of flow; (*d*) the increase in the share of military expenditures in particular and of government activities at large in the structure of the national product.

(*a*) Even with continuing peaceful relations in the world, immigration to the United States would probably have declined, certainly proportionately to this country's population and perhaps even in absolute volume. The proportion of *net* immigration to total population was at peak in the 1850's and, on the whole, declined to World War I (for the decade 1850-1860 it was close to 10 per cent of total population; for that of 1880-1890, it was 7.6 per cent; for the decade 1900-1910, it was 6.6 per cent). As our population grew and as the economic need for the type of labor provided by immigration declined, the net volume of immigration *retained* was bound to form a decreasing percentage of the country's total population. Continuation of this trend would in time have brought a decline also in the absolute volume of net immigration.

It may also be reasonably assumed that immigration would have been legally restricted, even had the world remained at peace. One important element in the pressure for restriction would have been the increased proportion of gross to net immigration, i.e., the tendency clearly manifest since the 1890's towards a gross inflow of people greatly in excess of what the country apparently could absorb. Unlike the earlier decades when, out of one hundred immigrants coming in not more than twenty returned, in the decade or two before World War I the proportion returning was running close to 40 per cent. Persistence of this tendency would have accelerated restriction of immigration, since such a large volume of temporary labor created social and cultural difficulties calling for some remedy. And one should add that restriction might have been the only readily available remedy, since any regulation of immigrants once *within* our boundaries would have run counter to all the traditions of the country's economic and social system.

This, necessarily conjectural, argument is strongly suggested by the historical record of the decades immediately preceding World War I. In so far as immigration was likely to decline and to be restricted, one might argue that the drastic reduction and restriction that followed World War I was but an acceleration of already existing trends, rather than a completely new pattern imposed by the changed international scene. Yet acceleration is too mild a term. Clearly the break in actual immigration trends was more drastic by far than would have been expected had the world remained at peace. A trend that might have emerged gradually over half a century or longer was compressed into a brief span of little more than fifteen or twenty years; and assumed a form that it might never have assumed, except for the major wars, the dislocations in their wake, and the other drastic changes in the international scene already indicated.

The effects of these upon the immigration flows are quite apparent. The First World War brought about a drastic reduction in immigration, and provided this country with the experience of managing its economy without a continuous inflow of people. Even though during the war quinquennium net immigration amounted to over half a million, it was a far cry from the 3.8 million of the preceding quinquennium. Dur-

ing the decade of the 1920's immigration was regulated by the
National Origins Act, a measure that reflected the exacerba-
tion of nationalist feelings during World War I and a fear of
the effects of participation in world conflicts. But during this
decade there was still a substantial flow of some 3 million of
net immigration, a third of the rate in the last quinquennium
prior to 1914. The drastic restriction came in the 1930's during
the major depression undoubtedly associated with the dislocations brought about by World War I. During this decade, total
net immigration dwindled to slightly over 200,000. Clearly,
the fear of wars; the emergence of authoritarian powers capable of controlling and distorting immigration streams in ways
completely unknown during the nineteenth and early twentieth
centuries; the experience with unemployment and the drive for
security—all brought about a drastic reversal in policy within
a relatively brief time span. It is highly unlikely that free
immigration will be resumed, although as one looks towards
the future a question may reasonably be raised as to the wis-
dom of complete abandonment of a policy of substantial immigration.

(b) On the surface, recent trends in the movement of goods
across the boundaries of the United States are a continuation
of trends manifest at least since the 1870's—of the continuous
decline in the proportion of imports, and of the somewhat less
consistent decline in the proportion of exports, both taken in
comparison with the relevant total of domestic output. But in
either case, there was a marked acceleration of this trend—
particularly in imports, the ratio of exports being temporarily
sustained by pressure upon this country for active assistance
during both World Wars and during the period of reconstruction immediately following these major conflicts. During the
decades from 1894-1903 to 1919-1928 the ratio of our imports
to total domestic output ranged from 5 to 6 per cent. During
1929-1938 that ratio dropped to 3.8 per cent. The ratio of
exports to domestic output, even disregarding the war decades,
was well over 6 per cent during the decades preceding the great

depression, dropping to 3.8 per cent during 1929-1938.[5] Furthermore, there were marked shifts and disturbances in the territorial spread of the international movement of goods and in the degree to which it was controlled by peacetime purposes related to economic progress. The relatively free movement of goods that characterized the decades prior to World War I, qualified, to be sure, by tariff policies, gave place, even in the peaceful years, to a movement necessarily inhibited by the existence of authoritarian states with inclination to control the flow of goods across their boundaries; and it was affected by the needs of either repairing the damages of past wars or preparing for future ones. Mere totals of the volume of international movements of goods or ratios of the latter to domestic output of the respective national economies do not reveal such shifts in the locus and composition of across-the-boundary flows.

While an analysis of the flows of goods across the boundaries, either into or out of this country, which would attempt to distinguish war-dominated sectors from others, cannot be undertaken here, two conclusions seem to be beyond reasonable doubt. First, as far as the purely peaceful flows are concerned, similar in character and economic significance to those that prevailed before World War I, the restriction in relative volume—relative to domestic production of this country—has been even more marked than the over-all ratios of foreign trade to total output show. In that sense, there was a catastrophic acceleration of the trend not dissimilar to that in immigration. Second, in the total flow of goods across boundaries, the war-dominated sectors increased strikingly; and partly correlated with this increase was an increase in what might be called international-policy-dominated sectors. The conspicuous example of the former are imports and exports of war materiel during major conflicts, or

[5] These ratios are calculated by using official figures on exports and imports, the latter inclusive of duty; and our estimates of gross national product (inclusive of imports). Estimates of gross national product are taken from the author's *National product since 1869*, N. Y., National Bureau of Economic Research, 1946. Both the numerators and the denominators are in current prices.

in preparation for them. A conspicuous example of the latter are lend-lease in various forms, including the recent decisions under the Marshall plan—dealing with the export side of our international transactions account; and what used to be called, during the war, "preclusive buying," and in recent years may be designated as "subsidy buying," on the import side of the account.

During a period in which one third of the years are marked by major armed conflicts, perhaps fully another third are years of immediate postwar recovery, and some of the remaining one third are tainted by war, the filling up of the channels of international movement of goods with conflict-dominated flows, to the exclusion or drastic restriction of peacetype normal flows, is inevitable. There are definite limits, at any given time, to the share of domestic output that *can* become engaged in across the boundary trade, without revolutionary changes in the economic and social institutions of the country. Given such limits and given retention of the institutions that set such limits, the pressure of war or politically dominated flows would necessarily result in the displacement and restriction of peace-type flows.

(*c*) World War I marked the transition of the United States from an international debtor to an international creditor. Whereas in mid-1914, this country owed the rest of the world somewhat over $3½ billion (net), its net *credit* at the end of 1919 was over $12½ billion; and even excluding government debts of some $9½ billion, there was a credit balance on the private international account of some $3 billion. In the 1920's, net assets on private account increased by another $5 billion, to yield, in 1929, a net credit balance of $8 billion. During the same decade the credit balance on government account also increased, from $9½ to somewhat over $11½ billion. During the 1930's the net credit balances had been substantially reduced, partly because of the default of some obligations but largely because of an influx of funds into the United States from other countries. In 1938 total foreign holdings, excluding inter-government war debts, were somewhat over $12 billion (on long and short term); but obligations were $9.2 billion, leaving a net balance of only $2.8 billion—a marked reduction from the net balance on private account of $8 billion in 1929. During the war our position changed further in the direction of reducing net credit on international account. Counting only non-government items, the position at the end of 1944 was marked by a gross claim of some $11 billion, a gross obligation of somewhat over $12 billion, and a net *debit* balance of about $1 billion. In the very recent years there has been a sizable export of capital abroad; so that at present, the United States is again a substantial creditor on the international account.[6]

These gyrations in the net balance of international indebtedness suggest three important conclusions. First, regardless of any temporary adverse balances, the United States after World War I has never ceased to be in fact a creditor country. Since it probably would have attained this position even had the world remained at peace after 1914, the demands of war and of postwar reconstruction only hastened this shift, accelerated rather than caused the trend. But as in the case of immigration and foreign trade, the acceleration was again very rapid and contributed to the failure of our institutions to adapt themselves quickly and effectively.

Second, because of deterioration in the position of most of the important creditor countries (particularly England, Germany, and France), the role of the United States as an international creditor was much more dominant than it would have been were the world to have remained at peace. This meant that the chief world creditor was a nation whose foreign transactions were but a minor element in its domestic economy. The

[6] For accounts of recent changes in the country's international indebtedness see Lewis, C., *Debtor and creditor countries: 1938, 1944*, Washington. Brookings Institution, 1945. An important analysis of the interwar period is contained in *The United States in the world economy*, United States Department of Commerce, Bureau of Foreign and Domestic Commerce, Economic Series No. 23, Washington 1943. A recent discussion is also Buchanan, N. S., and Lutz, F. A., *Rebuilding the world economy*, N. Y., Twentieth Century Fund, 1947.

severe fluctuations in the flow of credits from this country during the two decades between the two wars, may have been of some consequence to this country; but they were of even more drastic consequence to at least some debtor countries in the rest of the world. These characteristics of the recent decades cannot be interpreted as a continuation or acceleration of longer term trends that anteceded World War I: the foreign credit transactions of the United States had no such strategic importance in the network of international debts and claims during the nineteenth or early twentieth century.

The third recent aspect of our international accounts is also in the nature of a new and uncomfortable consequence of changed world conditions. Beginning in the 1930's, this country exercised a strong pull upon outside funds, as a refuge from possible monetary and political disturbances elsewhere. While such flows of "hot" money were probably not unusual in premodern periods of economic history, they were relatively unimportant in the Western World during the century between the end of the Napoleonic wars and World War I. Their reemergence in the 1930's was a clear consequence of serious economic and political maladjustments. And after our entry into the recent war, there were other inflows of funds here, governed not by peacetype economic needs but by political factors; balances were accumulated by some neutral countries because their products were needed by us during the war, and because the demands of war did not permit us to pay with goods of our own. In short, there was "politicization" of the flows of capital, similar to the militarization and "politicization" of the flows of goods, whether of commodities in foreign trade or of services on other real transaction accounts.

V. Post-World-War I Trends in Expansion and Conflict

If the recent third of a century was marked by drastic changes in the trends characterizing trans-boundary movements of the peaceful type, the breaks in the patterns of non-peaceful type of contact were even more marked. There was an end to the expansion of area under United States sovereignty, an end to the trend that was so important in determining the character of the country's economic growth in the nineteenth century. Of course, some unkind critic might point to the example of our occupation of former-enemy territory (e.g., Japan) as evidence of continued drive towards expansion. But even if by misuse of words these actions could be described as territorial expansion, there is a vast difference between this type of preventive measure which, on the whole, is a net burden on our economy, and the absorption of territory that characterized our nineteenth-century history and that provided the basis for unparalleled domestic growth.

Just as there was a reversal in at least the character of our territorial expansion, and upon a fairer interpretation, complete cessation of such expansion, so there was a reversal in the long standing policy of non-participation in major world conflicts. That this change can be explained quite simply by the absence of major world conflicts during the century elapsing between the Napoleonic wars and World War I, does not deprive the reversal of significance. Granted that the basic premise for such participation is the occurrence of world conflicts, and that, given the organization of the world into nations and the very huge economic size of the United States, it would be hard to think of a major world conflict in which this country might fail to participate. Nevertheless, such participation is a novel element in our history, and brings consequences some of which are not clearly appreciated, in spite of our apparent familiarity with wars in recent years.

In thinking of the economic consequences of such participation the first consideration is usually of the direct outlays involved. In these terms, the impact of World War I on this country was moderate. For 1917 through 1919, the three years in which such outlays were large enough to be included in the account, total war output in 1914 prices amounted to some $19 billion. For the same three years the nonwar output of our economy amounted to $108 billion.[7] We thus expended the equivalent of about one fifth of our nonwar output—not much more than our gross capital accumulation in many normal years. The same comparison for World War II (possible for totals in current prices alone) reveals the much greater effort in the recent conflict. For 1942-1946, total war expenditures amounted to $316 billion; during the same five years, nonwar output (gross of depreciation) amounted to $661 billion. Thus our direct war outlays were equivalent to 50 per cent of total nonwar output for these five years; and even this ratio should be raised because 1946, a year of proportionately low war outlays, was marked by a price inflation that disproportionately increased its weight in the total of five years. Thus, the recent conflict with its longer period of participation and its mobilization of a much larger relative share of total output for war expenditure has a much greater impact on our domestic economy than did World War I.

But the direct cost of participation in a war, especially to a country which, like ours, did not become a battlefield, is only part of the war's impact upon its domestic economy. A more important aspect is the opportunity cost. Even without direct participation in armed conflict, a country's economy responds to the pressures of war by a reorientation of its resources to new uses and by either complete cessation or drastic restriction of efforts directed towards normal, peacetype purposes. In the years prior to our entry in World War I, from 1914 through 1917, there was already a distortion of our domestic economy by pressure to supply the allied countries; a restriction of certain peacetype activities, e.g., residential construction; and inflationary price rises that were scarcely conducive to the consistent growth of our domestic economy viewed as a servant of long term, peacetime needs. Whatever might be put

[7] The estimates for World War I are from Kuznets, S., *National product in wartime*, N. Y., National Bureau of Economic Research, 1945; for World War II, from National Income, *Supplement to survey of current business*, U. S. Department of Commerce, Washington, July 1947.

on the other side of the scale, in the way of forced growth of some techniques and acceleration in the use of some resources during wartime, intensive economic participation in a war, whether or not accompanied by direct fighting, carries heavy net costs with it. It represents an interruption in that steady concern of the economy with the needs of consumers that is the vital basis for sustained economic growth. The technical accomplishments of a military production effort have dubious transfer value to peacetime; the opportunity costs represented by the diversion of economic effort to transient needs but dimly related to those of peacetime, are, by contrast, exceedingly heavy.

It is difficult to estimate this indirect cost of war. To use World War I as an example, how much was lost in the sense that it interrupted the normal immigration flows and reduced our population growth accordingly? How much did it cost us by accelerating expansion of capacity in some war needed industries, such as bituminous coal and steel, capacity unnecessary in post war years? How much loss was involved in reducing residential construction and wearing down the industrial structure of the country by limiting replacement? How much did the war cost us by imposing an unhealthy price structure and inhibiting a vigorous search by the community of producers for goods wanted by consumers, a search made unnecessary by the inflationary situation? Such questions cannot be answered adequately in quantitative terms. Yet one cannot avoid the impression that these opportunity costs were heavy. Is it unreasonable to argue that the drastic decline in the rate of growth of our economy, apparent when one contrasts the percentage increase in real national product during the years from 1914 through 1938, with the record for periods extending back to the Civil War, is in large part due to World War I and the dislocation it brought about in its wake? Is it unreasonable to suggest that, with a world at relative peace after 1914, our average rate of growth—as measured by total national product, would not have dropped from 20 per cent per quinquennium to 9.3 per cent; or the rate of increase in per capita output from 9.7 per cent to 2.6 per cent?[8] The opportunity cost involved in the reduction of these rates of growth by 3 or 4 per cent is vast indeed.

In inhibiting the growth of our domestic economy as a servant of peacetime needs, World War II is, by all signs, likely to constitute an even greater opportunity cost than did World War I. The form which this cost will assume may be different from that during the two decades from 1919 to 1939. In these earlier decades, the cost took the form of lower *total* productivity than otherwise might have been attained, and the loss emerged as one associated largely with the depression of the 1930's. We *may* escape that particular consequence because, in contrast to post-World-War I days, we are not making such an abrupt turn from a war to a peacetime economy. If the outlay of real resources on non-peacetype and lend-lease uses is kept at the proportions predicated in present plans, we may avoid a severe depression of the 1930's model and in that sense will not pay for World War II by a reduction in total output. But, from the point of view of economic development envisaged as growth in service of peacetime needs, there is little to choose between reduction of productivity that assumes the shape of an economic depression and a reduction of peacetype productivity accompanied by maintenance of high levels of total output *via* increase of outlays on military and defense purposes. Indeed, one might well argue that *if* we have to choose between these two evil consequences of major wars—dislocation and depression in a peaceful world as over against dislocation and high levels of production bolstered by military output in a warlike world—the choice is not necessarily in favor of the latter.

VI. TRENDS IN TRANSPORTATION AND COMMUNICATION

No explicit consideration has been given so far to the third group of factors affecting the economic relations of a country

[8] The comparison is between decades prior to and after 1914, and uses the estimates in Kuznets, S., *National product since 1869*, N. Y., National Bureau of Economic Research, 1946.

with the rest of the world, namely the technical and institutional means of contact. Clearly, the technology of transportation and communication played an important part in determining the flows across the boundaries—whether in a process of peaceful exchange or in one of forced invasion and defense. Without the striking changes that occurred since the early nineteenth century in the means of transportation, in international communication techniques, and in those institutional devices by which nations further peaceful intercourse or wage war, such huge peaceful flows and such vast and exhaustive conflicts as were recently experienced would have been impossible.

At first this technological development appears as a neutral factor facilitating equally the growth of peaceful and of warlike contacts. But the techniques of transportation and communication may develop, in some historical periods, in the direction of peaceful relations among nations and favor, in other periods, warlike relations. Since I am not familiar with any analysis of technological growth viewed from this standpoint, the present discussion of the developments during the last century can serve to yield only plausible impressions, of necessity broad and perhaps superficial.

We begin with transportation of men and goods across space. The first impression is that the technical progress associated with the origin and spread of the modern industrial system is at least as conspicuous in the field of transportation as anywhere else in the economy. Railroads, automobiles, and the application of internal combustion to air, represent crucial phases in this process, resulting in a revolution in transport greater perhaps than in any other field of production, either extractive or elaborative.

Second, this revolution in transportation made it possible to penetrate parts of the world hitherto untouched by the industrial system, and removed, or greatly limited, the blank areas on the world map. Before the advent of the railways, the vast continent of Africa was impinged upon by the Western powers only along its coasts and along some of its internal waterways;

and the growth to industrial maturity of such continental powers as the United States, Russia, and Australia was dependent upon the development of the railway. The matter is of importance in that conflicts of interest among major national units are, perhaps, more likely in a situation in which their boundaries or those of their satellites are contiguous, than in a world of isolated segments separated by areas that cannot easily be traversed by existing technical means.

Third, in so far as the technical revolution in transportation was possibly of greater magnitude than that in other types of production, it facilitated greater intercourse among nations —first and foremost a transportation problem. Facilitating such intercourse meant making it easier not only to augment the peaceful flows across boundaries, but also the warlike type of contact. Furthermore, in so far as the technical revolution in transportation called for heavy capital investment—a heavier investment per unit of service than of reproducible capital needed for extractive or manufacturing industries, it meant an increased economic investment in war far in excess of that needed in times when transport was primitive. When examining the apportionment of war expenditure between means of transportation (ships, planes, motorized equipment, etc.) and munitions proper, one cannot fail being impressed by the overwhelming dominance of the former; and one may reasonably conjecture that these proportions were not characteristic of at least land warfare of pre-industrial times.

Fourth, it may be argued that some recent technological changes in transport contributed more to the increase in the technical power of war contacts than of peaceful contacts. This argument is based upon a broad distinction between transport for peacetype uses as based upon assurance of proper facilities at either end of a bilateral contact, and transport for wartype uses which requires assurance of facilities at one end only. If men or goods are transported in peaceful migration and trade, transport facilities must be available with equal ease at the point of origin and at the point of destination; if men and goods are transported for purposes of war attack, there must

be facilities at the point of origin both for dispatch and for
return, but there need not be equal facilities at the point of
delivery or attack. The differences with respect to the factor
just noted between rail, motor, and air transport are quite
marked. The first can be used for warlike purposes merely as
a way of mobilizing resources for attack within the attacking
country—and so also can motor and air transport. But the
latter two, particularly air, can be used for attack within the
enemy country without any facilities for it in the latter, a feat
unattainable by railroads unless the enemy country obligingly
provides the facilities, and attainable by motorized transport
only over much shorter distances.

This argument in technical and military logistics should not
be pressed too far, particularly by a mere economist; after all,
even in wars, it is not enough to hit and run. Yet if such hitting
and running are done on a wide scale, the consequences to the
issue of an armed conflict may be decisive. And surely the old
saying that an army travels on its stomach is obsolete. In
present wars it travels on motorized wheels, and increasingly
so on wings; and while the stomach remains important, the
means of providing for it are much less of a problem than
those of supplying the wheels and the wings. One may, therefore, say that recent technological changes in means of communication did serve to aggravate the economic burden of warfare; and that by their technical nature, they served to increase
the scope of war contacts much more than that of peacetype
flows. The trend in this direction, as far as one can see, continues into the future, and it is irrelevant for the present
argument whether these technical changes in transport are in
themselves a consequence of greater attention to warfare than
to the problems of peace.

Communication is essentially transportation of information
and ideas, and in this field there has been an equally impres-
sive expansion of technical means of contact among nations.
Here, too, the more recent developments in the field, such as
radio, as distinct from the earlier (telephone, telegraph, mail,
etc.), are of a type in which it is possible for one link in the

contact to invade the other, without establishing full facilities at the far end. Here, too, invasion, as distinct from peaceful intercourse, has perhaps been facilitated by technical and institutional growth.

But in the field of communication the purely technical possibility of contact among nations is less important; more important is the existence or absence of common ground for the spread of information or ideas, of a peaceful or warlike type. Economic relations among nations, whether migration, trade, borrowing and lending, or warfare, assume some contact with respect to information and ideas governing the particular relation. It is not the technical means of communication but its content that determines its effect upon the volume and composition of economic relations. And the outstanding development with respect to the latter, as revealed by a broad look at the past century, has been the ever increasing number of nations drawn into the network of the modern industrial system and a corresponding spread of information and ideas that assign greater importance to *economic,* as over against religious and other sets of values. The main trend in communication was an acceptance by a rapidly growing proportion of the world of the values of a secular industrial economy with a consequent rapid extension of corollary institutions to facilitate economic intercourse among nations. The earlier isolation among national units, with their different historical and cultural heritages and with their completely different sets of values governing society, was rapidly giving way to at least a partial acceptance of values characteristic of our type of industrial society in which economic attainment is placed on a high, if not a completely dominant, level.

The result of this spread of secular economic civilization has been to facilitate peaceful flows of men and goods across boundaries. But it has also provided a basis for conflict which would not have existed without the common acceptance of economic values. To illustrate in terms of today—the ideological conflict between the capitalist and the communist nations is one based on acceptance by both of the importance of eco-

nomic performance, and of almost complete disregard by both
of performance on the scale of religious, aesthetic, or other
non-economic values. With this common base which permits
the capitalist society to appeal to some groups in communist
society and vice versa, the conflict may be of bitterness un-
imagined between e.g. an industrial nation of today and a
society like that of China or India prior to the modern centuries. It is because we are more of one world, in that our
judgments of social order are based upon similar if not identical criteria, that the opportunity exists for deep-seated conflict, backed by advanced economic means.

Thus an economist viewing the broadly changing scene in
the field of international communication is impressed not so
much by the growth in the technical means as by the trend
in the spread of common economic information, ideas, and sets
of values. He is impressed by the fact that, as the industrial
system spreads, it inevitably forces societies and nations drawn
into its orbit to adhere to a similar set of values, with a great
emphasis on economic attainment; that conflicts among national units are just as likely to emerge on this common basis
as on the basis of different systems of values; and that, when
they do emerge, they are likely to involve much greater economic outlays and thus constitute much graver economic problems than those among nations that fail to agree on the
importance of purely economic achievements.

VII. CONCLUDING COMMENTS

This paper presents a brief account of past trends in the economic relations of the United States with the rest of the
world and points out the contrast in these trends between the
century prior to World War I and the ensuing period. These
contrasts with respect to migration of men, the relative volume
of peacetype trade in commodities and services, the position
of the United States in the international capital accounts and
the character of its capital flows, the shift from peaceful territorial expansion to participation in major conflicts, and,

finally, the ways in which trends in the technological means of transportation and in the ideological conflicts as substance of communication have affected this country, are all readily apparent. The impacts of these changes in our economic relations with the rest of the world upon our domestic economy is equally apparent; at best, they mean slower growth in the future and an increased diversion of our resources to services other than welfare of domestic consumers; at worst, they mean a complete distortion of our economic and social system, and loss of most of our social and other achievements.

Throughout our discussion two omissions are apparent. One omission is common to any analysis of the past which adheres to facts, to the accomplished in disregard of the choices available at the time. In such an account an attempt to explain what has happened may easily produce an impression of simplicity and inevitability, i.e., that no alternative choices existed and that what has happened *had* to happen. This creates the illusory contrast between the simple past and the complex present; and worse, if the impression is accepted, it leads easily to an extrapolation of trends into the future in an aura of hopeless inevitability. There is no room here for a thorough discussion of the theory of historical causation, or for an analysis of the proper bases of historical extrapolation. One can only note that, in describing and accounting for the past, no attention was paid here to the alternatives at the time, and thus no indication given that at least some of these trends were a matter of choice, even though such choices were, as they always are, within a narrow range set by the heritage of the past. Any extrapolation of these trends, therefore, is also a matter of choice; and it would be foolhardy to identify the occurrence of an event with its inevitability, or the indications of a trend with its unavoidability.

The question of choices in history, and hence in economic policy, whether domestic or foreign, takes the form, most overtly, of alternative theories; and this leads to the second major omission of the paper. Our discussion, even if viewed merely as an account of the past, rather than an analysis of

the past as of choices among existing alternatives, is largely
limited to trends in material flows; and it thus overlooks the
impact of the view of the world and of the relation of the
given country to it. Such a view guides and determines long
range policy, either with respect to trans-national economic
relations or to the growth of the domestic economy proper. A
given country is member of the world concert of nations not
only in the sense that it trades with the others, exchanges
people or obligations with them, or engages in conflicts, overt
or hidden. It is also a member in that it either emulates other
nations or reacts negatively to them in scrutinizing their experience and policies with a view to either adaption or rejec-
tion in application to its own domestic economy.

This non-material aspect of economic relations between a
given country and the rest of the world cannot be studied
quantitatively. Yet one can see clearly that a nation, such as
the United States in the nineteenth century, which, in spite of
size and rapid progress, was not yet the economic leader of
the world, would look to the experience and policies of Great
Britain as the economic leader of the day, and be greatly
affected by the theory of economic growth and progress which
that leader advances or claims to exemplify. The United States,
in this case a follower country, would not necessarily accept
that theory without revisions that would suit the peculiar experiences and position of its own economy. But it may react
to the theory in a spirit of modified emulation; and evolve
a view of the world, and of its own relation to it, which would
provide the ideological basis for its own growth and for the
assumption of easy consent of the rest of the world to such
undisturbed growth.

In the nineteenth and early twentieth century, the United
States did appear to have a clear theory of economic growth
consonant with a peaceful world. This theory represented a
modification of that evolved in Great Britain. It had with the
latter the common element of stressing free adaptation of technological progress, by individual enterprise and within a framework of political democracy, to the production problems of an

economy. Another common element was the insistence upon free accessibility to scarce resources, without limitations by institutions that would not recognize the importance of private property and of entrepreneurs as the key elements in application of technical progress to economic problems. It differed from the English theory in being protectionist, in not accepting England's plan of serving as the workshop for the whole world with its corollary advocacy of fully free policy in international movement of commodities and resources. And the United States assumed that the rest of the world will give easy consent to such theory since the world would be a clear gainer from the rapid economic development that would occur under such conditions; gainer from the opportunities for free migration, from an expanded volume of foreign trade, from relatively free investment opportunities for any surplus funds that it might generate.

This was a theory of an important follower, rather than a leader, country, in a period in which there was wide acceptance of the theory as depicting a way of economic growth accessible to all would-be follower countries. With only some, albeit eventually important modifications, it was entertained by other countries that entered the orbit of industrialization during the century: Germany, Japan, and Tsarist Russia, to mention only the larger units.

After World War I the United States emerged as the economic leader of the world, and since that time changes in the international scene came thick and fast. Clearly, the theory entertained by this country, when it was in position of a fast growing follower in nineteenth century conditions and beliefs, would scarcely provide guidance when the country emerged to economic leadership; and when, particularly in recent years, the belief in feasibility of economic growth accompanied by free enterprise and political democracy has been shattered so gravely. Even disregarding the latter change, it is not clear that this country offered to the rest of the world a viable theory of economic growth, compatible with its own role as economic leader. No clear evidence emerged out of our domestic and foreign economic policies during the 1920's and the 1930's to serve as basis of formulating such a theory—to serve as guide both to ourselves and to the rest of the world towards a peaceful and economically progressive future.

The position of economic leadership involves responsibilities for formulating such a theory, since the organization of the world in competing nation-states forces other units to follow the leader—either by imitation or by opposition. Great Britain offered a theory which, if accepted, would assure some economic growth to the rest of the world and would at the same time serve to prolong, if not perpetuate, the industrial dominance of Great Britain. This theory was accepted, with the crucial exception that tariff barriers were erected and industrialization forced in countries that eventually brought about the loss of economic leadership by Great Britain. Some groping towards a theory compatible with economic leadership of this country, and preservation of a peaceful world within which the United States would be allowed to retain the major results of her economic advance, has been made in recent years. The partial abandonment of the tariff policy and the drive towards freer trade are one element in it. The consideration of economic investments in other countries is another element. But no consistent theory has emerged so far, and, in its absence, there seems to be too exclusive a reliance on negative elements. Too much emphasis is placed on preservation of already established economic superiority, and too little consideration of the elements that would be viewed as positive by the rest of the world. Yet a viable theory must combine the prolongation, if not necessarily perpetuation of a country-leader's own economic position, with assurance of adequate economic progress in the rest of the world, with the likelihood if not certainty that the economically leading country, in the very nature of prolonging her advanced position, will contribute effectively to advance in the rest of the world.

It is hardly surprising that such a theory has not yet been evolved. Recent changes have been numerous and rapid, and in such times there is always a marked lag in adaptation of our thinking, of our social and economic *mores*. The emergence of radically different principles of economic and social organization to serve as auspices under which economic growth in the rest of the world could be attained is, to say the least, a complication conspicuously absent during the nineteenth century. It is too early to say whether the sweep of industrialization accompanied by free enterprise and political democracy has already exhausted the areas of the world which, by their historical heritage and natural conditions, are potential participants; or whether there is still room for further extension of that type of growth. At any rate, careful study of the problem is vital as a basis for an adequate theory that would combine a sound view of potentialities of economic growth both in our country and in the rest of the world—growth in the service of satisfying ultimate human wants, not of power politics of competing nation-states. The existence or absence of such theory would, in the long run, mean much in determining the future impact of international relations on our domestic economy.